D0146180

WITTGENSTEIN

RETHINKING THE INNER

WITTGENSTEIN
RETHINKING THE INNER

Paul Johnston

London and New York

First published 1993
by Routledge
11 New Fetter Lane, London EC4P 4EE

Simultaneously published in the USA and Canada
by Routledge
29 West 35th Street, New York, NY 10001

© 1993 Paul Johnston

Typeset in 10 on 12 point Baskerville by Witwell Ltd, Southport

Printed in Great Britain by
T.J. Press (Padstow) Ltd, Padstow, Cornwall

All rights reserved. No part of this book may be reprinted or
reproduced or utilized in any form or by any electronic,
mechanical, or other means, now known or hereafter invented,
including photocopying and recording, or in any information
storage or retrieval system, without permission in writing from
the publishers.

British Library Cataloguing in Publication Data
Johnston, Paul
Wittgenstein: Rethinking the Inner
I. Title
192

Library of Congress Cataloging in Publication Data
Johnston, Paul
Wittgenstein: rethinking the inner / Paul Johnston.
p.   cm.
Includes bibliographical references and index.
1. Wittgenstein, Ludwig, 1889-1951. 2. Philosophical anthropology.
3. Self. I. Title.
B3376.W564J64   1993
128—dc20   92-33980

ISBN 0-415-09177-2

For Steve, always a true friend

But I wouldn't say now 'Thinking is hard'. There is I believe a stage in philosophy where a person feels that. This material I am working at is as hard as granite but I know how to go about it.

Wittgenstein, 1949

CONTENTS

PREFACE

The contemporary follower of Wittgenstein finds him or herself in a strange position in that Wittgenstein is widely regarded as one of the greatest philosophers of this century and yet the central thrust of his work is emphatically rejected by the current philosophical community. As A.C. Grayling puts it, 'apart from work done by Wittgenstein's relatively small band of disciples, *most* of what has happened during and since his time consists exactly in what his writings proscribe: namely, systematic investigation of the very "problems of philosophy" which he says will vanish when one attends properly to language'.[1] The implication of this is that Wittgenstein is not as great a philosopher as had been thought and Grayling hints that, although he may have been a great philosophical personality, he was not in fact a great thinker. The one area of Wittgenstein's work which is still in some measure accepted is the so-called private language argument, which is treated as separable from Wittgenstein's implausible and perverse methodological claims. This has paradoxical consequences. On the one hand, the argument appears as a philosophical jewel in a sea of nonsense, and, on the other, the argument itself starts to look odd, for if it is so important, why is it so irrelevant to the rest of modern philosophy? Doubts as to the validity of the argument have certainly emerged and one suspects that it too may eventually be rejected as interesting but ultimately flawed.

This book takes a very different approach. First, it is based on an acceptance of Wittgenstein's methodological claims and takes these to be central to the proper understanding of his work. Second, it argues that the private language remarks are not part of a restricted argument about the possibility of a certain kind of language, but form the basis for a radical new approach to the whole topic of the Inner. The book starts by investigating what it is about the Inner that makes it seem so philosophically problematic. It then considers, in Chapters 2 and 3, what have traditionally been seen as the two basic aspects of consciousness – sense-experience ('impressions') and thought ('ideas'). This leads on to consideration in Chapter 4 of how language operates in relation to the Inner, and I argue that it is here the distinctiveness of Wittgenstein's approach becomes most apparent. The attempt to understand the Inner throws new light on our relation to language and this in turns enables us to give an account of the Inner which does justice to its richness and complexity. Chapter 5 emphasises the variety of concepts which make up the Inner and seeks to undermine our tendency to view it in terms of a distorting uniformity. Chapter 6 then explores the fundamental question of the Inner–Outer picture itself and seeks to pin down what it is that lies behind our use of such a strange and philosophically confusing notion. The final chapter considers two opposing objections to Wittgenstein's account; first, the suggestion that his stress on criteria involves a denial of the Inner, and, second, the converse claim that, in accepting the notion of the Inner, he embraces an outdated anthropocentrism which uses special concepts in relation to humanity and so fails to treat it, like any other natural phenomenon, as something to be explained in purely causal terms.

Various people have helped in the preparation of this manuscript. I am grateful to Malcolm Budd, Mike Egan and Stephen Mulhall for their comments, criticisms and suggestions; to what extent they have been able to improve the book, each will have to judge for himself.

THE PROBLEM OF THE INNER

The expression 'Who knows what is going on inside him!'
The interpretation of outer events as consequences of
unknown, or merely surmised, inner ones. The interest that is
focused on the Inner, as if on the chemical structure from
which behaviour issues.

For one needs only to ask 'What do I care about inner events,
whatever they are?!' to see that a different attitude is conceivable. – 'But surely everyone will always be interested in his
own inner life!' Nonsense. Would I know that pain, etc., etc.,
was something Inner if I weren't told so? (*RPP2*, para. 643)

The concept of the Inner is both familiar and mysterious. Lying
at the heart of all our psychological concepts, it is invoked
whenever we wonder what is going on inside someone's head or
try to assess exactly what lies behind a particular look or smile.
But what exactly is the Inner? Where, for example, is it located?
Here we encounter a difficulty. It is clear that the Inner is not
literally inside the individual, and yet it would make little sense
to locate it somewhere outside her. The attempt to describe the
contents of the Inner creates further problems: consciousness
seems an ever-shifting mass of fleeting experiences and it seems
impossible that words should ever capture it. Even in the case of a
particular experience the task seems little easier, for here too one
is tempted to say that the only way to know the experience is to
have it. Thus, although inner experience is the very essence of
human life, it seems impossible to describe or define it. What we
feel and think seems inherently private, knowable only to the
individual herself. But this suggestion has the implausible

implication that communication is impossible: the fact that we can talk about what we feel suddenly seems a paradox. Furthermore, the individual seems inexorably pushed towards solipsism, for is not the world of consciousness the only one she really knows? And is not that world exclusively hers, an inner realm into which no one else can ever gain admittance?

These questions, and a host of related ones, lie at the heart of Wittgenstein's later work. Having himself come close to solipsism in the early 1930s, he spent nearly twenty years struggling to come to grips with the problem of the Inner, and as he did so, he developed a radically new approach to psychological concepts, one which challenges both traditional ways of thinking and more recent ideas. Before we look directly at Wittgenstein's claims, however, it is important to grasp exactly what it is about the Inner that makes it so problematic. One way of doing this is to consider certain oddities about psychology, the science which studies the Inner. As Wittgenstein noted in his final lecture series at Cambridge,[1] the most striking of these is that the psychologist can never directly observe the phenomena she is supposedly studying. All she can actually observe are the manifestations of the Inner, not the Inner itself. The alternative, and the only means of *direct* access, would be introspection, but this is even more problematic. First, it would involve a circularity; to observe thinking, for example, one would already have to know what it is. Second, the results of any such inquiry would immediately be questionable, for why should one person's conclusions hold for everybody? For example, if someone says she always has an image when she thinks, this may be true of her but would not necessarily apply to everyone else's thinking. A final problem is the difficulty of separating the act of observing the experience from the act of having it. 'If you go about to observe your own mental happenings, you may alter them and create new ones, and the whole point of observing is that you should not do this' (*WLPP* p. 235). Thus it seems impossible to study the Inner either from the outside or from the inside: 'the science of mental phenomena has this puzzle: I can't observe the mental phenomena of others, and I can't observe my own in the proper sense of "observe" ' (ibid.).

As these remarks illustrate, there seems to be something peculiarly elusive about thinking and about the Inner in general.

2

Baffled by this elusiveness, we may be tempted to fall back on the idea that the Inner consists of specific but indescribable experiences known to the individual through her own personal acquaintance with them. But what sense does this conception really make? The first problem with it is the clash between the notion of privacy and the fact that we can – and do – discuss our feelings and experiences: if our inner worlds are in principle inaccessible to others, how is it we still manage to discuss them? The natural answer is that our words offer a picture or translation of our thoughts; although our inner world is private, it can nonetheless be represented in a way comprehensible to others. At first, this idea seems plausible, for we do indeed talk of trying to put our thoughts into words and of trying to find precisely the right word to capture our meaning. But how can we translate something the other person cannot possibly know into terms which she is supposed to understand? How can the other person make a connection between the word and some object which must of necessity remain perpetually hidden to her? Furthermore, is it really the case that there is a process of comparison and translation every time someone says what she thinks?

As these questions suggest, understanding the Inner and in particular its relation to language is not as straightforward as it might at first appear. Although the idea that we translate our thoughts into words seems self-evident, pinning down this process seems much more difficult. In fact, Wittgenstein argues that the very idea of translation makes no sense. His first point is that it only makes sense to talk of translation if it is possible to distinguish between accurate and inaccurate accounts. In the case of translating thoughts into words, however, this creates a difficulty, for, if the individual's inner world is *ex hypothesi* inaccessible to others, how can the accuracy of her 'translation' be checked? The natural response is to say that the individual can check it herself, but what does this actually mean? Suppose she finds a mistake – how can she be sure that her second translation is more accurate than her first? Maybe she only thinks she made an error! Or maybe neither of her translations is correct and some third version is the true one. The problem is that, in her search for correctness, the individual never reaches firmer ground – each of her statements is only backed up by her belief that it is correct, so that intrinsically all are on the same level. Faced with a number of possible translations, the individual can only adjudicate between them in terms of which strikes her as correct at that particular moment. Lacking an independent standard, the individual's self-assessment is an empty charade. Since she has no means of distinguishing what *seems* right to her from what *is* right, the notion of accuracy, and hence that of translation, cannot get a grip. But if this is so, why doesn't this problem arise whenever anyone translates anything? The answer is that the existence of a public practice provides a context within which seeming right and being right are distinguished. Within the practice, there are rules of translation and procedures for checking whether or not these rules have been correctly applied. It is the existence of these rules and procedures which allows a distinction between accurate and inaccurate translation and so justifies our claim to be translating as opposed to simply setting down whatever feels right at the time.

The thrust of this argument is to refute the idea that the individual's expression of her thoughts is the translation or representation of a private process inside her. It also undermines the very notion of private inner events. The reason for this is that, if the individual's statements cannot be seen as reports, the only possible means of access to the supposed inner events has been ruled out. Since neither we nor she can distinguish between her believing a certain event took place and that event actually taking place, the notion of these events as independently existing occurrences is undermined. In fact, the only thing that plays a role in the language-game, and hence the only thing that can matter to us, is what the individual says or is inclined to say. The idea of independently existing thought processes on which she reports can be dropped. It is important, however, to note that this is not because the individual is unreliable, but rather because it makes no sense to treat her statements and her thoughts as two separate entities standing in a one-to-one correlation. The impossibility of a check implies a completely different set of conceptual relations. As Wittgenstein notes, ' "it seems to me I have multiplied correctly" does not mean "I have multiplied correctly". But apparently, if it seems to me I have compared, I have compared' (ibid., p. 11). What this shows, however, is that talk of a comparison is misplaced. If the individual's statements cannot be wrong, their claim to validity cannot lie in their being

4

an accurate translation or projection of 'what went on inside her'.

The importance of this argument is hard to exaggerate, for it undermines our natural picture of the Inner and calls for a general rethinking of our approach to psychological concepts. The argument challenges our most basic presuppositions about how we should understand the Inner and, if these are overthrown, it is by no means clear what we should put in their place. The temptation is to switch to behaviourism but rather than solving the problem this only suppresses it. Despite the mysteries and uncertainties surrounding it, the Inner plays a crucial part in our lives and, from a Wittgensteinian perspective, the point is to understand that role, not to deny it. As well as opening up a whole new set of problems concerned with the Inner, Wittgenstein's argument also raises far-reaching questions about how language works; for, if representation is ruled out, how does language operate here? If the individual speaks in a ruleless vacuum, how can her words have meaning? Paradoxically, however, it is precisely these words that can mean most to us. Unravelling these problems will take up the rest of this book and, as we shall see, the connection between language and the Inner is of crucial importance. However, before exploring Wittgenstein's positive account, it is worth considering the initial argument in more detail and one way to do that is to consider the example of inner speech.

One striking feature of inner speech is that at first glance it seems a blatant counterexample to Wittgenstein's claims. The natural inclination is to see it as a faint copy of outer speech – one talks as it were less and less loudly until one is speaking so softly there is no outer noise, only a sound in the imagination. Here there would seem to be no problem of translation, for *ex hypothesi* the individual's report on her inner monologue simply gives voice to words which she has already used, only internally rather than externally. But even here the same problem arises, for in the absence of an independent check, there is no means of assessing the accuracy of the individual's statement and hence it cannot be construed as a report.

'He is an accurate reporter of what *The Times* says' has good sense, you check it by reading *The Times*. And he can check it by reading *The Times*. But 'he is trustworthy about what he really says to himself' won't do for us and it won't do for him: in this case to seem to yourself to have said X is the only meaning I can give to 'I have said X.' (*WLPP*, p. 250)

Paradoxically, this implies that, when the individual tells us what she said to herself, her statement cannot be seen as the reproduction of anything. Her words are not a report on a separate but private inner process, rather they must stand or fall on their own merit; if they have an interest, this cannot lie in their being accurate because in this context the notion of accuracy cannot get a grip.

In an attempt to avoid this conclusion, it is tempting to try to justify the individual's statement by looking for some other criterion against which it can be checked. One possibility would be to find some physical correlate of normal speech which also occurred when the individual talked to herself. Suppose, for example, we discovered that normal speech was accompanied by certain movements in the larynx and found that similar movements could be correlated with the individual's account of her inner speech. This would seem to confirm the individual's account and so give sense to the idea that her statements are the outer projection of an inner process. One objection to this is that there is no guarantee that any such correlations exist. A more fundamental objection is that the reference to larynx movements introduces a new criterion and hence a new concept. Since this is so, the two accounts cannot be seen as confirming each other, indeed, in calling both the concepts 'inner speech' we are simply inviting confusion. Consider the situation if the two criteria diverge. If we treat the new criterion as authoritative and say the individual was mistaken about what she said to herself, we would be abandoning our current concept of 'inner speech'. If, however, we give the individual's account priority, we would no longer be able to claim that the physical data offer an independent confirmation of what she says. In fact, since the two criteria are independent, there is no reason why we shouldn't keep both. If, for example, there were larynx movements, but the individual had no account to offer, we might say that inner speech occurred but that the individual did not talk to herself. Conversely, if she had an account but there were no larynx movements, we might describe the situation by saying that she spoke to herself and no inner speech occurred. Examples of where the two criteria diverge bring out a more general point, for inner speech of which the individual was unaware or inaccurately aware would have a quite different interest from what we currently call inner speech. As things stand, our interest is in the individual's own account of what she said to herself; in other words, it is precisely an interest in an account where there is no difference between it seeming so to the individual and it actually being so. For this reason, it is pointless and quite misguided to seek a new criterion to justify our existing concept. If what we currently call 'inner speech' does not involve any criteria independent of the individual, the introduction of one can only create a completely new language-game. Any such game would not provide objective evidence of what really goes on inside us; rather it would replace our existing concept with a new one of a completely different kind.

Instead of seeking an independent confirmation of what the individual says, Wittgenstein urges us to recognise the distinctive grammar of inner speech. Rather than viewing it as a hidden version of outer speech, he argues that we should treat it as a completely different concept but one which has a tie-up with outer speech. To underline this point, he describes a case where the differences are much more obvious.

> Imagine *this* game – I call it 'tennis without a ball': The players move around on a tennis court just as in tennis, and they even have rackets, but no ball. Each one reacts to his partner's stroke as if, or more or less as if, a ball had caused his reaction. (Manoeuvres.) The umpire, who must have an 'eye' for the game, decides in questionable cases whether a ball has gone into the net, etc, etc. This game is obviously quite similar to tennis and yet, on the other hand, it is *fundamentally* different. (*LW1*, para. 854)

It is also possible to imagine a further variant on this game – 'inner tennis', where the two players play tennis in the imagination, that is to say, imagine they are playing tennis and describe to each other the shots they have attempted and how successful they have been in executing them. Each of these games is related to tennis and yet fundamentally different from it. Indeed, in the second case, the game is no longer even a form of exercise. Furthermore, it presupposes a quite different set of qualities, e.g. sincerity and a realistic appraisal of one's own tennis ability. For these reasons, and in contrast with the case of inner speech, there is little temptation to say that inner and outer tennis are exactly the same thing. The fact that the practical consequences are so much clearer makes it more obvious that the inner version of an outer activity involves a completely new set of conceptual relations.

To reinforce Wittgenstein's argument about inner speech, let us consider the special case of calculating in the head. The advantage of this example is that it's an everyday occurrence with a certain practical importance. It also has plenty of detail. As with inner speech, the natural inclination is to treat it as unproblematic and to argue that calculating in the head and calculating on paper are exactly the same thing. There are, however, obvious and important differences. In the one case, the individual manipulates signs on a piece of paper according to generally recognized rules, and, since this activity is public, every stage of it can be observed and checked by others. In the case of calculating in the head, however, all that we can observe is that the person concerned concentrates and gives an answer. But how should we describe the latter? On the one hand,

> there is a wish to say; 'And that is the description: he sits, knits his forehead, looks tense, and comes out with an answer'. But to this one also wants to say 'No, no. He did something else: he can tell you what.' (*WLPP*, p. 251)

Unfortunately, this 'something else' is rather elusive. The only way to describe it is in terms of the concept of calculating, but even here all the description amounts to is the mysterious claim that the inner activity is somehow the same as the outer one. But what does the same mean here? Simply stressing the notion of identity is no use, for the supposed privacy of the Inner creates a gulf which calls everything into question. Although the individual may claim to be calculating, how can we (or *she*) know that this is the correct description of her activity? Furthermore, what can possibly justify her taking a word used to describe an outer activity and suddenly applying it to an inner one?

To answer these questions, it is best to approach the issue from the perspective of a third party. It is important to remember, however, that the problem is not that the individual is unreliable, but that it makes no sense to treat her statements as reports on an independent process. As Wittgenstein puts it, 'I cannot accept his testimony because it is not *testimony*. It only tells me what he is inclined to say' (*PI*, para. 387). So what do we actually know about what does occur? Imagine we *didn't* calculate in our heads but came across someone who claimed she could, what would we make of her claim? Treated as a report, it could only appear as highly dubious. Since in principle we cannot have access to the inner process, we would only have her word for it that it occurred in her head rather than in her feet or that it involved the same symbols as calculating on paper or indeed that the symbols it involved formed a proper system. Furthermore, the same questions that arise for us also arise for her: how can she be sure that she hasn't made a mistake and isn't claiming to be calculating in the head when actually calculating in the foot or when not calculating at all? If her statements are genuine reports, the possibility of error cannot be excluded, and yet, strangely enough, the idea of her getting it wrong seems to make no sense. Thus the real nature of her inner activity remains surrounded in mystery. Although she may claim that she calculates, this provides neither us nor her with indisputable evidence about the supposed inner process; since no one can check her statements, all these tell us is what she is inclined to say is occurring, not what is actually occurring.

In view of these difficulties, we might decide to reject her claim. It is significant, however, that, if we leave to one side the question of what actually occurs inside her, her statements may be still be useful. If, for example, her answers tally with our calculations on paper, she might serve a useful function as calculating machine. Despite denying that her statements describe an inner process, we might still make use of them. Indeed, we might say 'Who cares what goes on inside her (or if nothing does) as long as she produce the right answer?' In view of this, we might agree to call what she does 'calculating' not because she says so but because the results of her activity connect up with our practice of calculating. Furthermore, if she could also state the stages of the calculation leading to the result and, in the middle of her activity, tell us the stage she had reached and the answer so far, this would make the parallel with calculating even closer and so give further reason for calling what she does calculating. It is important, however, to recognise that the decision to call this new activity 'calculating in the head' is simply a matter of convenience: what the phrase does is highlight a connection between two quite distinct things. It might, for example, be likened to finding a set of lines on a wall and describing them as 'a drawing of a Greek temple with bits missing'.

> This doesn't mean that it was connected with an actual drawing of one; it means only that it could sensibly be described as 'a drawing with bits left out'. What he (the man who calculates) does can conveniently be described as 'he does something rather like what he would be doing if he had read a sum off'. (*WLPP*, p. 270)

Thus, if we did decide to say that she could calculate in her head, this would not be because her statements were accurate reports of a process which turned out to be identical to our process of calculation. Rather it would reflect the fact that at various points her statements connect up with our practice of calculating.

Against this, someone might argue that we would have no choice but to recognise that what she does is the same as what we do, that we would be compelled to accept it is a genuine case of calculation. But why? What she does is *not* the same as what we do, and whether we extend the concept of calculating on paper to take in inner calculation is matter of decision, not compulsion. Of course, it's true that there are occasions when we find extending a concept in a certain way highly inviting. For example, in describing the picture of a burning house, one could either say that the smoke is coming out of the house or simply that it is above it. Some people may find it natural to use the first description, indeed, they may even feel 'compelled' to use it, but if they are, that is simply an interesting fact about them (*WLPP*, p. 151). From a conceptual point of view, however, talk of compulsion is misplaced. If we could not calculate in our heads and came across someone who said she could, we might find it natural and convenient to extend our concept of calculation to take in this new phenomenon. On the other hand, we might decide to call it 'unreal calculation' or decide not to call it calculation at all.

So far, our discussion of calculating in the head has ignored its most striking feature – the individual's claims about her own experience. As we have seen, the individual uses the word 'calculating' in a radically new context, and yet she claims that it is exactly the right word to describe what she is doing. So what justification does she have for this? In one sense, none whatsoever, for nothing in the previous employment of the word justifies its use in relation to an experience. In fact, the new use is a spontaneous and in a sense arbitrary extension of the concept. The key point, however, is that other people may share the inclination to put the word to this new use. Paradoxically it is through the use of new and apparently nonsensical phrases that people are able to convey their experiences to each other. Here the mark of their sharing an experience is the inclination to use the same apparently nonsensical phrase to express it. Consider, for example, the phrase 'I feel a presence'. Here two quite heterogeneous elements are put together, for we did not learn the word 'presence' in connection with feelings. Furthermore, when someone is present, we don't usually talk of feeling a presence. It would make no sense therefore to suggest that we learn the word 'presence' and then discover that there is a feeling associated with it that can also occur when no one is physically there. Nonetheless, people do say 'I feel a presence' and this is 'a spontaneous growth and a growth of something: you learn "feel", you learn "presence" too; then one day you combine them. Poets do it. One man uses such a phrase, then thousands use it' (*WLPP*, p. 270). What happens here is that the individual takes up a phrase learnt (and used) in one way and gives it a new use as an expression of experience. The words she uses do not function by accurately representing what went on inside her, nor are there any rules for their use; rather she uses a certain phrase and her doing so characterises her experience as being of a certain kind. When she says 'I felt a presence', it is her use of that phrase which enables us to say she had a specific experience, viz. the experience expressed by the phrase 'I felt a presence'. The outer expression constitutes the criterion for the inner experience and here that expression consists in the individual's taking up a phrase that she has been taught in one way and giving it a radically new use.[2]

This way of using language is characteristic of the first-person use of psychological concepts, and to emphasise that such statements function as expressions of experience and not as reports of ineffable processes, Wittgenstein referred to them as *Aeusserungen* or utterances. The point of this is to indicate that this type of statement has a quite different grammar from that of a description. In the latter case, our statements involve the application of generally agreed criteria, specifying what it means to say that a certain process or event is occurring, and whether those criteria have been applied correctly can in principle be checked by others. In the case of the Inner, however, the individual does not learn rules or generally agreed criteria; her statements are not based on evidence and cannot be assessed by others for their accuracy. On the contrary, they are like signals. Their interest lies in the fact that the individual is inclined to make them, for it is her use of a particular phrase that characterises her as having had a particular experience. In contrast with outer events, the experience cannot be separated from its expression: what the individual says and does is crucial, since this provides the only possible criterion for distinguishing between different inner states. For example, we should say that something different happened (a different experience occurred) when the individual says 'I calculated and the answer was 340' and when she says 'The number 340 floated into my mind'. Similarly, if the individual gives the right answer to the sum but offers as her path to the answer some nonsense (e.g. she says 'a, m, n, therefore 340'), we might decide not to call this calculating and to mark the difference between it and the normal case by saying that the individual only 'quasi-calculated'.

This account of the Inner, and the way language functions in relation to it, also has implications for memory; indeed, one could say that the Inner involves a different concept of memory. Normally when we talk of remembering something, it is possible to verify the correctness of the memory. We say 'I attended a lecture this morning' or 'I remember attending a lecture this morning' and our memory claim can (at least in principle) be corroborated or refuted by other people. If, however, someone says 'I remember going through every stage of the calculation in my head', there is no possibility of a check and therefore no way of distinguishing between her thinking she did so and her actually having done so.[3] However, this does not mean that the individual is wrong to say she remembers; rather it shows that here remembering has a different sense. This may seem to suggest that the individual can say anything she likes, but that is not so. What we are interested in is what the individual is *sincerely* inclined to say, not what answer would now suit her best. In this context, therefore, the key distinction is not between an accurate and an inaccurate statement but between a sincere and an insincere one. To put it another way, the only measure of accuracy is sincerity. The individual's statements about what she experienced in the past are on the same level as those about the present; both can only be made sense of as expressions of experience, not as accurate or inaccurate reports.

Against this, one might argue that, without the notion of accuracy, the memory claim is useless; surely we want to know what actually happened in the past, not just what the individual is inclined to say happened. This objection misses the whole point of Wittgenstein's argument, for it assumes that what actually happened and what the individual says happened are two distinct things. As we have seen, however, the grammar of psychological statements means that the latter constitutes the criteria for the former. If we see someone with a concentrated expression on her face and want to know 'what is going on inside her', then her sincerely telling us she is trying to work out the answer to a complicated sum tells us exactly what we want to know. The question of whether, despite her sincerity, her statement might be an inaccurate description of what she is (or was) doing does not arise. The source of confusion here is a failure to recognise that psychological concepts have a different grammar from that of concepts used to describe outer events. What makes the Inner seem so mysterious is the misguided attempt to understand one kind of concept in terms of another. In fact, our concept of the Inner, what we mean when we talk of 'what was going on inside her', is linked not to mysterious inner processes, but to the account which the individual offers of her experience. By contrast, if the individual could indeed report on events inside her, there is no particular reason why this should be of interest to us. ' "Why should what happens within you interest me?" (His soul may boil or freeze, turn blue or red: what do I care?)' (*RPP1*, para. 215). As processes or events, what goes on inside the individual is of no interest, or rather is of a purely medical or scientific interest. On the other hand, if someone tells us 'I was thinking about my friend N', this is interesting because it tells us something about the person concerned. The possibility that she is making a mistake is not allowed for in our concepts, for that is not what such concepts are about.

From this perspective, the example of calculating in the head is slightly atypical because the concept is more directly practical than many of the other concepts of the Inner. This, of course, is one reason why it is such a good example, for the fact that its consequences are what matters to us makes it easier to approach it in a less prejudiced manner. Even in this case, however, the key point is that what the individual says has a use despite the fact that it is not a report; what matters is not that the individual accurately reproduce an inner process but that her mental arithmetic prove itself. Furthermore, it is not only the results of calculating in the head that can be useful, other aspects of the individual's utterances may also be of use. For example, when the individual offers an account of stages she went through in doing a sum in her head, this may tell us something about her mathematical competence. She may, for example, have taken a particular short cut or may have made a mistake of greater or lesser stupidity. The account has a use quite independently of whether or not it accurately reproduces some supposed inner event.

Despite these points, there may still be a desire to claim that inner processes do take place and simply are the same as their outer analogues. For example, in the case of calculating in the head, one may still want to say that it just is the same process as calculating on paper. One way to counter this inclination is to imagine our reaction to a group of people who made claims of this kind where we do not. Suppose, for example, that a group of people (or one person) claimed they could take their pulses mentally. Asked what their current pulse rate is, they concentrate for a minute or two and then give the correct answer (as independent measurement confirms). They say they do exactly the same thing in their heads as we do outwardly, and, indeed, they employ the same terminology as we do, e.g. they say 'I'm looking for my pulse', 'I've now found it and begun measuring', 'I've lost count, I'll have to start again', etc. So what should we make of these claims? One response would be to say that it can't be the *same* thing because taking one's pulse involves a physical process. However, calculating also involves a physical process, so if this is a reason for rejecting the idea of taking one's pulse mentally it is also an argument against calculating in the head. So what conclusion should we reach? Are the two activities the same or are they not? As Wittgenstein says in the *Philosophical Investigations*, 'Say what you choose, so long as it does not prevent you from seeing the facts' (*PI*, para. 79).

Another way to undermine the notion of a specific inner process is to note that there is no guarantee that different people will say the same thing. For example, it is conceivable that one group of people should say 'I calculated in my head', while another spontaneously use a different expression, e.g. 'I calculated unreally' or 'I calculated and I didn't calculate'. To ask which of these phrases is correct would be misguided, for the question as to whether all these people do the same thing and have the same experiences is answered not by looking for processes behind the utterances, but by looking at the utterances themselves. If someone said she calculated in her foot, her saying this would itself give us reason for saying that her experience was different from ours. Similarly, if her account of her mental arithmetic had the form 'a, m, n, therefore 340', we should certainly have doubts about saying that she was calculating. The type of judgement involved here is of the same kind as that we might make if we came across different groups of people engaged in activities similar but not identical to our own. Suppose, for instance, we came across two groups of people who played chess-like games. One group plays as we do but has a rule which says that a move is only permitted if accompanied by the statement 'I now move this piece'. The other group plays as we do but rejects what we would otherwise call good moves if the pattern created by the move is aesthetically unpleasing. In the first case, we might treat the difference as inessential and say the people do indeed play chess. In the other case, however, we would probably say the people played a significantly different game. Similarly, if someone claimed to calculate unreally rather than in the head, we might treat this difference as insignificant. On the other hand, if she talked of testing numbers until one felt right, we might object to calling this calculating even if it infallibly generated the right number.

The variety of ways in which calculating in the head might be expressed show how the phenomenon can be looked at in many different ways. Indeed, despite our obsession with inner processes, there is no reason why it has to be seen as a process at all. As Wittgenstein points out, it could easily be seen under a completely different aspect.

> One teaches someone to calculate in his head by ordering him to *calculate*! But would it have to be like that? Might it not be that in order to get him to calculate in his head, I don't have to say 'Calculate', but rather: 'Do something else, only get the result' or 'Shut your mouth and your eyes and keep still, and you will learn the answer'.
>
> I want to say that one need not look at calculating in the head under the aspect of calculating, although it has an essential tie-up with calculating.
>
> Nor even under the aspect of 'doing'. For doing is something that one can give an *exhibition* of. (*RPP1*, para. 655)

Far from treating it as the same as calculating on paper, it would be possible to view calculating in the head as a completely different activity, only one which has the useful feature of providing a paperless way of finding the answer to a sum. Alternatively, it might be seen not as an activity at all, but simply as a capacity people have or can be trained to have. In fact, it would even be possible for a group of people to reject the connection with the Inner altogether. In their case, the individual would be taught to say (or might spontaneously say) 'I calculated unreally' and anyone who talked of something going on inside her would be laughed at or treated as mentally retarded. However, even if the inner process is disposed of in this way, this does not mean that all that is left is the outer process, the behaviour, for in addition to the behaviour, there is also the language-game we play with the utterance (*RPP1*, para. 659). Wittgenstein's attack on the notion of inner processes does not imply that only the Outer matters; on the contrary, by bringing out the true nature of utterances he underlines the fact that we aren't just interested in behaviour. We don't just want to know that the person's body was in such-and-such a position and her features arranged in such-and-such a way. Rather we are interested in her account of what lay behind this behaviour; we want to know whether her restless actions and thoughtful look were because she was having difficulty working out a sum or because she was worried about losing her job.

To sum up, our talk of calculating in the head can be seen as having two components. First, it involves a natural extension of the concept of calculation to cover a new phenomenon, viz. the individual's ability to give the result of a sum without making any calculation on paper. Second, it involves a new use of the terminology of calculation, viz. the individual's use of it to express her experience. In pointing this out, Wittgenstein is not seeking to deny that we calculate in our heads; his aim is simply to undermine the idea that what lies behind this concept is some mysterious mental process which somehow corresponds to calculation on paper. Similarly, in the case of inner speech, the thrust of his argument is to undermine the tendency to treat the Outer as the model for the Inner. The difficulty is that the existence of certain connections encourage us to treat the Inner as a hidden version of the Outer. In fact, however,

> one cannot say: writing in one's notebook or speaking is *'like'* silent thinking; but for certain purposes the one process can *replace* the other (e.g. calculating in the head can replace calculating on paper). (*RPP1*, para. 583)

The force of Wittgenstein's remarks is not to reject the idea of inner experience, but to undermine an incoherent account of the nature of that experience. His aim is to question the approach we are naturally inclined to take and to guide us towards a new way of seeing these phenomena and the concepts they involve. In fact, his claims open up a whole new range of issues. As Wittgenstein himself notes,

> if someone were now to say: 'So, after all, all that happens is that he *reacts*, behaves, in such-and-such a way,' – then this would once again be a gross misunderstanding. For if someone gave the account: 'I in some sense *calculated* the

result of the multiplication, without writing etc.' – did he talk *nonsense* or make a false report? It is a different employment of language from that of a description of behaviour. But one might indeed ask: Wherein resides the importance of this new employment of language? Wherein resides the importance, e.g. of expression of intention? (*RPPI*, para. 652)

The locus classicus for Wittgenstein's attack on the traditional conception of the Inner is, of course, the private language argument (*PI*, paras 243ff.). However, the idea that these remarks are a self-contained whole is somewhat misleading, as is the suggestion that their main concern is with the nature of language. As our discussion of calculating in the head has illustrated, the importance of Wittgenstein's remarks on privacy is that they point to the need for a complete reassessment of our conception of the Inner. For this reason, the 'private language argument' cannot be isolated from the rest of Wittgenstein's work, indeed, it might well be said to raise more questions than it answers. The arguments which undermine the idea of privacy should be viewed not as the completion of a philosophical task but as its delineation; although they contain the seeds of a positive account, they also raise a vast array of new problems which the rest of the *Philosophical Investigations* (and Wittgenstein's other writings) are devoted to solving.

In the private language remarks, Wittgenstein focuses on the example of sensations and he considers the idea of a language whose words 'refer to what can only be known to the person speaking; to his immediate private sensations' (*PI*, para. 243). *Ex hypothesi* such a language would be incomprehensible to anyone other than its creator, for no one else could know what its words referred to. Clearly this clashes with the fact that we do talk about our sensations; leaving this point to one side, however, Wittgenstein spells out in more detail what a private language would have to involve. The sensation words in it would be defined by the individual forging a private link between the name and the sensation. For example, if she wanted to keep a diary about the recurrence of a certain sensation, she would do this by associating the sensation with the sign 'S' and writing the sign down on every occasion on which the sensation occurred. This procedure differs from normal ostensive definition in that the individual would not be able to point to what she is defining, since the sensation is of course private. Instead she is assumed to point as it were mentally, forging the link between sign and its referent by concentrating her attention on the sensation she is trying to name. In this way, the private linguist impresses upon herself the connection between the sign and the sensation; although for everyone else the sign is meaningless, for her it has a meaning.

As this sketch makes clear, the private linguist's case rests on the possibility of a private ostensive definition. According to Wittgenstein, however, this involves a fundamental misunderstanding of the nature of ostensive definition. One way of illustrating this point is to note the ambiguity in the idea of giving something a name. Typically when we talk of giving something a name, what is involved is naming a pre-defined object, e.g naming a ship or giving a name to a child. With ostensive definition, however, what is at stake is something quite different – not the naming of a pre-defined object but the definition of a concept. For this reason, pointing is not enough. Instead rules for the use of the concept must be laid down, for it is only by specifying what is to count as the same thing that the nature of what is being pointed to is determined. If someone points to an object and says 'That is X', this might be the definition of a colour, a quantity or an entirely new concept. Only when the person explains how we should use this sample, in what way other objects should be compared with it and adjudged the same, is a particular concept actually defined. Thus giving a name to something is the culmination of the defining process; the person giving the definition points to a sample, but this act only defines a word if the rules for using the sample are clear. This point, however, is completely ignored by the private linguist who treats defining as if it were simply a question of naming. What she forgets is that 'a great deal of stage-setting in the language is presupposed if the mere act of naming is to make sense' (*PI*, para. 257). In this sense, her fundamental error is to believe that 'once you know *what* the word stands for, you understand it, you know its whole use' (*PI*, para. 264).

Thus the first stage of Wittgenstein's argument is to stress that an ostensive definition only makes sense where there are rules for using the sample it introduces and hence where there is a practice of using that sample. In the case of the private linguist, however, there are neither rules nor a practice. The private linguist supposedly undertakes to use the word in a particular way, but she doesn't specify what that way consists of. Is it to be assumed that she invents the technique of using the word or does she find it ready-made? (*PI*, para. 262). The real problem, however, is not simply that she fails to lay down rules but that in principle she could not do so. This is because the concept of a rule only makes sense where there is a practice of following the rule and a practice is necessarily public, something which more than one person might in principle engage in. Contingently there may be only one person in the practice and its rules may be known to her alone, but unless others can in principle learn the rules, there is no basis for saying that the individual is following a rule rather than just doing what seems right to her at the time. The point is that, without publicly checkable procedures, she cannot distinguish between following the rule and merely thinking she is following the rule. Since this is so, all her supposed private rule-following can amount to is doing whatever seems right to her at the time. By contrast, where we can properly speak of rule-following, there are established ways of determining whether or not something is in accordance with the rule. These procedures create the logical scope for distinguishing between the individual thinking she is following the rule and her actually doing so. For the private linguist, no such distinction is possible, so that whatever mental feats she may perform, her would-be ostensive definitions cannot fulfil their function. As Wittgenstein puts it in his lectures,

> Nothing I can do in myself can make it a rule. Perhaps if I concentrated my attention, I'd sooner learn some sort of rule. But if it were a private *rule* it would have to be public. Being a rule means being an instrument that is checkable, and by an agreed technique. (*WLPP*, p. 247)

To reinforce this argument, let us consider the private linguist's case in more detail. Suppose she claims to have set up rules which give her a 'subjective justification' for using the word S as she does. She might, for example, claim that she has some sort of table (or dictionary) in her imagination and that when she believes she is experiencing S, she compares the sensation with her memory of sensation S and applies the word when the two are the same. But how can she determine whether or not she is remembering S correctly? In other words, how can she distinguish between the 'comparison' showing the two are in fact the same and her simply believing that this is what the comparison shows? When the private linguist says 'I believe it is S again', one might reply 'Perhaps you only believe you believe it' (*PI*, para. 260). Since neither she nor we can check the supposed justificatory process, it makes no sense to treat it as a justificatory process at all. Instead of a process of independent verification, all we have is a procedure whereby if the private linguist says it is justified, it is and if not, not. At the end of the comparison, the private linguist is exactly where she started, for all she is left with is her inclination to say that she was again experiencing S. Since the supposed 'justification' is on exactly the same level as the initial impression, it is a sham; it is 'as if someone were to buy several copies of the morning newspaper to assure himself that what it said was true' (*PI*, para. 265).

What is misleading here is the idea of a subjective justification, the notion that the individual can establish the correctness of her judgement by, for example, consulting a table in her imagination. As Wittgenstein points out, however, a check in the imagination is not a real check because it does not actually involve appealing to something independent. It might be compared to testing the structure of a bridge by imagining it being subjected to increasingly heavy weights. This might be called testing the bridge in one's imagination but it would not justify a particular choice of dimensions, for the imaginative exercise does absolutely nothing to show the bridge will actually hold up. Like the private linguist's ostensive definition, the imaginative exercise is modelled on a real activity and uses its vocabulary; the difference, however, is that it does not have the same consequences. It is like one hand trying to give the other money.

> My right hand can write a deed of gift and my left hand a receipt. – But the further practical consequences would not be those of a gift. When the left hand has taken the money from

> the right, etc., we shall ask: 'Well, and what of it?' And the
> same could be asked if a person had given himself a private
> definition of a word, I mean, if he has said the word to himself
> and at the same time has directed his attention to a sensation.
> (*PI*, para. 268)

The private linguist apes the process of ostensive definition but
does so in the absence of the context which gives that process its
sense. She claims to be laying down rules and setting up a
practice, but no rules are actually specified and, if she tries to
check her 'rule-following', the only answer she can ever get is 'if
you think you're right, you're right, and if not, not'.

All this would seem to show that the sign S is useless. From the
start, it was clear that it cannot be used to communicate, for *ex
hypothesi* others cannot understand it. Furthermore, we have
seen that it cannot even be of use to the private linguist herself,
for she cannot distinguish between being inclined to apply it and
being justified in applying it. Suppose, however, that we did
discover a use for it. We might, for example, discover a correlation between the individual saying 'I'm experiencing S again'
and a rise in her blood pressure. This would be useful insofar as
it would enable us to tell that the individual's blood pressure was
rising without using any apparatus. The key point, however, is
that it would make no difference whether or not the individual
was correct in thinking she recognized the sensation. What we
would actually have correlated with the rise in blood pressure is
the individual's saying (or being inclined to say) 'I'm experiencing S again'. In a sense therefore it does not matter whether the
sensation is the same or not. Or more accurately, since the only
criterion for the occurrence of the sensation is what the
individual says, the only possible grounds for calling it the same
are the individual herself saying so. Thus where the sign S does
have a use, this is not because it refers to a private event, indeed,
the latter plays absolutely no role in the language-game, it is 'a
mere ornament, not connected with the mechanism at all' (*PI*,
para. 270). The relationship between the sign and the sensation
is quite different from what the private linguist imagined; rather
than marking the occurrence of an inner event, use of the sign is
in fact the only basis for our talk of a particular inner event
having occurred.

The above line of thought is summarised in Wittgenstein's famous beetle in the box argument. There Wittgenstein notes that, since the inner object is in principle inaccessible to others, there is no way of knowing that two people are experiencing the same thing. Consequently, if we accepted the private linguist's account, we would have to admit that 'pain' might refer to a something different in each person. However, if others can never know the object to which the name supposedly refers, then the use of the word cannot involve reference to that object. In that case, however, the whole idea of the private object drops out of consideration.

> Suppose everyone had a box with something in it: we call it a 'beetle'. No one can look into anyone else's box, and everyone says he knows what a beetle is only by looking at *his* beetle. – Here it would be quite possible for everyone to have something different in his box. One might even imagine such a thing constantly changing. – But suppose the word 'beetle' had a use in these people's language? If so it would not be used as the name of a thing. The thing in the box has no place in the language-game at all, not even as a *something*: for the box might be empty. No, one can 'divide through' by the thing in the box; it cancels out, whatever it is. (*PI*, para. 293)

Thus the idea that the word designates a private inner object is empty: if our sensation words have a use, they must function in some other way than the private linguist imagines.

As the above arguments illustrate, Wittgenstein's attack on the private linguist has various elements; to illuminate their interrelation, he compares the notion of a private ostensive definition with a design for a motor he was once shown (*RPP1*, para. 397). According to this design, the motor would be located inside a hollow roller with both its crankshaft and its cylinder attached to the wall of the roller. At first glance the construction seems possible, but as Wittgenstein points out 'it is a rigid system and the piston cannot move to and fro in the cylinder. Unwittingly we have deprived it of all movement' (*Z*, para. 248). There are, however, two ways of seeing the fault in the construction. The direct way is to note that the cylinder could be rolled from outside regardless of whether or not the 'motor' was running.

The indirect way is to notice that the device is a rigid construction and not a motor at all. Similarly there are two ways of recognising the error in the idea of a private ostensive definition. The direct method is to note, as in the beetle in the box argument, that private objects are irrelevant to our use of sensation words. As far as our actual use is concerned, the private inner object could be present, absent or constantly changing, it would make no difference; the only thing that can play a role in our language-game is what is accessible to us and that is the individual's utterances. The indirect way of seeing what is wrong with the idea of private ostensive definition is to realise that it is not in fact a definition at all; the connection between the word and its purported referent is rigid, for the criterion for S having occurred is that the private linguist believes it has occurred. The private inner object is an illusion. S does not refer to an independent entity; rather it is the use of S that provides the criterion for saying that a specific experience has occurred.

Wittgenstein's investigation of the concept of a private language shows why our traditional approach to the Inner won't work; however, it also contains the seeds of a more fruitful approach. As we saw, the first objection to the private linguist's account of sensation language is that it rules out the possibility of communication; the natural starting point therefore in the search for an alternative to it is to ask how it is that we actually can talk about sensations. Take pain words as an example. How do we learn to use these? According to Wittgenstein, we learn them against the background of certain instinctive types of behaviour. The words

> are connected with the primitive, the natural, expression of the sensation and used in their place. A child has hurt himself and he cries; and then adults talk to him and teach him exclamations and, later, sentences. They teach the child new pain-behaviour. (*PI*, para. 244)

The important point here is that from the first there is a connection between the inner experience and its outer expression. Without this connection, there would be no way of bringing language and the experience into relation with each other. We could not, for example, learn pain words by guessing which of the inner processes connected with falling down they refer to; 'for in that case this problem might arise as well: on account of which of my sensations do I cry out when I injure myself?' (*RPP1*, para. 305). In fact, what happens is that the child behaves in a particular way and on this basis is taught to say it is in pain. In this way, a verbal component is added to its behaviour, and later this component itself is developed into more complex language-games of pain-expression. From 'it hurts', the child moves on to expressions such as 'My foot hurts' or 'I have a stabbing pain in the back of my ankle'. Later still, the concept of pain is extended to the non-physical, so that the individual can, for example, describe her pain by saying that she feels as if she has lost all that was most precious to her. As Wittgenstein emphasises, however, to recognise the origins of the language-game is not to embrace behaviourism. ' "So, you are saying that the word 'pain' really means crying?" – On the contrary: the verbal expression of pain replaces crying and does not describe it' (ibid.). Although the outer expression provides the basis for the language-game of the Inner, the essence of that language-game is that it's not a language-game about behaviour.

These comments bring out the special role language plays in relation to the Inner. In this context, use of a word does not involve learning rules; rather it builds on a natural reaction. The individual does not apply the word on the basis of criteria, but applies it on the basis of having been taught to use it on the appropriate occasion. Mistaken use of an expression is akin not to the misapplication of a rule but to the inappropriate use of a signal. What is striking, however, is that we do not just use pre-ordained signals, but go on spontaneously to develop new possibilities of self-expression. For example, the individual takes the word 'throbbing' which was originally used in connection with something that can be seen to be pulsating and uses it to describe her pain even when no pulsating motion is visible. Here the relationship between the words and what they refer to is quite different from in the case of an outer description. In this case the relationship is criterial: the individual's pain is characterised as being of a particular type because of the words she uses, and the words she uses are the 'right' ones because she endorses them as such.[4]

These points underline, on the one hand, the importance of utterances and, on the other hand, their difference from statements based on observation. One consequence of this is that while there are criteria for the individual saying someone else is in pain, there are no such criteria in her own case. If one person says another is in pain, she can typically support his statement by pointing to aspects of the other person's behaviour which are accepted as criteria for pain. In her own case, however, she does not observe something which then leads her to say she is pain nor can she justify this statement by pointing to evidence for it. Instead she simply repeats an expression she has been taught or spontaneously develops a new one of her own. This does not mean, however, that she can use words completely arbitrarily. If someone says 'I'm in pain' and yet is obviously enjoying herself, she will taken to have misunderstood the meaning of the sign she is using. The same is true if she claims to have a dull continuous pain, when her features are periodically distorted with spasms of agony.

As the example of pain utterances illustrates, the individual's use of an expression is not the end of the language-game but its beginning (*PI*, para. 290). Whereas initially her pain-behaviour consisted simply of crying, etc., it now has a verbal component and this can itself become the basis of ever more sophisticated language-games. Once pain has a verbal expression, new options open up to the individual, new types of 'pain-behaviour' become possible. For example, the individual may specify the nature of her pain, characterising it as a throb, a dull ache, repeated stabs of pain or whatever. Other more elaborate statements are also possible; for example, the individual may say she feels as if she had a knife in her ribs. Such examples are particularly interesting, for, although the person concerned may never have experienced what it is really like when this happens, the phrase may still give expression to her pain, and it may give others an idea of what she is feeling even if they too have never had the misfortune of a knife wound. What is also striking is that here the individual's use of language is not rule-governed. The individual learns a word and then combines it with others in a new apparently arbitrary way; mysteriously, however, other people are still able 'to understand what she means'.

Our ability to use language in this way is an unexplored

26

philosophical puzzle and we shall return to it in more detail in Chapter 4. For the moment, however, there are several important points to note. The first is that our use of language to express the Inner presupposes certain natural reactions which we share. The reaction may involve behaving in a certain way and in a particular context (e.g. crying when hurt) or it may involve putting together words and phrases in new ways; in either case, however, using language does not involve applying pre-given rules. The individual does not connect up her experience and her words, and, if she had to, one might ask how she knows that the words she uses are indeed the right ones to express what she feels. The point, however, is that the content of what she feels is given by her words; there is no need to make a connection between the two because the one is the criterion of the other.[5] The second key point is that language extends the individual's possibilities of expression and hence her possibilities of experience. A dog, for example, cannot hope that its dinner will be served punctually at nine o'clock nor can it be appalled at the outrageously kitsch decoration on its bowl. To have these experiences, one must be able to speak. Thus it is through the acquisition of language that the individual acquires more complex possibilities of expression and hence the possibility of a more complicated inner life. Only as her 'behaviour' develops do certain concepts (and certain experiences) become accessible to her. While an adult can experience the tragedy or the irony of a particular situation, a child cannot.

This approach to the Inner involves a completely new way of understanding our psychological concepts. It also involves rejecting the confusing picture which treats the Inner as though it were a substance whose changes, states and motions the individual observes and reports on. In contrast, Wittgenstein's approach emphasises that what interests us is the attitudes and behaviour of human beings. The pain-behaviour of others, for example, matters to us, and it is on this basis that the language-game is built up. What happens is that the individual reacts in a certain way (e.g. cries after falling over) and we teach her to use a linguistic expression. We call the words she then uses 'sensation words' because of the type of basis they have and because of their role in the language-game. 'Primitive pain-behaviour is a sensation-behaviour; it gets replaced by a linguistic expression. "The word 'pain' is the name of a sensation" is equivalent to "I've got a pain" is an expression [Aeusserung] of sensation' (*RPP1*, para. 313). Wittgenstein's emphasis on behaviour should not, however, be seen as a form of behaviourism. On the contrary, the concept of the Inner expresses the distinctive nature of our interest in human beings. The whole point is that we do not treat each other as bodies which happen to behave in particular ways but as conscious individuals who act. The notion of the Inner does not refer to some separate reality but expresses our relation to each other and a particular way of understanding human action. Our interest in others is expressed as an interest in 'what is going on inside them'.[6] When doing philosophy, however, we misinterpret this picture and are left struggling with the confused idea that what is essential to pain is a mysterious and private inner event. Against this, Wittgenstein urges us to recognize that we are interested in people's utterances not as reports on mysterious occurrences about which we are for some reason curious, but as expressions of what the individuals concerned feel. We are interested in them not because they are accurate reports on inner processes but because they are what the individuals are inclined to say.

To reinforce these points and to encourage us to change the way we think about the Inner, Wittgenstein introduces the idea of the soulless tribe. The purpose of this idea is to show that the usefulness of psychological concepts is not dependent on their referring to some kind of inner reality. Suppose, for example, that we conquered a race and for whatever reason maintained that its members had no inner life. We treat this claim as an accepted fact and laugh at anyone who holds otherwise; the suggestion that anything goes on inside these people is treated as we treat the idea that a stone might be in pain. Despite this, we still want these people to work for us and are interested in various aspects of their behaviour. We might therefore teach them concepts similar to our psychological concepts despite believing that nothing 'went on inside' them. Take the case of depression.

> I'm interested in that in the slaves. It's important that he can say 'I'm depressed': he won't work well. (So) I teach him to

give me a signal from which I can predict his behaviour. I observe his behaviour and predict. Then I can teach him to signal for me so then I can predict – but he does it *without observing himself*. I, in my observations of him, single out 'He bares his teeth' or 'He waves his arms' or 'He gets red in the face'. For a purpose I group behaviour which offhand differs, and I distinguish behaviour which offhand looks alike – you go by what follows, e.g. he bares his teeth in rage, in friendship, to clean them. (*WLPP*, p. 281)

Here the idea of depression as a private inner state is treated as irrelevant. What is important is that we have a practical interest in how the individual acts and on this basis pick out certain types of behaviour in particular contexts. We then teach the individual to use a particular signal on that occasion. However, what unites these occasions is not some inner event; rather the signal is fashioned for certain practical purposes and it is our interest in the individual that determines how different types of behaviour are classified. Thus different actions are treated as the same (e.g. shaking one's fist and stamping one's foot), while what is apparently the same is treated as different (e.g. baring one's teeth in anger and smiling).

The signal for depression is not of course the only signal we might teach these people. For example, we could teach them a signal for pain and it might then be useful to develop this signal by incorporating into it reference to a particular part of the body. Learning the new signal would not involve connecting a phrase up to a specific inner feeling; rather the phrase would be taught as a substitute or extension of the slave's reaction of clasping her foot when it has been injured. If they lacked this sort of reaction, we might simply encourage them to name a part of the body 'at random' and, if it turned out to be the case that the named part was often the part which was malfunctioning from a medical point of view, we might use this as the basis for talk of pain location. From the traditional perspective, this presents matters precisely the wrong way round, for the natural inclination is to treat the individual's reaction of clasping her foot as based on knowledge of where the pain is. But in what sense does the individual know where her pain is? Although this looks like an empiricial claim, it is actually conceptual, for the point is that the basis for ascribing a location to pain is what the individual says. If she says her hand hurts, then the pain is in her hand even if the doctor tells us that the cause of her suffering is a nerve trapped in the neck. One factor that obscures this point is the fact that the area we say is painful often turns out medically to be the part of the body where something is going wrong. However, even with us this is not always the case. Furthermore, where there is a discrepancy, we treat the individual, not the doctor, as the authority on where the pain is located. It is conceivable, however, that other people should have a different conception. For example, there could be people who feel pain (and different types of pain) but who never speak of pain in relation to a particular part of the body. If asked where they feel pain, they stare blankly or reply 'How can we know where the pain is? Only the doctor can discover that'.

The reference to a location constitutes an important difference between the pain-signal and the depression-signal; it would be wrong, however, to infer that depression is simply a non-localised form of pain. This claim makes the two signals look alike but at the expense of ignoring the essential differences between them. The point is that when one of the slaves gives a pain-signal, 'I do something to a part of his body. A depression signal is given and what I do is different (and it doesn't go with bodily signs, i.e. with bodily signs which can be opposed to other bodily signs)' (*WLPP*, p. 282). What matters are the differences between the signals – their different functions and consequences. Assimilating them blurs the categorial differences and only serves to introduce a superficial, and hence confusing, unity. As well as the signals for pain and depression, there are others we might teach the tribe. For instance, it might be useful if the slave could be taught to say what she is about to do before doing it, e.g. to say 'throw' before throwing. On the basis of this, we might teach her to say 'I'm about to throw' or 'I intend to throw'. We would also be interested in the needs and desires of these people for these too might affect their work. We might therefore teach them to say 'I want food' or 'I want to drink'. Thus we would have four types of signal, each with its own function and interest.

(A) A word like 'pain' used in connection with some part of the body, usually a hurt part. This goes with medicine for the part, anaesthetics, etc. (B) 'Depression'. I expect bad work, but I don't, e.g. do anything to his eyes if he weeps. (C) 'Wish' – used with the names of food, etc. This goes with giving him 'what he wants', etc. (D) 'Intention' – with a verb of action which I then expect. (*WLPP*, p. 40)

The interesting feature of these signals is that none of them makes any reference to something going on inside the members of the tribe. Furthermore, our teaching of these signals leaves no scope for the suggestion that there is something in common to all cases, viz. an experience. On the contrary, what is striking is the diversity of uses the signals have. What would happen then if we suddenly introduced the Inner/Outer picture? The main effect would be to obscure the differences between the signals by making all the utterances look alike.

> The picture has a sort of equalizing influence. We are now to say that the man when he gives those various signals is simply observing various phenomena. When we treated them simply as signals they seemed to have nothing in common.
>
> (ibid., p. 41)

Against this, one might want to object that there is surely a truth of the matter and that the picture of the Inner captures what really goes on. For example, in the case of intention, it might be argued that when one of the slaves has an intention, something must surely happen inside her. But who says anything happens? The signal was not taught as a signal that something was happening inside her, indeed, the whole game with the signal makes no reference to any happening – it is as if one were to ask what happens when grass is green or 2 + 2 = 4. In fact, nothing can force us to say that something is going on inside these people; the signals we have taught them are perfectly comprehensible without any reference to the notion of an Inner.

One difficulty here is that lying seems to make reference to an inner state essential, otherwise it seems there is no way of distinguishing between false claims to be in pain and genuine ones. However, this doesn't follow, for if these people say they are in pain when they are not, we shall simply conclude 'that sometimes they give pain signals without all the appropriate antecedents and consequents' (ibid., p. 283). The basis of the distinction between feigned and genuine pain is whether or not the signal is embedded in the appropriate type of behaviour. For example, we would talk of feigned pain where members of the tribe say they are in pain when an unpleasant task needs doing but 'miraculously' recover when lighter chores are at hand. Similarly we should treat their behaviour as non-genuine when threats or incentives are sufficient to make them work quite normally. Thus we would have no problem distinguishing between feigned (or merely apparent) pain-behaviour and genuine pain-behaviour, and the basis of our distinction would not be the occurrence or non-occurrence of a particular inner phenomenon.

The purpose behind all this talk of the soulless tribe is not to suggest that we might one day come across such people, but to show that our psychological concepts could be seen and treated in a very different way. What would happen, though, if the members of the tribe themselves spontaneously began to use the Inner/Outer picture? Suppose they began to talk of things going on inside them, would we have to believe them? Here, as in the case of calculating in the head, nothing could compel us to say they have an Inner or a soul. We might treat their claim to have experiences as a joke, like a parrot saying 'I love you' or 'I've got a headache'. The more important question, however, is what would be involved in treating them as having souls. This raises the fundamental issue of the basis and significance of our picture of the Inner and we shall tackle this issue in Chapter 6. So far, however, our aim has simply been to outline the problem of the Inner and sketch Wittgenstein's solution to it. That solution doesn't involve rejecting the Inner, or indeed our picture of the Inner: all it rejects is a confused interpretation of that picture. The force of Wittgenstein's claims is to call for a radical rethinking of our approach to the Inner without suggesting that talk of the Inner is an illusion or error. In the rest of this book, we shall examine what this implies for our understanding of various aspects of the mind and consciousness, and in the course of doing this, we shall also explore the basis and significance of the Inner/Outer picture itself.

THE WORLD OF THE SENSES

What actually is the '*world*' of consciousness? There I'd like to
say: 'What goes on in my mind, what's going on in it now,
what I see, hear. . . .' Couldn't we simplify that and say 'What
I am now seeing'? (*LW2*, p. 95)

Wittgenstein's arguments on privacy show that a reassessment of
our approach to the Inner is necessary; however, the attempt to
carry out this task clashes with some of our deepest philosophical
prejudices. The main source of resistance is the feeling that
Wittgenstein's approach denies the essence of our experience.
The notion of consciousness, for example, seems to force the idea
of privacy upon us, for the natural way to view it is as an inner
realm made up of a continuous succession of private experiences.
On this approach, the difference between the various psychological concepts is that each corresponds to a different 'content of
consciousness'. But what does this actually mean? If we consider
specific cases, the idea of a content of consciousness suddenly
seems less plausible. Take belief, for example. What is the
content of consciousness when someone believes something? The
natural suggestion is that believing something involves having a
mental image which corresponds to the belief. The problem,
however, is that images are often ambiguous, and with some
beliefs it is far from clear what image would correspond to them.
The alternative suggestion that the proposition itself is present to
the mind is just as unclear. Indeed, it is hard to see how we could
explain what being present to the mind means without recourse
to the notion of an image, and yet believing that the earth is

round does not involve constantly having a image of this proposition nor occasionally having one.

The example of belief shows both that the idea of a content of consciousness is far from clear and that the most obvious candidate for such a content is an image. In fact, the notion of an image exercises a pervasive influence over our understanding of consciousness and has dominated philosophical thinking about it since the beginning of modern philosophy. When Hume, for example, divides experience into ideas and impressions, he takes the example of the mental image as his model for an impression and treats ideas as copies of these impressions. In this way, sense-impressions, and more particularly visual sense-impressions, come to be treated as the paradigm of inner experience. What lies behind the idea of consciousness as a succession of experiences is the idea of a succession of images; in its essence, the inner realm is a realm of pictures, real and imagined – the world of consciousness is a space peopled with impressions (*RPP1*, para. 720). The best way therefore to explore the notion of consciousness is to examine the idea of sense-impressions and in particular the concept of vision. This will enable us to confront the suggestion that Wittgenstein is denying a key aspect of our experience and by demystifying the notion of consciousness will show how the concept of the Inner can be treated in a clear but non-reductive way.

So what do we experience when we see something? What does seeing 'consist in'? The natural answer is to say it consists in being aware of a series of inner pictures and that these pictures are created in us by objects in the outside world. Presented in this way, vision seems straightforward, but, when one tries to think through this account, a multitude of problems arise. Even the fact that we see with two eyes creates difficulties, for surely we should experience two visual impressions each slightly different from the other (*RPP1*, para. 952)? Furthermore, how is that when we describe our visual impression we leave out the edges of the visual field (*RPP1*, para. 1094)? If visual experience did consist of inner pictures created in us by outer objects, what we really ought to see is a two-fold image surrounded by darkness corresponding to the edges of our eye sockets. Plainly, however, that's not how it is. These initial difficulties lead on to other more fundamental problems, for in some circumstances there may be a tension between the individual's account of her experience and an account in terms of sense-impressions. For example, someone may describe the colour of the table in front of her as brown despite the fact that a variety of colours are reflected in its shiny surface. In such cases, what should we say about her sense impressions, that they were multi-coloured or that they were uniform? Similarly, what should we say if she describes the wall in front of her as uniformly yellow despite the fact that it is partly in shadow and so looks almost grey? 'Am I to say, [she sees] a uniformly yellow surface, which admittedly is irregularly shadowed? Or: yellow and grey patches?' (*RPP1*, para. 442). This sort of difficulty goes to the heart of the inner picture approach, for it brings out a tension between the inner picture as embodiment of the individual's experience and the idea that it is a replica of the outer object. Furthermore, the difficulty cannot be avoided by saying that the individual had the relevant sense-impressions unconsciously, for the whole point of sense-impressions is that they are the constituents of the individual's experience, hence they only exist insofar as the individual is aware of them.

Further problems with the inner picture account arise if one considers the notion of a visual impression. For example, the way our gaze wanders over a scene may be crucial to the impression it makes on us and yet this effect cannot be captured in a picture and therefore not in an inner picture either. Again this difficulty is critical, for how can there be aspects of visual experience which defy representation in terms of the content of that experience? And yet, there are many cases where it would be impossible for an inner picture to capture our visual experience. For example, no picture could capture the experience of watching a fast-running river, for even a film of what the individual saw might fail to capture the particular impression (menacing, exhilarating or whatever) that the rushing water made on her (*RPP1*, para. 1080). These examples show that there are cases where our impression cannot be captured in a picture, but there are also other difficulties, for even when impression can be represented in a picture, there may be no one picture that corresponds to it. For example, after glancing at another person, an individual will generally be unable to describe the location of each hair on the other person's head (*WLPP*, pp. 110–11). She might therefore accept various slightly different pictures as representing what she saw. In that case, however, which of these corresponds to her inner picture? And how should we describe that picture? It would seem odd to say that it was blurred and yet the alternative is also ruled out, for, just as it makes no sense to talk of an unconscious sense-impression, so too we cannot claim that there was a definite picture but one the individual cannot specify. For similar reasons, the possibility of misperception also creates difficulties. Suppose someone mistakenly reports that she saw four people standing in a group when in fact there were three. What should we say of her inner picture that it contains three people or four? If we say three, the inner picture won't correspond to her visual experience and, if we say four, it won't correspond to the visual reality.[1]

The various phenomena associated with aspect perception create similar problems. Indeed, even the quite simple case of seeing a piece of writing raises difficulties, for in such cases what should we say about the visual impressions of those who can read as opposed to those who can't? The two groups of people certainly describe what they see differently, so presumably their inner pictures are different and yet this clashes with the fact that they are replicas of the same object. Furthermore, even if the impressions are different, how can this be expressed in terms of their supposed content, the inner picture? For example, how could a picture represent the fact that one person saw (and read) the word 'Wittgenstein', while the other saw a strange sequence of black marks? More elaborate cases of seeing an aspect under-line these problems. Take the case of the duck–rabbit figure. This ambiguous drawing can be seen either as a duck or as a rabbit, so two people could be looking at it and one could say she was seeing a rabbit, the other a duck. How can these different visual experiences be represented in terms of the inner picture each sees? On the one hand, the inner pictures must differ, since the experiences are different. On the other hand, they must be the same, since they are copies of the same object. Similar problems arise when the aspect changes, for what should we say then? The essence of aspect perception is that what is seen (the duck–rabbit picture) remains the same while the individual's visual exper-ience changes. But, if this change corresponds to a change in the inner picture, what does this change consist in? And how does the new picture relate, first, to the previous one and, second, to the unchanged outer picture?

As these examples show, vision is by no means as straightforward as it seems, and, far from constituting an indisputable model of it, the inner picture account only serves to generate puzzles of its own. Paradoxically, the conception of consciousness as a series of inner pictures does not work even for the area from which it was drawn. It would be wrong, however, to think that science might provide the solution to our difficulties. The problem in trying to understand both consciousness and vision is not that we lack information, but that we cannot organise the information we already possess. For example, in the case of seeing, we offer an account (the inner picture model) which is both internally incoherent and at variance with the way we actually use the concept. Further scientific discoveries about what happens when we see may explain various aspects of our visual ability (e.g. why certain illusions fool us and others don't), but they cannot tell us anything about our visual experience itself, for *ex hypothesi* what we do not already know cannot be part of our experience. For example, the fact that the retinal image is upside down does not show that what we really see are upside-down images, for, whatever the mechanics of the eye, our experience is of a world the right way up. Thus the scientific and the conceptual tasks are distinct. The philosophical problem centres on the concept of seeing and on the paradox that we use this concept and yet cannot give a coherent account of it. The solution is to attain an *Uebersicht* or overview of the concept; as we shall see, this involves adopting a new approach to the Inner and abandoning the picture of consciousness as a cinema of the senses.

To clarify the concept of seeing, Wittgenstein focuses on the phenomenon of seeing aspects, for it is here that various problems about vision come to a head. He introduces the topic by noting that, if someone is asked what she sees, her response can be of two kinds. On the one hand, she may simply say 'I see *this*' and offer a description, drawing or copy to illustrate what she sees. On the other hand, she may say 'I see a likeness between these two faces' and in this case there will be no drawing that corresponds to the likeness, nor will she necessarily be able to offer a further description. As these differences indicate, the word 'see' can be used in two ways, and in each case the object of vision ('what is seen') belongs to a different category (*PI*, p. 193). The second case, however, seems paradoxical, for someone may see the two faces (and be able to copy them) and yet not notice their similarity. Furthermore, when she notices the similarity, she may be said to have a new visual experience and yet the source of her experience won't have changed. How then should we understand this second type of seeing? And how is it related to the first?

To answer these questions, Wittgenstein examines the phenomenon of aspect perception; in particular, he considers our reaction to pictures such as the one below.

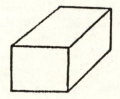

As he notes, this picture could be interpreted in a variety of ways, e.g. as a glass cube, as an inverted open box, as a wire frame, as three boards forming a solid angle, etc. However, not only can we interpret the picture in several ways, we actually claim to see it a different way in each case (*PI*, p. 193). This suggestion seems to introduce a foreign element into our visual experience; the interpretation seems an idea rather than a perception. We may therefore be inclined to claim that the interpretation is an indirect description of our experience. But what is the direct description? It seems there is none. Suppose we argue instead that there are a number of visual experiences and that each corresponds to a way of seeing the picture and hence favours a particular interpretation (*RPP1*, para. 9). This would seem to explain why the individual invokes the interpretation in describing her experience. But what does it mean to say the experience favours a particular interpretation? And, crucially, how is that experience identified? The problem is that once the interpretation is treated as external to the experience, we lack any criterion to justify our talk of different visual experiences. This is important, for it shows that, far from being an indirect expression of the experience, the reference to an interpretation is essential: 'the inclination to use that form of verbal expression is a characteristic utterance [*Aeusserung*] of the experience' (ibid., para. 13). The experience of seeing the figure as an inverted cube is characterised by the individual saying 'I'm now seeing the figure as an inverted cube'.

Having made that point, however, aspect perception still looks extremely puzzling; for how can the individual's visual experience change, while its object remains the same? One tempting explanation is that what we see remains the same, but our interpretation of it changes. Unfortunately, as the example of the duck–rabbit figure illustrates, this approach cannot work.

This figure can be seen either as a duck or as a rabbit. Someone who has only ever seen it in its rabbit aspect will simply treat it as a picture of a rabbit; asked what it represents, she will point to other pictures of rabbits or to real rabbits or she might even imitate a rabbit. What she won't say, however, is 'Now I am seeing the picture as a rabbit'; instead she will simply report her perception in the normal way. The difficulties of aspect perception only arise either if someone who is familiar with both aspects says 'She sees the picture as a rabbit' or if the individual herself suddenly sees the other aspect and says 'Now it looks quite different, now it's a duck!' The essence of this latter phenomenon is that the individual has a new visual impression despite the object before her remaining unchanged. It is tempting therefore to claim that what changes is the individual's interpretation of her experience, but this suggestion won't work, for the grammar of seeing as is quite different from that of interpreting. In particular, seeing a picture in a certain way is a state and has the same kind of duration as seeing itself. It makes sense, for example, for someone to say 'I looked at the picture for five minutes and saw it as a duck for the first minute, then as a rabbit for about a minute and a half and then as a duck for the rest of the time'. In contrast to this, interpreting is an action and involves using the picture in some way, e.g. taking it for a particular character in a sign language. For this reason, it has a quite different kind of duration. If someone said 'For five minutes, I interpreted the picture as a duck, then I started to interpret it as a rabbit', we could only understand her as meaning that she spent five minutes trying to apply it one way, then switched to the other. This brings out a further difference between seeing as and interpreting, for an interpretation is a hypothesis and may turn out to be wrong. For example, in a picture-language message we might interpret the duck–rabbit as a duck when it was intended to represent a rabbit and so misunderstand the message. With seeing as, however, there is no hypothesis and hence no possibility of error. When someone says 'Now I am seeing it as a rabbit', her statement is no more capable of being wrong than the statement 'Now I am seeing red'. Thus in several important respects aspect perception shares the grammar of vision. Like seeing, it is a state and has continuous duration. Furthermore, as with other perceptual utterances, the utterances which characterise it are immediate expressions of experience not capable of being right or wrong.[2]

These points suggest that aspect perception is not a case of interpreting, but in that case how should it be characterised? As we have seen, the first thing that draws our attention to this phenomenon is the experience of aspect-dawning. This is the reaction of surprise characterised by the individual explaining that it is as though she had seen something new without what she is looking at having changed. For example, she says 'It's the same picture, but now it looks completely different' or 'Now it's a duck, before it was a rabbit'. These utterances are paradoxical insofar as they seem to express both a new perception and a recognition that the the object of perception (and in a sense the perception itself) is unchanged. Together these features distinguish aspect perception both from genuine perception and from hallucination. Despite having the same form as perceptual reports, the utterances used in aspect perception do not report a change in the outside world; rather, as the word 'now' indicates, what is elsewhere the report of a perception is here the expression of an experience. Furthermore, the experience ushers in a state which can endure. As Wittgenstein puts it, the interpretation strikes the individual and she clothes the figure with it (*RPP1*, para. 33). Aspect perception can therefore be seen as consisting of two related phenomena – the phenomenon of aspect-dawning and that of continuous aspect perception. Of the two, it is the latter that is the more important, for if we can grasp what is involved in seeing an aspect, there should be no difficulty in understanding what happens when the aspect changes.

If we try to understand these phenomena in terms of an inner picture, we rapidly run into problems. Suppose, for example, we try to explain the change of aspect by saying that the inner picture depicts first a duck then a rabbit. This captures the sense in which the individual sees something new, but at the price of ignoring the sense in which what she sees stays the same. Furthermore, it is far from clear what it actually means, for what is the difference between the inner picture when it depicts the duck and when it depicts the rabbit? In fact, the demands being made on it are contradictory, for the picture before the change must differ from the picture after and yet both must correspond to the original drawing. What this brings out, however, is the underlying incoherence of the inner picture approach. The problem is that the inner picture is modelled on the concept of an outer picture and yet also contains elements from a totally different domain. 'This makes this object into a chimera; a queerly shifting construction. For the similarity to a picture is now impaired' (*PI*, p. 196). This comes out most clearly in the case of aspect perception, for there the inner picture is supposed to represent both the drawing itself and the various ways of seeing that drawing. However, these two elements belong to quite different categories, and while the colours and shapes of what is being seen can be captured in a picture, the aspect under which it is being seen cannot. Thus aspect perception forces us to abandon the idea of an inner picture, and, as well as raising puzzles on its own account, it makes us reconsider the concept of seeing itself.

How then should seeing as be understood? Here Wittgenstein takes as his starting point a simple drawing which can be seen in a wide variety of ways.

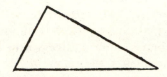

As he points out, this can be seen as a triangular hole, as a solid, as a geometrical drawing, as standing on its base, as hanging from its apex, as a mountain, as a wedge, as an arrow, as a pointer, as an overturned object which is meant to stand on the shorter side of the right-angle, as a half-parallelogram and as various other things. So what should we make of this plethora of aspects? The first point is that the aspects we see are all aspects the figure might on some occasion have *permanently* in a picture (*PI*, p. 201). However, we don't simply recognise that the picture could be used to represent such-and-such a thing, rather we actually see it as that thing. So what does this distinction involve? The answer is a difference in the way we relate to the picture. Consider what someone who did not see aspects would be like. The aspect-blind person would see what we see in the sense of being able to describe (and copy) the geometrical properties of the picture, but *ex hypothesi* she would not claim to see it in a particular way. This suggests that the only difference between us and her is that we make certain utterances she doesn't. However, this difference itself shows that her whole relation to pictures is different from our own. As our utterances indicate, we stand towards pictures in some respects as we do towards the object they depict. For example, if a human face is depicted (even in a few bare strokes), we can study its expression and react to it as the expression of a human face. Rather than guessing what the picture might represent (or be used to represent), we relate directly and immediately to it. Furthermore, the directness of the relation implies a special sensitivity. A tiny change to the line of the mouth may totally alter the impression the picture makes upon us, and yet in geometrical terms the picture before and after the change will be essentially the same. What aspect perception brings out therefore is the special nature of our relation to pictures. The importance of aspect-dawning is that it draws attention to the wider phenomenon of continuous aspect perception. Against the background of the latter, the former loses its mystery, for the change of aspect in an ambiguous drawing is simply the correlate of the unchanged aspect in an unambiguous drawing.

So far we have argued that the key to continuous aspect perception is the idea that we relate to pictures in a different way than someone who does not see aspects, but what exactly does this mean? What are the signs that someone is relating to a picture in this way? In the case of ambiguous pictures, the individual's utterances are a key criteria, but, as the case of unambiguous pictures shows, these tie with other aspects of our reaction. Take the example of a picture of a cavalry charge.

> I see the picture of a horse: I know, not merely that it is a horse, but also that the horse is running. Thus I can understand the picture, not just *spatially*, but I also *know* what the horse is now about to do. Imagine someone seeing a picture of a cavalry charge but not knowing that the horses don't stay in their various places! (*RPP1*, para. 873)

The claim that we see the horses as running summarises our reaction. Furthermore, it does not simply mean that we know that the picture represents horses in motion. Rather 'one is trying to say something else. Imagine that someone reacted to such a picture by a movement of the hand and a shout of "Tally ho!" Doesn't that say roughly the same as: he sees the horse running?' (*RPP1*, para. 874). If we wanted to convey the impression the picture made upon us, a stuffed horse standing in a galloping position would be quite wrong; rather the best 'representation' would be a galloping horse itself. In our case, when we look at the picture, we do not simply note a pattern of shapes and colours; rather we relate to it as the representation of a specific object and treat it almost as if it really was the object it depicts.

Take another example. Suppose we are looking at a picture of a balloon floating up into the sky. If the picture is well executed, we might express our reaction by saying 'You can feel the lightness of the balloon. It's as if the next breath of wind will blow it right out of the picture.' This, and similar utterances, justify the claim that we see the balloon as floating rather than simply know that this is what it is supposed to represent. An aspect-blind person's reaction would be quite different. She would be just as aware as we are of the marks on the paper but *ex hypothesi* would relate to these simply as marks. For example, she would note the roughly circular object on the paper and might agree that it could represent a balloon but would add that it could also represent a thousand other things. Furthermore, she would not understand the idea that the picture might represent something independently of its having a certain use. In a sign language, the figure might represent a balloon, or in a diagram it might indicate the shape of a hole to be made, but on its own it would simply be a form of a particular kind. These examples illustrate the difference between our relation to pictures and that of the aspect-blind and in this way justify the claim that we see pictures differently from them. Furthermore, this account clarifies the phenomenon of aspect-dawning, for what happens there is that we relate to the picture first as one object, then as another.

The concept of aspect perception highlights a particular type of reaction, but one might ask why this reaction is so important? In what contexts does the ability to see aspects matter? The most obvious answer is aesthetics, for the basis of visual art is our ability to relate directly to visual representations. In fact, the concept of seeing aspects is important throughout the arts, for just as understanding a picture may involve seeing its elements in a certain way, so too appreciating a piece of music may involve hearing it in a certain way. In each case, the ability to see an aspect is crucial, for the absence of a direct response to the medium would abolish the very possibility of its artistic use. The aspect-blind person for whom a picture was simply an amalgam of shapes and colours would lack both the desire and the ability to participate in our artistic practices. Without the ability to see aspects, she would lack the kind of sensitivity on which visual art is based. Another rather different area where the ability to see aspects can be important is geometry, for understanding a proof may require the individual to see a diagram in a certain way. The point here is that understanding the diagram involves seeing it three-dimensionally, i.e. as though it were the object it represented. The demonstrations we use in geometry would be no use to someone unable to do this or to someone for whom the aspects continually changed.

Both of these examples come from fairly specialised contexts, but it would be wrong to limit seeing aspects to these areas. Pictures play an extensive role in our lives and the real importance of aspect perception is what it shows about our relation to pictures in general. Take the example of someone looking at a picture of an animal transfixed by an arrow. Here too our reaction – and our visual experience – is significantly different from that of the aspect-blind. If asked what we can see, we answer with a definite description ('it's a picture of an animal transfixed by an arrow'); by contrast, the aspect-blind would be indifferent between a variety of descriptions. The difference in response would also come out if we had to represent our visual experience. While we might get the length of the straight lines wrong or misrepresent the shape, our copy would always be similar to the original at least in one respect, viz. that it depicted a transfixed animal. Thus there are certain errors we would not make. With the aspect-blind person, however, errors would be random, i.e. unconnected with the 'sense' of the picture. Differences of this kind justify the claim that, while we see a picture of an arrow going through an animal, the aspect-blind person sees a pair of disconnected straight lines. The fact that we treat the picture as representing an animal transfixed by an arrow characterises our attitude to it, and this is the justification for calling it a case of seeing rather than simply knowing what the picture is supposed, or can be used, to represent.

Wittgenstein's analysis of aspect perception brings out the particular nature of our relation to pictures, but not all pictures have the same role in our lives. While we use some pictures as a means of conveying or recording information, there are others we enjoy even when they represent something that never occurred or never could occur. Here there is a contrast between our relation to working drawings (e.g. an engineer's blueprint) and our relation

45

to paintings. In the former case, there is generally no question of seeing as. Using such drawings may indeed involve a process of interpretation, a process of decoding the information contained in them. Here what is important is not what the individual experiences when looking at the drawing, but her ability to use it, e.g. to construct the object it depicts. With a painting, however, it is our reaction that matters; someone who simply knew what it represented but couldn't see it as representing the object in question would be unable to appreciate its artistic merit. These two types of case illustrate contrasting possible reactions to pictures and make clear that we do not have to assume that people will always relate to pictures as we do in the second case. If they do not, we shall expect different things from them. Not only will they talk about the picture in a different way from us, but pictures will play a different role in their lives. Thus talk of the inner experience of seeing aspects gets its point from the outer manifestations of that experience, from the particular reaction which justifies our saying that someone sees an aspect.

Having made these points, however, we have still not fully determined the concept of seeing as, for it is not clear what we should say about its duration. Even if we do relate to a portrait almost as if it were a living being, when do we do so and for how long? And in the case of an ambiguous picture surely we are aware of the aspect when it changes in a way we are not when we simply come across the picture in the normal course of events? For example, although it makes sense to say 'I now see the picture as a duck', it is less clear what would be meant by saying 'I have been seeing the picture as a duck continuously for the last half hour'. To justify the latter remark, we should have to think of the individual as continuously occupied with the picture, as it were, continuously meditating on its duck aspect. This problem does not arise with aspect-dawning, for the reaction of surprise locates the experience at a particular moment in time. By contrast, it is less clear what sort of duration concept we should use in relation to seeing as, for when someone sees a face as looking in a particular direction, 'what corresponds to the continuous seeing as – is that this description, without any variation, is the right one and *that* only means that the aspect does not change' (*RPP1*, para. 863). When the aspect dawns we experience it in an acute way, but 'in the chronic sense the aspect is only the kind of way in which we again and again treat the picture' (*RPP1*, para. 1022).

To complete our analysis of aspect perception, we can therefore make a further distinction and note that, although our relation to pictures is characterised by aspect perception, we are not always conscious of the aspect. In other words, the picture does not always 'live' for us. While there are some occasions on which we are immersed in a picture and its expression, there are others when the picture is in front of us but our mind is on other things. We might decide therefore to say that someone will only be said to be seeing a picture as the object it depicts when she is preoccupied with it, for it is the experience that occurs in this context that generally interests us. In the case of the duck–rabbit,

> one asks oneself: how can the eye – this *dot* – be looking in a direction? – *'See, it is looking!'* (And one 'looks' oneself as one says this.) But one does not say and do this the whole time one is looking at the picture. (*PI*, p. 205)

As this remark suggests, the question of duration can be used to make a further distinction within the category of aspect perception. We could, for example, distinguish between seeing as and regarding as. If we are asked to describe a picture, we will always answer in terms of the object it represents and hence in this sense we may be said always to regard it in this way. However, we are not continuously preoccupied with the picture and hence in that sense do not always see it as what it depicts.[3]

Having made these points, it is important to note that there are different types of aspect and hence different types of seeing as. For example, while it takes imagination to see a triangle as a piece of broken glass, none is need to see the aspects of figures such as the one below.

Here the aspects are purely optical. The change in aspect could be illustrated simply by pointing first to a black cross then to a white cross (or vice versa). Even someone lacking imagination or unfamiliar with the idea of using pictures as representations might be said to see an aspect of this kind. Another type of aspect perception which differs from both of the above is that involved in seeing the schematic cube as a cube, for there the aspect is three-dimensional, whereas with the double cross it is not. In the latter case, the experience does not have to be described as that of seeing a black cross against a white background, but could simply be expressed in terms of seeing a black cross and a white surrounding. Furthermore, the two aspects could be illustrated by painting crosses on a sheet of paper, i.e. in terms of a two-dimensional representation. By contrast, the experience of seeing the schematic cube as a cube can only be explained three-dimensionally, e.g. by pointing to a real cube.

The different types of aspect perception also have different kinds of prerequisite. For example, to be able to see the aspects of the duck–rabbit one must already be conversant with the shapes of these two animals. With the double-cross, there is no such condition. Similarly, to see one side of a triangle as the base, another as the apex, one must be well acquainted with these terms and have mastered the technique of applying them. In this case, the individual must possess certain abilities before she can be said to have a particular experience. The reason for this is that the criteria for saying she sees the triangle in this way are the fine shades of her behaviour in relation to triangle, i.e. her ability to make certain applications of the figure quite freely. Thus 'the substratum of this experience is mastery of a technique' (*PI*, p. 208). This may sound odd: how, one wants to ask, can mastery of a technique be a logical condition of having an experience? Certainly, no such condition is presupposed for someone to be able to have a toothache. All this means, however, is that we are not dealing with the same concept of experience here – rather it is a different though related concept (ibid.). Thus, not only does the notion of seeing aspects involve a modification of the concept of seeing, it also creates the possibility of experiences which belong to a different type from those we tend to consider fundamental. Rather than denying the possibility of such experiences, we should recognise that the concept of experience is much broader – and less uniform – than we are inclined to think.

Wittgenstein's discussion of aspect perception resolves the puzzle about the two types of seeing, for it shows that vision is by no means as straightforward as the inner picture account makes it out to be. What we see does not belong to one homogeneous category but involves different types of concept, each of which is an object of sight in a slightly different sense. In particular, the aspects of a picture belong to a different category from the colours and shapes which make up that picture. While someone who is seeing a schematic cube can tell another what she sees by drawing it, she cannot describe *how* she is seeing it (or explain what happens when the aspect changes) without recourse to a three-dimensional model. Similarly, if someone is seeing the duck–rabbit as a rabbit, she could describe her visual experience by saying 'I can see these colours and shapes' (she gives the details) 'and besides something like this' (she points to a rabbit or pictures of rabbits). As Wittgenstein notes, the difference in the type of explanation 'shows the difference between the concepts' (*PI*, p. 197). It also indicates why we hesitate to call aspect perception 'seeing', for seeing as might almost be said to involve seeing a concept. However, this should not be seen as a difficulty; rather it underlines the fundamental point that our psychological concepts shade into each other with some phenomena straddling the boundaries. Thus aspect perception has similarities both to perception and to thought. Someone looking at a puzzle picture and unable to make out what it represents sees all there is to see; what she suddenly sees when the aspect dawns is not some hidden detail of the drawing but the internal relation between it and a particular object. The experience of aspect-dawning is similar to that involved in a flash of insight and yet it is also similar to seeing, for in this case the new insight takes the form of a new visual experience.

The complexities of vision, and the way in which seeing and thinking intersect, can be illustrated by considering the case of recognition. Take the example of someone recognizing an acquaintance in a crowd, perhaps, after looking in her direction for some time. In Wittgenstein's words, 'Is this a special sort of seeing? Is it a case of both seeing and thinking? Or an amalgam of the two as I should almost like to say?' (*PI*, p. 197). In the flash of recognition, what we see changes – an anonymous crowd suddenly becomes an old friend surrounded by people. We have a new experience and one which is simultaneously a new visual experience and a thought ('That's N'). The two aspects of the experience cannot be separated from each other and therefore the attempt to isolate a purely visual component of the experience makes no sense. This point can be generalised, for the context in which we see something (and our reaction to what we see) may be inseparable from the rest of our visual experience. Compare, for example, the experience of seeing a lion in a zoo and that of seeing one loose in the street. Do we see the same thing in the two cases? Clearly in one sense we do. However, the impression the lion makes may be quite different in the two cases: the wretched zoo animal may be almost unrecognisable in the ferocious beast tearing down the street. Correspondingly the accounts we offer of our visual experience may also differ – for example, our estimates of its size may vary or in the second case our impression may as it were be all jaws and claws. The general point here is that describing our visual impression involves giving an account of what we saw, and thus any type of difference in that account could be used to justify talk of a difference in visual experience. For this reason, one might almost say that the exclamation 'What was that?' itself expresses a particular visual experience (*LW1*, para. 557), for the surprise and uncertainty which this exclamation expresses will also characterise the individual's account of what she saw. Like recognition itself, the experience of non-recognition might be said to be half thought and half visual experience.

The example of recognition brings out the importance of the individual's representation of what she saw, and this helps to explain the looseness of the concept of seeing, for what this reflects is the elasticity of the notion of a representation. Although we tend to think of a drawing as the best representation of our visual experience, aspect perception shows that this is not always so. Indeed, in some cases even a three-dimensional model may not capture our experience. For example, in the case of the schematic cube, even a model would not show whether we see the cube as coming out towards us or extending back away from us.

In this case, we can only convey our visual experience through words or gestures. This recourse to gestures may suggest that the visual experience is strictly speaking inexpressible or at least only expressible in a vague and approximate way. However, as we saw in Chapter 1, the notion of a private, inexpressible experience makes no sense. In fact, here as elsewhere, the only basis for talk of a specific experience is what the individual says or does; in this case the experience is characterised either by her saying 'I see the drawing as a cube projecting towards me' or by her conveying this with gestures. This point holds even in cases where the individual cannot find adequate words to describe what she saw, for the difference between her and us is not that she knows what the experience was and we don't. Rather the difference lies in her grammatical position as the person who had that experience. It is she who describes her impression and who says whether the description is adequate. Until and unless she completes her description, all that we (and she) know and can say about her visual experience is that it was indescribable or that it can only be described in the vague terms she has already used, e.g. as an impression of something large or threatening or whatever.

The key therefore to understanding vision is to recognise that the content of the individual's visual experience is given by her account of what she saw.[4] By contrast, the idea of an inner picture only stands in the way of understanding, for it blinds us to the variety of possible visual concepts and fosters a misguided and distorting dogmatism about what we 'really' see. For example, many philosophers, notably Bishop Berkeley, have argued that we don't really see depth. Instead they claim that what we actually see is two-dimensional and that spatial relationships are simply hypotheses supplied by the mind or the brain. According to Wittgenstein, however, this is misguided: the fact that we naturally describe our visual experience in three-dimensional terms is itself enough to justify the claim that our visual experience takes this form. In order to imagine someone who did see two-dimensionally, we should have to imagine someone who really did have to translate what she saw into a series of hypotheses about objects confronting her. Such a person's account of her visual experience would consist not of descriptions of objects in space, but of descriptions of forms combined with hypotheses about their spatial relationships. But this is clearly not the form our visual experience takes. We say 'I can see a person standing near the tree at the bottom of the field' and not 'I can see a person-like shape which I estimate must be 100 yards away if it is indeed a person and that person is of average height'. To make these points is not to claim that we see depth in exactly the same sense as we see colours and shapes; like the aspects we see, depth does not belong to the same category as colours and shapes, and hence is an object of sight in a different sense. In part, the attempt to deny that we see depth may reflect a sensitivity to this difference. Where it goes wrong, however, is in the quest for a pure concept of seeing, for this search can only result in an empty and confusing dogmatism.

In marked contrast to this sort of approach, Wittgenstein emphasises the variety of descriptions of what is seen. Rather than seeking to pin down the truly visual, he notes the multiplicity of possible visual concepts and the variety of differences which could be used as criteria for a difference in visual experience. For example, he compares the different impressions created by reversing a simple pattern and writing a word backwards.

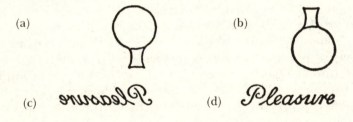

Here Wittgenstein notes that there is 'a different difference' between our impression of (c) and (d) and between those of (a) and (b) (*PI*, p. 198). In the latter case, the two impressions are simply different, whereas in the former there are qualitative differences – for example, (d) looks neater than (c), (d) is easy to copy, (c) is hard. This underlines the error in treating the visual impression as simply a replica of the object, for geometrically similar patterns may make quite different visual impressions on us. We react differently to the familiar pattern of a word and to that same pattern reversed, and it would seem odd not to describe this difference as a difference in the visual impression the pattern makes. Indeed, in expressing our reaction we typically use the vocabulary of vision, for example, we say 'Before the word looked reassuring, now it just looks ridiculous'. Of course, one could try to define a concept of seeing which excluded such 'subjective' elements, but from what has been said, it should be clear, first, that this would be no easy task, and, second, that this would introduce a new and rather artificial concept of seeing rather than providing the key to the one we already have.

As a final illustration of the way we tend to misrepresent our own use of the concept 'seeing', it is worth considering the way we describe our perception of other people, for it is interesting that we claim to see joy, fear, etc. in the other person's face and behaviour. Against this, the 'purist' will argue that we don't really see the fear, but rather see an expression or piece of behaviour and infer from this that the person concerned is frightened. But what's wrong with the normal way of putting it? After all, that's how we use the concept 'seeing'. Furthermore, the only grounds for talking of a process of inference is the dogmatic belief that there must be one. As it is, no such process is detectable and we would certainly find it difficult to define even approximate rules for such inferences. In fact, our use of psychological terms to describe other people enables us to pick out subtleties of difference which we could not describe in other terms. For example, we say 'the frightened look on her face gave way to a certain wariness' and yet we cannot say exactly how her expression changed. Thus our visual impression can only be expressed in terms of the psychological concept, and it would therefore be odd to say that the 'real' content of our impression was something we could not specify. Resistance to this claim arises from tensions between different aspects of the concept of seeing. For example, if someone could not recognise a smile as such, we would not for that reason say her vision was impaired. In one sense, she sees exactly what we do; in another sense, however, she sees the face differently from us and might well be said to be 'blind' to its expression. However, the tension between these two claims should not be seen as a problem. This is simply how we use the concept of seeing and, since the concept evolved for use rather than for philosophical inspection, it is hardly surprising that it does not display a tidy unity. According to

Wittgenstein, there is nothing wrong in saying we see the glance that one person throws at another, but this does not mean we see it in 'just the same sense' as we see shapes and colours. 'Our naif, normal, way of expressing ourselves does *not* contain any theory of seeing – it shows you, not any theory, but only a *concept* of seeing' (*RPP1*, para. 1101).[5]

These examples illustrate the point that vision is not the simple concept our philosophical preconceptions lead us to believe. As our investigation of aspect perception, recognition and other phenomena shows, many types of visual concept are possible. The apparent simplicity of the concept shatters; instead the concept

> makes a tangled impression. Well, it is tangled. – I look at the landscape, my gaze ranges over it, I see all sorts of distinct and indistinct movements; *this* impresses itself sharply on me, *that* is quite hazy. After all, how completely ragged what we see can appear! And now look at all that can be meant by 'description of what is seen'. – But this just is what is called description of what is seen. There is not one *genuine* proper case of such description – the rest being just vague, something which awaits clarification, or which must just be swept away as rubbish. (*PI*, p. 200)

The example of seeing shows, not that consciousness is full of ineffable experiences, but that our concepts have a complexity we tend to underestimate. The mystery of consciousness reflects our uncertainty and confusion in trying to make sense of concepts we use everyday. The path to understanding, however, lies not in introspective analysis of the experience but in careful exploration of the grammar of the concept. The key is to recognize the essential link between the Inner and the Outer, between the experience and its manifestation.

So where does this leave the idea of a world of consciousness? As we noted earlier, we tend to think of this world as a private realm made up of experiences, the paradigm of which is the mental image. Our discussion of vision, however, has shown that this is misleading even with regard to the supposed paradigm case. Seeing something does not consist in having an inner picture;

rather the individual sees something and her description of what she saw provides the criteria for saying she had a particular visual experience. In fact, one might even argue that it is slightly odd to talk of experience here, for generally when we ask someone what she saw, we do so because we are interested in finding out about the outer world, not because we have any special interest in what she experienced. One might therefore contrast seeing (and other forms of perception) with 'genuine' experiences such as feelings and sensations, for in these cases our primary interest is indeed in what the individual experienced.[6] Far from providing a paradigm for private inner experience, the case of vision underlines Wittgenstein's points about the role of the Outer as the criteria for the Inner. Furthermore, it undermines the idea that what we really experience is not the world itself, but a private replica of that world within us. By treating all experience as indirect, this claim abolishes the very distinction on which it is supposedly based. It ignores the fact that seeing, hearing and feeling something for oneself is precisely what we call directly experiencing it. Someone who listens to tales of the sea and imagines herself on similar adventures might be said to have an indirect experience of ship-board life. By contrast, there is nothing indirect about the experience of someone who admires a landscape; her gaze is directed outward, not inward – the source of her admiration is the field itself, not some copy of that field within her.

Against this, one might still claim that some of our experiences are indescribable and that no amount of words can convey their real content. Take colours, for example: surely seeing red is a specific experience and one which cannot be explained or described? What makes us want to say this though? If we compare a colour-blind person and someone who is not colour-blind, we shall certainly say they have different visual experiences, however, the basis for saying this is not a comparison of what goes on inside them, but the fact that one can play a game which the other can't. Learning the game involves learning to distinguish between objects in terms of the public paradigm of red and someone who can do this will be said to know the difference between having an impression of red and having an impression of some other colour. By contrast, someone who cannot learn the game is thereby excluded from having the corresponding impressions or experiences. Furthermore, since the ability to play the game is the criterion for having the experience, no amount of explanation will help her. The bedrock of the language-game is the ability to use certain samples to distinguish between objects and it is at this level that explanations come to an end. What is specific is the language-game, not the experiences; or rather, what makes the experiences specific is their relation to specific articulations of the language-game.

Despite these points, we may still be inclined to argue that someone who was only familiar with certain colours would need to be given something new if she was to know what the other colours were like. But what would she have to be given? Suppose new coloured patterns had to be introduced into her brain, what role would these play in her action? If we are to judge that she now knows what the new colour words mean, she will have to be able to correctly point out objects of those colour, etc. What is important is that her seeing-behaviour includes new components (*RPP1*, para. 616). However, the new element is not some private experience, but her ability to make distinctions in terms of the public paradigm or sample for that particular colour. Although the individual may now be said to have a new set of experiences, the basis for saying this is that she can now play a game which she previously could not. In fact, the claim that red is a specific experience exemplifies the reaction on which our language-game is based, for the whole point of colour concepts is that they pick out what we see as significant differences between objects. If therefore we wanted to explain what was specific about red, we would have to describe our game – e.g. point out that we treat pink as a mixture of red and white or that we talk of reddish yellow but not of reddish green. Similarly, to show what was specific about colour, we would have to describe our game with colours. 'The naming of colours, the comparison of colours, the production of colours, the connexion of colours and light and illumination, the connexion of colour with the eye, of notes with the ear and innumerable other things' (*RPP1*, para. 628). Wittgenstein does not deny that the world of consciousness is made up of specific experiences, but points out that this can easily lead to confusion. The experiences may be specific but they are not private; indeed, what justifies our talk of them is their relation to the public language-game.

At this stage, it might be argued that we have still avoided the hardest case, for we have not yet discussed mental images. Maybe the realm of the imagination is the real inner world. If seeing doesn't consist in experiencing an inner picture, surely imagining does. Even here, however, the idea of the inner picture runs into difficulties. One problem is distinguishing between seeing and imagining. The traditional way of making this distinction is in terms of vivacity, but this transforms the categorial difference between impressions and images into an experiential difference. Doing this makes the difference contingent, which means that in principle it would be possible for someone's impressions to be *less* vivid than her images. This would presumably mean that her images interfered with her visual impressions, but in that case what she is suffering from is not an over-vivid imagination but hallucinations. As this suggests, seeing, imagining and hallucinating are distinguished not by their content (or by the quality of their content) but by their role in our lives. The difference between the various concepts is grammatical, not experiential. The 'similarities' in their content arise from the connections between them, for what can be seen can also be imagined or hallucinated and what in one context represents what the individual saw can elsewhere represent what she imagined or mistakenly believed was there. Thus the basis of all three language-games is the concept of seeing. Only after the individual has learnt to describe what she can see does she learn to describe what she can 'see in her imagination', and the rules of this new language-game distinguish it both from seeing and from hallucinating. The reason images cannot interfere with perception is not that they happen to be less vivid, but because of their grammar. If a normally-sighted person cannot see what is in front of her, this very fact indicates that she is suffering not from an over-vivid imagination but from an hallucination.

One way of bringing out the categorial differences between seeing, imagining and hallucinating is to note the different conceptual relations each has. For example, they can be distinguished by reference to the notion of perception, for while seeing tells us something correct about the world and hallucinating something incorrect, imagining does neither. Similarly, the grammar of seeing connects it with looking, examining and finding out, while imagining plays a quite different role.

Another way of expressing the differences between the three concepts is to note their different relation to the will. Someone can change what she is seeing by moving her head or by shutting her eyes, but she can usually change what she is imagining simply by thinking of something else. The fact that an image may as it were take possession of us does not undermine this point, for even with an obsessive image our relation to it is not the same as to something we can see. In the latter case, the very question of banishing does not arise and therefore we cannot even try to banish it. Similarly, while the sight of a lion might give grounds for fear of a mauling, being obsessed by the image of one would not: someone who took steps to protect herself would be said to be suffering from an hallucination not from an obsessive image. We can summarise these differences by noting that imagining is voluntary, while seeing and hallucinating are not. It is more akin to something we do than something that happens to us; as Wittgenstein puts it, when we imagine something we are not observing and, since it is the product of our thoughts, what we see does not surprise us (Z, para. 632). The same grammatical difference can be underlined by noting that we can order someone to imagine something but not to see something; while the order 'Imagine a red object' makes sense, 'See a red object' would at best mean find a red object and look at it.[7]

These points show the different roles the three concepts play, but they may seem to leave unanswered the question of what actually happens when someone imagines something. However, the only answers to that question are tautological; we can put forward paraphrases of the concept ('The individual sees a picture in her imagination', 'She sees something which she knows isn't there, which doesn't interfere with her visual perception and which she can still see with her eyes closed', etc.), but none of them actually gets us any further. What is wrong here is the idea that we have to explain imagination, for our problem is not that we don't know what imagining is, but that we can't find our way round with this concept and can't relate it to the other concepts of experience. In fact, even the idea of an inner picture is only a pseudo-explanation, for the picture cannot be treated as an independently existing entity. If it were, this would clash with the grammar of imagination, for it would suggest that the individual might misidentify her mental image, i.e. believe she was having an image of N when actually the picture was of someone else. Similarly there might be occasions when she would have to say 'I have a mental image, but I can't make out what it is'! However, this is clearly not how our concept of imagining works: what the individual says she is imagining *is* what she is imagining. The individual does not discover a resemblance between her image and an object; rather she says she has an image of such-and-such and her saying so establishes that she is imagining that particular object. The inner picture is not independent of the individual's utterances and, insofar as it plays a role in our language-game, it does so simply as another paraphrase of our concept of imagining.

One factor which gives the inner picture account its force is the fact that pictures can be used to represent both what we see and what we imagine. However, this does not mean that either the visual impression or the visual image are themselves a kind of picture. In fact, both concepts function in a very different way from that of a picture. For example, whereas all pictures have edges, it is far from clear what would be meant by talking of the edge of a mental image. Similarly, a mental image need not be determinate in every respect, whereas, even if a picture is blurred, that blurredness must be represented in a determinate fashion. Thus questions which make sense in relation to a picture do not necessarily make sense in relation to a mental image. As Wittgenstein puts it,

> the image is not a picture, nor is the visual impression one. Neither 'image' nor 'impression' is the concept of a picture, although in both cases there is a tie-up with a picture, and in each case a different one. (Z, para. 638)

Seeing and imagining are related, but not similar. The individual uses exactly the same terms to describe both what she sees and what she imagines, but the context in which the description is given and the role it plays is different in the two cases. In fact, in the case of imagination there could be a concept which was similar to ours in practical terms but which had a different form of expression. For example, there might be people who drew and modelled 'out of the imagination' but who denied that they saw anything while making the drawing or model. Instead of saying 'I can now see N before me' or 'I now have an image of N', these people might simply concentrate and say 'I can now say what N looks like'. This concept would play a similar role to our concept of imagining, but the connection with seeing, and *a fortiori* with the notion of an inner picture, would be excluded. Of course in our language-game we do talk of having a visual image, but this is not a private object which the individual describes nor something which provides independent grounds for her statements. On the contrary, it is the individual's utterances which provide the criterion for the claim that she has a particular image. Thus Wittgenstein does not deny that the individual 'sees an image inside her'; rather he shows what this phrase means and by doing so clarifies how the concept actually works.

In this chapter, we have concentrated on vision, since this is the form of perception we tend to take as the paradigm of experience in general. In principle, however, the world of consciousness is a world of sounds, smells, tactile sensations and tastes just as much as of sights. But the other senses tend to take second place in philosophical considerations, and this is hardly surprising since, as we shall see later, following the traditional conception through is even more difficult in their case than it is with vision. What is it though that brings together the senses and characterises them as group? One answer is to say that they all tell us about the external world, indeed, as we noted earlier, this is one way of distinguishing between seeing and imagining. In *Zettel*, however, Wittgenstein describes the general claim as partly right and partly wrong (*Z*, para. 477). He argues that the claim is correct insofar as it points to a logical criterion, i.e. insofar as it is a remark about the grammatical status of sense-impression statements. The danger, however, is that can be misinterpreted as an empirical remark. For example, one might argue that experience teaches us both that it will rain when the barometer falls and that it is raining when we have certain sensations of wet and cold or such-and-such visual impressions (*PI*, para. 354). This would make the link between our sense impressions and external phenomena contingent, and one might justify this by pointing out that our senses sometimes err and that therefore there cannot be a necessary link between particular impressions and the occurrence of, e.g. rain. The effect of this, however, is to imprison the individual in the world of the senses; if all we ever experience are appearances, how can we move beyond these to the world itself? If our senses simply give us information, how is the something about which they give us information defined? The solution to this problem is to note that the logical order is in fact the opposite to the one suggested above. We do not move from the concept appearance of rain to the concept rain. Rather we start with the occurrence and from there move to the idea of appearances or sensations. First we teach someone to say 'It is raining', then she learns 'It seems to be raining'. We learn to talk about wetness in connection with water, and it is a late and paradoxical use of the concept if the individual one day says 'I have a sensation of wetness despite being totally dry'. Thus our senses do not teach us that there are objects; rather 'that we speak of material objects characterises the concept "sensations" ' (*WLPP*, p. 306).

Wittgenstein's claim that the notion of a sense-impression is secondary to that of the external world is controversial and worth looking at in more detail. According to Wittgenstein, what we learn first is the use of descriptive words, e.g. we learn 'That's a chair', 'That's red', etc.; only later do we learn 'That seems to be a chair' or 'That looks red to me'. This does not mean that we begin by learning a false certainty; rather Wittgenstein's point is that doubt only enters the game at a later stage. Only after someone has mastered the use of the word 'chair' can she be in doubt as to whether her application of it is correct. Only after she has learnt 'That is a chair' can she learn to say 'That seems to be a chair' or 'I have the impression that a chair is there even though I know one isn't'. Similarly, the individual learns to use the word 'red' in connection with a public paradigm and demonstrates her mastery of the word by pointing to the appropriate sample. It is only later that reference to a perceiving subject enters the language-game. When it does, the language-game gets a new joint, for 'the red visual impression is a new *concept*' (*Z*, para. 423). Even at this stage, however, the person who says 'It looks red to me' must still be able to demonstrate that she understands the concept by pointing to the right paradigm, i.e. by pointing to something indisputably red.[8] Far from being primary, the notion of a sense-impression is a refinement of the original language-game, not its basis.

If we now ask why the language-game should come to be modified in this way, the answer is not hard to find, for on occasion we may be just as interested in what the individual thought she saw, heard, felt, etc. as in what actually happened. It is useful therefore to supplement the language of description ('The object was red') with the language of sense-impressions ('I had an impression of something red'). One effect of this change is to allow us to present the language-game in a completely new light, for the concepts originally used to describe the outer world can now be used to populate an inner world. This new inner world will necessarily parallel the outer one, for its function is to mirror the outer world and give an account of what we believe happened which may or may not correlate with what actually happened. As Wittgenstein puts it 'the description of the subjectively seen is more or less akin to the description of an object, but just for that reason does not function as a description of an object' (Z, para. 435). The two types of description have similar forms, but they play quite different roles in the language-game.

As these remarks show, Wittgenstein does not reject the metaphor of the inner world, but he does emphasise how easily it can be misinterpreted. This point can be underlined by considering the philosophical idea of sense-data, for this idea seeks confusedly to build on the parallels between sense-impressions and the descriptions of objects. Thus 'sense-data are conceived after the pattern of physical objects; they are the furniture of a subjective space; there is a visual book in the visual room' (WLPP, p. 78). Here it is significant that we once again come back to vision, for as we shall see later, it is only with regard to visual sense-impressions that the sense-data approach has any measure of plausibility. Even with regard to vision, however, the approach quickly runs into difficulties, for the attempt to treat sense-impressions as a type of object founders on the rock of their grammatical differences. The parallel 'In my visual field I see . . .' and 'In this room there are . . . ' does not really work, for questions that make sense in one context do not in the other. For example, the statement 'There are three tables in my visual field' does not allow of the response 'And how many are there to the right of your visual field?' Similarly the suggestion that two sense-data men look the same height but aren't makes no sense. As these examples show, the grammar of 'appearances' is not the grammar of objects and therefore any account of impressions cannot treat them as such.

The only plausible alternative is to treat sense-data as 'perspectives', for at least this approach holds out the possibility of translating our current talk into a more 'philosophically correct' language. Instead of learning to say 'I see a table', a child could be taught to say 'I am experiencing view D of the table'. Even here, however, the 'sense-data' would not be private, for the basis of the game would have to be a public definition of these experiences. For example, each of the different views of the table might be defined in terms of a separate picture and the child would be taught to use the view vocabulary by reference to these sample pictures. This seems to define a coherent possibility, but it is one that is parasitic on the game we currently play and which contains a host of difficulties. How, for example, would the innumerable possible views of table be reduced to a finite but generally applicable set of perspectives? Furthermore, how would the individual apply the pictures defining the perspectives, for if she tilts the picture is it still a picture of the same view? (*WLPP*, p. 318). Thus the mechanics of a language of perspectives are by no means clear, but even if one could set up such a language, it is hard to see what point there would be in so doing. The possibility of paraphrasing our actual language in this way would not show that perspectives were 'the real furniture of the universe'. In fact, the notion of sense-data and the accompanying idea of a world of sense-impressions (the idea that the chair and table of the external world are paralleled by a visual chair and table in the inner world) simply offers a new way of looking at our language-game. Like the basic idea of a sense-impression, it turns the description of the Outer into the description of an Inner and shifts the focus of interest from descriptions of the external world to the individual's expression of her experiences. The idea of the visual room does not embody a new insight into what we really experience; rather it introduces 'a new way of speaking, a new comparison; one might almost say a new sensation' (*PI*, para. 400).

It is no coincidence that, in our discussion of sense-data, we again returned to vision, for it is only in this case that the idea of sense-data has even the remotest plausibility. To illustrate this point, let us consider the example of touch. In this case, we are much less inclined to talk of sense-data, and there are good reasons for this, for touching is not articulate in the way seeing is. Suppose, for example, someone is being taught to identify objects simply by touch. When she is asked 'How does the object feel?', she may reply by describing the tactile qualities of the object, e.g. saying 'it feels rough'. More generally, however, she will describe her feeling in terms of an object, e.g. by saying 'it feels like a book'. In contrast with vision, there is no temptation here to talk of an intermediary sense-data – it is hardly plausible, for example, to suggest that we infer the presence of a book from our awareness of a rectangular tactile sense-datum. One reason for this is that there is nothing in the case of touch which can play the role of a picture in the case of vision. In particular, the individual cannot represent her perception in terms of discrete snapshots. Without this possibility, however, the whole idea of a sense-datum crumbles. What tactile sense-data, for example, go to making up someone's awareness that she is holding a sphere? Although the individual may know what she is holding, there is no plausible way of breaking this down into component sense-data. By exploring the object with her hands, she may find out what it is, but independently of any reference to an object, there is generally no meaningful answer as to what tactile sensation she is having at one particular moment.

Against this, it might be argued that the individual could make a model of what she is feeling, but even this process would fail to isolate a specific sense-datum as opposed to an overall impression. The model would show what the individual believes she is holding, but it would not show how individual sense-data added up to yield this impression. One source of difficulty here is that with touch, the impression of the object comes from movement; to know, for example, that the object she is touching is unchanged, the individual has to keep moving the position of her fingers. One implication of this is that sensations of touch do not have the same kind of duration as those of seeing or hearing. The succession of tactile sensations yield an impression, but changes in the impression could not be plotted moment by moment on a graph in the way the impression of an increasingly loud noise or of an increasingly bright colour could. Thus, although the sense-data theorist lumps all the senses together, there are important differences between them. Furthermore, as our exploration of touch has shown, it is only really with vision that the idea of sense-data gets much of a grip. As Wittgenstein notes, 'some do speak of "tactile sense-data". But that people speak of them at all is something of a stunt. And when they come to describe them things get very odd' (*WLPP*, p. 318).

The other senses present different sets of problems for the sense-data theorist, but having considered vision and touch we shall leave the others to one side. Instead, we shall consider a rather different question, for if the sense are so different, what holds them together? Why do we treat seeing, hearing, tasting, touching and smelling as in some sense the same? The answer to this is not to be found by immersing oneself in the sense-impressions themselves but rather by noting the role of the senses in our lives. As we saw, one way of characterising that role is to note that the senses tell us about the external world. This distinguishes sense-impressions from other psychological concepts such as pain or intention and also from the experiences involved in imagining and in hallucinating. Furthermore, the fact that they fulfil the same role creates analogies and connections between the senses: 'what holds the bundle of sense-impressions together is their mutual relationships. That which is "red" is also "sweet" and "hard" and "cold" and "sounds" when one strikes it' (*RPP1*, para. 896). The common function of sense-impressions also means they can have similar kinds of properties, in particular, notions of intensity and hue can be applied to each of them. Just as a light-source can be unbearably bright, so too a sound can be unbearably loud. Similarly, a noise, a sight, etc., can all be barely perceptible. As for hue, this highlights the fact that each of the various sense-impressions can involve mixtures of qualities, e.g. what we see may be reddish-brown or what we taste bitter-sweet, etc. However, the analogies between the senses are not uniform. Although seeing and hearing are similar in the sense of being the most articulate of the senses, one could also claim that seeing and feeling are similar, for in a dark or semi-dark room, it is feeling and not hearing that replaces seeing. Thus the senses are different but linked; what connects them is not a uniformity of content or form but a common role.

To sum up, the aim of this chapter has been to undermine the idea that the world of consciousness is a private inner world. The world we are aware of is the real world of tables and chairs, not a phantom world of sense-data and indescribable impressions. The metaphor of an inner world (the idea that to every sight and sound there corresponds the individual's impression of that sight and sound) is an acceptable and useful one, for it allows us to focus on the individual's experience independently of whether or not that experience correctly reflects what happened. However, it should not be taken to imply that the real furniture of the universe is mental events. Furthermore, there is nothing ineffable about our experiences. Of course, if we apply the grammar of objects to them, they seem mysteriously insubstantial, but if we recognise their distinctive grammar, the mystery dissolves. Having made these points, however, we have still only explored one aspect of consciousness, for we have talked about impressions, but not about ideas. In the next chapter, therefore, we shall consider that other key aspect of our inner life – the mystery of thought.

3

THE MYSTERY OF THOUGHT

'Thinking is a mental activity.' – Thinking is *not* a bodily activity. Is thinking an activity? Well, one may tell someone: 'Think it over!' But if someone in obeying this order talks to himself or even to someone else, does he then carry out *two* activities? So thinking can't really be compared to an activity at all. For one also cannot say that thinking means: speaking in one's imagination. This can also be done without thinking. (*RPP2*, para. 193)

The world of consciousness has always been seen as the world of the senses but also of course as the world of thought. Although sense-impressions, and in particular images, are the paradigm content of consciousness, it is thought and thinking that constitute its essence. But how can thought be described? If anything, it seems even more puzzling than perception, for the mind seems capable of almost magical feats. In an instant, it can leap any distance and, using its predictive powers, it can defy time and peer into the future. Thought also possesses a strange unpredictable quality. In a flash of inspiration, a problem which has troubled us for days may suddenly become clear, and yet paradoxically, spelling out the solution may take hours, days or even months. So what is it to think? What does thinking actually involve? Despite its importance, it seems impossible to pin down the exact nature of thought: anything we point to seems dead and empty in comparison with the process of thought itself. Similarly, although we may be able to describe a procedure which corresponds to the behaviour of someone acting intelligently, this seems to leave out the essence of the activity.

The procedure is something mechanical, the mere husk of thought – what makes it a manifestation of thought is that it is applied 'thinkingly'. Thus the essence of thought seems indescribable; it seems the only mystery thought cannot penetrate is its own.

These mysteries deepen if we consider the question of what thinking consists of. Here there are only two real candidates – images and inner speech – and each has its virtues. On the one hand, images are undoubtedly involved in some of our thought processes and seem to connect up with other more specific phenomena, e.g. with the flash of insight expressed in the phrase 'I suddenly saw the solution'. On the other hand, inner speech seems more suited to capture the complexity of thought. Furthermore, although the flash of insight is sometimes contained in an image, it may also take the form of a brief phrase, e.g. when someone pushing against an unyielding door suddenly thinks 'Why not pull?' Despite these attractions, both approaches run into difficulties. Take images first. One problem here is the implausibility of claiming that we always experience an image when we think or act in an intelligent way. Someone who is reading, for example, may only experience the odd image, if any, and yet this does not show that reading does not involve thinking. Another problem is that not all thoughts can easily be represented in pictures. This is true not only of abstract ideas but also of everyday thoughts. For example, it is unclear what images correspond to the thought 'It's a pity I didn't stay at the meeting longer because, although it was boring, I might have got the opportunity of having a quiet word with N'. The really fundamental objection, however, is that this approach fails to capture the dynamic quality of thought. In comparison with thought, any picture or image seems dead – in itself it means nothing, for it has to be applied if it is to have a sense. Thus, even if we could see all the images passing through another person's mind, we still wouldn't know her thoughts, for we wouldn't know what she was using those pictures to think. The images, it seems, are not the thoughts, rather the thoughts are what give those images life.

The idea that thinking consists in inner speech runs into precisely the same problem, for here too we would need something to give the words of our inner speech life. Otherwise one could only report the words of the conversation and the external circumstances under which it was carried on, but not also the meaning that these words had for the speaker. If someone said to himself (or out loud) 'I hope to see N soon', it would make no sense to ask: 'And which person of that name did you mean?' For all that he did was to say these words.

(*RPP1*, para. 180)

In fact, since thinking is what gives sense to both inner and outer speech, there would be a strange circularity in trying to explain the former in terms of the latter. On the contrary, the natural conclusion is that thinking is something over and above speech. Like mental images, our words seem dead unless backed up by thought. Even if we could hear another person's inner speech, we would still need to know what she meant by her words – who she meant by N, whether she was being sarcastic, how serious she was, etc. Thus there must be more to thought than either images or inner speech, but what? What sort of explanation can capture the flow of thought, the dynamic quality that makes it the essence of consciousness?

The extent of these difficulties can be underlined by considering the idea that thinking is a process. This seems unobjectionable, after all, we say such things as 'Don't talk without thinking' and this seem to suggest that intelligent speech involves two activities, one outer, one inner. Similarly, since inner speech is not itself thought, it would seem natural to treat thinking as a process that accompanies inner speech and gives it meaning. However, even this basic idea is replete with difficulties. For example, the idea that thinking is an activity which accompanies others implies that it could also occur in an unaccompanied form. However, when we try to isolate thought from what it accompanies, nothing is left. The relation of thought to its manifestation is not like that between the words of a song and the music, but like that between the expression with which the music is played and the music itself. Just as it is impossible to sing a tune with expression and then repeat the expression without the tune, so too the thought embodied in a sentence cannot be repeated without repeating the sentence (*PI*, para. 332). This creates a paradox. On the one hand, we want to say that thinking is a process that distinguishes mechanical from non-mechanical action, and, on the other hand, we seem to be forced to admit that no such special process actually exists.

The same problems arise with regard to the concept of meaning, for here too we encounter the paradox of a process which is essential and yet undetectable. As Wittgenstein notes, 'the puzzle is: that I can speak mechanically and non-mechanically, but I can't find anything that's essential for the difference' (*WLPP*, p. 296). Furthermore, as with thinking and its expression, there is a conflict between the desire to treat meaning as something independent of the words we utter and our sense that the two are inseparable. On the one hand, when we utter a meaningful sentence, it seems that some act or process of meaning imbues these sounds with sense. On the other hand, no such act or process can be separated off from the actual use of language. There do, however, seem to be certain experiences associated with meaning, and yet these only introduce further complications. For example, when we repeatedly utter a word in isolation, we seem to experience its gradual loss of meaning. Despite this, it seems that meaning cannot simply be shifted from one word to another, for the attempt to say one word with the meaning of another seems somehow absurd. Indeed, even if we set up a code replacing an English sentence with some other sequence of sounds, we may still feel that the coded sentence somehow fails to contain the meaning in the way the English sentence does – the coded sentence seems empty in a way that a normal sentence is not. Thus meaning seems just as confusing as thinking itself.

One way of trying to give an account of meaning is to stress the experiences we have just mentioned. For example, one might argue that every word is associated with a particular feeling and that this constitutes its meaning. On this account, the difference between a meaningful sentence and a nonsensical one is that the speaker (and her audience) experiences a certain depth or resonance in the former case but not in the latter. Our relation to ambiguous words seems to support this account, for such words do seem to have a different feel in each of their meanings. Indeed, we may experience the link between the word and its meaning so intensely that it strikes us as strange that one word can serve two masters – how peculiar that we use the same sign and the same sound for the site of a riverside stroll and for the place where we get our money, and how odd that an English colloquial expression for drunkenness should be an American synonym for being angry. Despite its attractions, however, no account of this kind can explain meaning, for it has the wrong kind of grammar. As in the case of thinking, reference to an experience fails to capture the dynamic quality of meaning; indeed, it transforms meaning into something that happens to us rather than something we do. It also runs into another kind of difficulty, for, despite our strong inclination to talk of an experience of meaning, it seems impossible to specify its content. 'It's as if one were expressing an experience, but then could not think what the experience really was' (*RPP1*, para. 105).

As with thinking, we may try to avoid these difficulties by sticking to the basic idea that meaning is an activity or process. This avoids the danger of making meaning something passive but does little to avoid other – now familiar – difficulties. For example, if meaning is a process that accompanies our speech, why can't it occur unaccompanied? Furthermore, what does the process consist in? There is no plausible answer to this question, but even if introspection did uncover some putative meaning-process, there would be no way of being sure that it always occurred when we spoke. This would yield the strange conclusion that we might occasionally leave out the vital process and so believe that we had spoken meaningfully when in fact we hadn't. Similarly, it raises difficulties about our relation to others, for how can we be sure that this process which we occasionally observe in ourselves always takes place in them? And yet, despite this, we constantly and confidently talk of them saying and meaning things. This undermines the idea of a special act of meaning: if we can recognise the speech of others as meaningful without knowing that an act of meaning has occurred, then such an act cannot be the essence of meaning. Thus, once again we are left with a paradox, for, although we cannot isolate a special process of meaning, we seem constantly to refer to it – we say 'I didn't mean that' or 'What I really meant was' or we ask 'What do you mean when you said . . .?' etc. Like thinking, therefore, meaning seems a mysteriously elusive activity, a strange but crucial something about which we can say little.

The mysteries surrounding these concepts increase if we

consider a phenomenon Wittgenstein called 'the lightning speed of thought'. This refers to the way thinking sometimes seems to occur in an accelerated form. A puzzle, for example, becomes clear in a flash or we suddenly see the solution to a complex problem which has long troubled us. Here thought seems to outstrip language and hence

> it is natural to ask if the same thing happens in lightning-like thought – only extremely accelerated – as when we talk and 'think while we talk'. So that in the first case the clockwork runs down all at once, but in the second bit by bit, braked by the words. (*PI*, para. 318)

The example of a flash of insight may make this seem an unusual phenomenon, but the lightning speed of thought is actually a very common feature of our lives. When we meet a friend, for example, one glance at her face may tell us exactly what she is going to do or say. The thought that she is about to do or say such-and-such can occur wordlessly and in an instant, but if so, what does it consist in? And how is the instantaneous thought related to the thought in its expanded form? Although the explanation comes after the thought itself, we treat it as somehow contained in the flash of inspiration. How can this be? Here there seem to be two quite disparate things – on the one hand, the explanation the individual now gives and, on the other, an experience in the past which is somehow supposed to contain that explanation.

The same difficulty arises with regard to meaning, for the lightning speed of thought manifests itself every time we say 'I meant . . .' or 'I thought you meant . . .'. Here the explanation we later offer does not consist of something we said to ourselves at the time of speaking; rather it seems somehow to be contained in our experience at the time. One way of trying to capture this phenomenon would be to say that we experience a 'germ of meaning', i.e. that we have an experience which grows into the later explanation of meaning. On this account, when someone says that she meant (or understood) a word in a particular way, she is reporting the occurrence of a particular experience. What happens is that, when the word is uttered, she experiences the germ of meaning and her later explanation is simply an interpretation of that experience (*RPP1*, para. 94). But there are other problems this account must also tackle, for, as the philosopher and psychologist William James noted, the phenomenon of the lightning speed of thought occurs in relation to the future as well as the past. Just as the individual can explain what she meant, so too she knows what she is going to say even before she has said it. If, for example, someone is interrupted, she will generally be able to explain what she was going say (what she was meaning to say). Here it is as if the sentence was complete before it was uttered, and yet the explanation the individual offers isn't simply a public expression of what she has previously said to herself silently.

The ability of thought to run ahead of itself is no less mysterious than the idea that a complex thought can be contained in a momentary experience in the past. In this case, the individual is assumed to have already thought the sentence before saying it, and yet this process seems to take little or no time at all. So how is this possible? And in what sense and in what form is the thought there before it is uttered? Again, we seem forced back to the idea of a germ, an experience which contains what we are about to say. Interestingly, this connects up with a common phenomenon, for it seems plausible to argue that when the individual has 'a word on the tip of her tongue' she is experiencing precisely this germ. As Wittgenstein puts it,

> the idea forces itself on one, of the gap of which James speaks, which only this word will fit into, and so on. – One is somehow as it were already experiencing the word, although it is not there. – One experiences a growing word. – And I might of course also say that I experience a growing meaning, or growing explanation of meaning. (*RPP1*, para. 254)

The idea of a germ seems to capture the essence of our experience, but it also provokes a host of questions, for what does it actually mean? How can someone experience the meaning of a word, let alone a 'growing meaning'? And how do these peculiar experiences relate to the practical purposes of communication? Here, as with thinking in general, one mystery seems to lead to another.

To clarify these mysteries, let us start by looking at the problem of the lightning speed of thought and, in particular, the problem

in relation to meaning. According to Wittgenstein, the best way
to do this is to consider what someone who did not experience
meaning would be like. As we saw in the preceding chapter, he
uses a similar idea to explore aspect perception, indeed, he
explicitly notes that a key aim of his exploration of seeing aspects
is to clear the ground for an examination of the problem
of experiencing meaning (*LW1*, para. 784). The concept of
meaning-blindness is intended as 'an imaginary construction
line' – it enables Wittgenstein to test various ways of understanding the experience of meaning, for any inaccuracies or confusions will manifest themselves in an inability to flesh out the
picture of the meaning-blind man. In fact, in his attempts to get
to grips with this problem, Wittgenstein makes several false
moves and only gradually does a clear, coherent account emerge.
One consequence of this is that the concept of meaning-blindness
takes on a different sense as each way of understanding the
experience of meaning is explored. To make sense of these
fluctuations, we shall therefore stick closely to Wittgenstein's text.

The starting point for Wittgenstein's discussion is the problem
of the lightning speed of thought in relation to meaning.

> If you say 'As I heard this word, it meant . . . for me' you refer
> to *a point of time* and *to an employment of the word.* – The
> remarkable thing about it is of course the relation to the point
> of time. (*RPP1*, para. 175)

As Wittgenstein notes, however, this phenomenon is not restricted to meaning alone. On the contrary, it occurs with respect
to past expressions of intention in general; for 'if you say "I was
wanting to go on . . ."' – you refer to *a point of time* and to *an
action*' (ibid., para. 176). Since these two phenomena are linked,
if one is inaccessible to the meaning-blind man, both must be: if
he does not say 'I meant' nor will he say 'I was going to'. But how
should we understand this inability? What should we make of the
difference between us and the meaning-blind?

Wittgenstein's first idea is to treat the meaning-blind man as
someone whose thought processes are more explicit than ours. In
him, the mysterious flux of consciousness ('the continuous
coming to be and passing away' in the domain of consciousness
(*RPP1*, para. 294)) is eliminated. On this approach, what is
characteristic of the meaning-blind man is

that he has his intentions in the form of thoughts or pictures and hence that they would always be replaceable by the speaking of a sentence or the seeing of a picture. The 'lightning speed' of thought is missing in him.

(*RPP1*, para. 178)

This suggestion appears to define a coherent concept of meaning-blindness and the difference between us and the meaning-blind seems clear. However, as Wittgenstein continues his investigation, certain problems arise; in particular, this approach seems to undermine the idea of the meaning-blind man as an agent. One feature of *our* action (and speech) is our ability to offer explanations for it and yet such explanations do not always consist in giving voice to what we had already said to ourselves. By contrast, the meaning-blind man can only offer an explanation where this reproduces something he said to himself or an image he had. But if this is so, how can we still see him as a normal agent? Is our assumption

supposed to mean that he often moves like an automaton; walks in the street, perhaps, and makes purchases; but when one meets him and asks 'Where are you going?' he stares at one as if he were sleep-walking? – He won't answer 'I don't know' either. Or will his proceedings strike him, or us, as planless? I don't see why! (*RPP1*, para. 178)

The problem here is that Wittgenstein wants the meaning-blind man to be able to express present intentions in the normal way, but only wants him to be able to express past intentions when he explicitly has them in the form either of an image or a piece of inner speech. A consequence of this, however, is that the meaning-blind man cannot offer a continuous account of his past and hence the intentionality of his actions is undermined.

If someone asks him 'Where are you going?' I want to assume that he answers just as we do. – But will he also say 'As I left the house, I was meaning to go to the baker, but now . . .'? No; but ought we to say that on that account he set out on this way as it were sleep-walking? (ibid.)

In comparison with us, the thoughts of the meaning-blind man seem to come in fits and starts – every now and then he has intentions as we do, but in between he seems to lapse into a strange automatism. Noting this point, Wittgenstein is struck by a further doubt, for if this conception of meaning-blindness makes sense, isn't it remarkable that

> in all the great variety of mankind we do not meet such people as this? Or are there such people among the mental defectives; and it is merely not sufficiently observed which language-games these are capable of and which not? (*RPP1*, para. 179)

As these points suggest, this first conception of meaning-blindness is flawed. In fact, it still contains the problem with which we started: despite appearances, the lightning speed of thought hasn't been eliminated at all. Suppose, for example, the meaning-blind man intends to go and see his friend N; since all his intentions are explicit, having this intention will involve him saying to himself 'I will now go and see N'. But who does he mean by N? Presumably the meaning-blind man will be able to answer this question, but in that case even his explicit intention has the problem of the lightning speed of thought built into it. In explaining what his intention statement meant, the meaning-blind man is doing precisely what he is not supposed to be able to do. The only way to avoid this problem would be if we assumed that the meaning-blind man's thoughts were always fully explicit, but this idea does not make sense, for whatever he says to himself it will always be possible to seek further elucidation of what his words mean. Thus Wittgenstein's first conception of meaning-blindness goes both too far and not far enough. On the one hand, the meaning-blind man's inability to offer continuous explanations of his actions undermines his intentionality. On the other hand, the explanations he does offer still embody the puzzling phenomenon of the lightning speed of thought.

To avoid these problems, Wittgenstein tries another approach. This time instead of emphasising the experience at the time of speaking (or acting), he seeks to eliminate it. Instead of stressing the experience in the past, he emphasises the fact that the individual is now inclined to offer a particular explanation. On the previous approach, the difference between us and the meaning-blind man was that he always had an image where we only sometimes have one. Now he is someone who never experiences anything at the time of speaking and therefore has no temptation to treat the explanation he now offers as somehow inherent in an experience in the past. If, for example, he says 'I hope to see N soon', he will understand the question 'Who do you mean by N?', but not the question 'Who did you mean by N?'. This approach eliminates any reference to a past experience and so avoids the problem of the lightning speed of thought. By implication, it suggests that our reference to the past is simply a misleading metaphor, the use of a peculiar picture. Consideration of what actually happens when we talk seems to support this analysis.

> If someone says to me 'N has written to me', I can ask him 'which N do you mean?' - and must he refer to an experience in speaking the name if he is to answer me? - And if he now simply pronounces the name N - perhaps as an introduction to a statement about N - can't I equally well ask him 'Whom do you mean?' and he equally well answer? (*RPP1*, para. 181)

As this remark suggests, it is implausible to argue that we always have a special experience when we say something or hear something said. Furthermore, since nothing that occurs at the time of speaking can possibly contain every explanation we might later give, there seems little point in postulating an experience at all. If anything we could possibly experience is at best a 'germ', something from which the explanation later develops, why not drop all reference to the experience and focus on what really matters, i.e. the explanation the individual later gives?

These points can be reinforced by considering the nature of our interest in meaning and understanding, for that interest is not an interest in the occurrence of particular inner experiences or processes. Consider, for example, the sentence 'I must go to the bank and get some money'. If we ask someone how she meant the sentence or how she understood it, we would not usually expect her to start describing all sorts of experiences, images and feeling. On the contrary, the question 'How did you understand the sentence?' essentially means 'How would you explain this sentence, what action would you expect when you hear it, etc.'? (*RPP1*, para. 184). Here it would be no use an individual assuring us that in her case meaning and understanding did consist in having certain processes occur within her; for we would still test whether she had understood something by asking her to explain what was said, etc., not by seeking to establish whether certain events occurred within her (*RPP1*, para. 302). Thus, where a word (e.g. 'bank') has several meanings, meaning or understanding it a certain way cannot be a question of having a particular experience – any experiences are as it were covered up by the use, the practice of the language-game. While there may be experiences associated with understanding and meaning, these play no part in the practice of communication: 'and that merely means: here such experiences aren't of the slightest interest to us' (*RPP1*, para. 184).

So where does this leave Wittgenstein's account of the meaning-blind man? Unfortunately, it is still not clear exactly how this concept is supposed to work. At one stage, Wittgenstein suggests that our talk of experiencing meaning is an illusion (*RPP1*, para. 193). This would suggest that the meaning-blind man is simply someone spared the illusion. However, Wittgenstein immediately questions this idea. 'Is it (in the end) an illusion, if I believed that the other's words had this sense for me at that time? Of course not!' (*RPP1*, para. 201). Although reference to an experience in the past may be irrelevant, reference to the past is not. Recognising that the experience of meaning is irrelevant to the use of language, Wittgenstein had assumed that the meaning-blind man was missing out on very little. However, this conflicts with the fact that 'we sometimes say that some word in a communication meant one thing to us until we saw that it meant something else' (ibid., para. 202). As this remark suggests, the reference to the past is crucial, for how the individual understood something at the time (as opposed to now) may explain a particular reaction on her part. For example, the individual heard that N had died, believed that this meant her friend and then she realised she was mistaken. So at first she looked upset, then she was relieved, etc. (ibid., para. 204).

But what should we say about the meaning-blind man in relation to this sort of situation? Should we say 'that [he] is not in a position to react like that? Or that he merely does not assert that he then experienced the meaning – and so, that he merely does not use a particular picture?' (*RPP1*, para. 205). It would certainly seem odd to argue that he never reacts in this way (i.e. never responds to what is said to him), but the alternative is equally unsatisfactory. The reference to the past cannot be treated as the use of a misleading picture because the only interest of the explanation is as an account of what the individual thought at the time. Furthermore, in the cases where we do use a picture, this simply underlines the essence of the reaction itself. Take the example of the flash of insight. *Ex hypothesi*, the meaning-blind man will not use the picture 'The whole course of thought was before my mind in a flash', but why should this stop him having a flash of insight? Why shouldn't he still say 'Now I've got it!'? (ibid., para. 206). However, if we allow him this reaction, his thought takes on precisely the property we were seeking to eliminate. If he sees the solution to a puzzle and begins to give it, he must surely be said to know the answer to the puzzle from the very beginning of his sentence. In that case, however, he is no different from us – he too can understand something 'in an instant'. Thus, Wittgenstein's second conception of meaning-blindness is just as flawed as his first conception; the reference to the past can neither be eliminated nor simply treated as the use of a particular picture. If the meaning-blind man can think at all, his thinking, like ours, will manifest the lightning speed of thought.

The failure of these two approaches at least has the merit of clarifying the problem, for it shows that the real task is to understand how reference to the past can be real and yet not a reference to an experience at the time of speaking. To explore this point, Wittgenstein considers the simple sentence 'I give you my full confidence'.

> If someone who is saying this pauses after the word 'you', I am perhaps able to continue; the situation yields what he wants to say. But if to my surprise he now goes on: 'a gold watch' and I say 'I was prepared for something else' – does that mean: while he was saying the first words I experienced something that may be called that way of taking the words?? I believe that this can't be said. (*RPP1*, para. 209)

If, however, there was no special experience as the other person spoke, what justifies the individual saying 'I was prepared for something else'? The answer is nothing. We assume the individual will be able to tell us what she was expecting, but she does not infer this from anything that was going on inside her at the time. Rather her statement is an utterance and has its importance in the context of our treatment of the individual as a conscious being. The point is that we assign the individual a special role in explaining her actions and this involves assuming that she will be able to give an account of what she meant, thought and intended. In this case, for example, it is assumed that she will be able to explain why the continuation surprised her. If she cannot, her apparent reaction of surprise will be treated as an oddity, perhaps as purely physical reaction. If, however, she could never explain her reactions, we would no longer treat her as a normal person, but as someone who was ill or suffering from a mental disorder.

The claim that the individual's explanations are not based on evidence may seem to suggest that she can say whatever she likes, but this misses Wittgenstein's point, for it ignores the fact that we distinguish between sincere and insincere utterances. We assume that the individual will be able to offer explanations of her past words, deeds, reactions, etc., but the account we are interested in is a sincere account: if the individual's later deeds (or her own confession) show that she just said what suited her best at the time, we shall have no hesitation in saying that she was lying. This underlines a general point, for the individual's account must of course tie in with how she acted before, at the time and afterwards. If she reacts to a statement with surprise and then says 'You said exactly what I expected you to say', we won't know how to put the utterance and the reaction together. On some occasions, we might decide to believe her despite the conflicting evidence, and on others we might make the opposite decision. The key point, however, is that what matters is not some mysterious experience which somehow contains the explanations the individual later gives, but the individual's special role as elucidator of her own words and deeds. Although her statements use the past tense, it is the past tense of the Inner and so has a different grammar from the past tense used to describe events and occurrences.

Here it might be objected that this seems a rather odd sort of past tense, for, if the account of the past simply rests on what the individual is inclined to say, how can it be of interest? Why isn't this supposed disclosure empty talk or mere fantasy? (*RPP1*, para. 218). Asking this question involves misunderstanding the nature of our interest in the Inner, for exactly the same question could be asked in relation to the individual's utterances in the present tense. Furthermore, if we are to treat the individual as an agent, we must assume that she can offer this type of explanation. For example, if we are to treat the sounds she utters as speech, we must see some intention as lying behind them and this involves assuming that she can explain her words, i.e. say what she means and what she meant. Similarly, if we are to treat the individual's behaviour as voluntary, we must assume that in general she can explain it, i.e. say what the intention behind it was. In the case of meaning, the speaker's privileged position in the language-game reflects the assumption that she is saying something, and this assumption is justified not by the occurrence of some special process but by the fact that at any time the speaker can be stopped and asked to explain what she means. The distinctive status of the speaker's claims is underlined by the fact that the possibility of error is irrelevant. It wouldn't matter if the individual said 'It *seemed* to me that I meant' because the subjective element would make no difference (*LW1*, para. 100); what interests us is the explanation the speaker is inclined to give and so the possibility of a mistake is excluded.

This may seem to leave unanswered the question as to whether use of the past tense is justified, but the question itself is misleading, for this is simply how we use the past tense in this context. What needs to be recognised is the distinctiveness of the Inner. The impossibility of checking the individual's account of the past (and of the present) is not a weakness, but a reflection of what makes these concepts important to us. A 'real' past tense which did not rely on the privileged position of the speaker/ agent would have a completely different interest. Instead of giving the individual's account of her experience, it would simply give us more information about the Outer, e.g. tell us that such-and-such a change took place in her brain. Furthermore, it is important to note that within the grammar of our current psychological concepts we do make a distinction between the past and the present. For example, if someone says something and clarifies her statement by saying 'What I mean is . . .' rather than 'What I meant was . . .', the implication is that she is amending her statement rather than simply elucidating it.

Although her statement does not refer to something that happened at the time of speaking, it makes a significant difference whether she presents the explanation as one she would have offered at the time or as something that has occurred to her since.

> He asks 'What did you mean when you said . . .?' I answer the question and then I add: 'If you had asked me before, I'd have answered the same; my answer was not an interpretation which had just occurred to me.' So had it occurred to me earlier? No. – And how then was I able to say: 'If you had asked me earlier, I'd have . . .'? What did I infer it from? From nothing at all. What do I tell him when I utter the conditional? Something that may sometimes be of importance.
>
> (*RPP1*, para. 1134)

Although the individual gives the account now, she distinguishes within that account between what she thought, meant and intended at the time and what she now thinks, means and intends; and this distinction has an obvious importance. When the individual says she would have offered the same explanation had she been asked earlier, the other person

> knows, for example, that I haven't changed my mind. It also makes a difference whether I reply that I was 'only saying these words to myself' without meaning anything by them; or, that I meant this or that by them. Much depends on this.
>
> (*RPP1*, para. 1135)

Thus the use of the past tense is both appropriate and necessary. Indeed, if we did treat the explanation as coming after the words, we would undermine the notion of a speaker altogether. The individual would be transformed into a speaking machine from which words spontaneously issued. *Ex hypothesi*, her words would be as much of a surprise to her as to anyone, and, if that were so, why should we treat her as better placed to interpret them than anyone else?[1]

One feature of this account is that it rejects the idea that our talk of meaning is based on the occurrence of special inner processes. This may seem implausible, but consider the parallel case of understanding. Suppose someone is told that it's seven o'clock, doesn't react and then suddenly exclaims 'Seven o'clock. Then I'm already late. . . .' Here the inclination is to say that a specific process must have occurred when the individual suddenly realised what the words meant. But what does this process involve? What happens when the individual repeats the words 'Seven o'clock!'? Significantly, all we can do in response to this question is paraphrase the idea that the individual suddenly grasped what had been said (*RPP1*, para. 214). This encourages us to argue that the process of understanding is indescribable, whereas in fact there is nothing further to describe. The actions of the individual provide the criteria for claims about how she understood something, and it is only on the basis and in relation to these criteria that we talk of something going on inside her. Suppose, for example, that we tell two people to turn left and one of them turns left and the other turns right. How should we describe the difference between them? We may certainly say that something different went on inside each of them, but the key point is that the basis for saying this is the way each acted. The 'inner process' is not independent of the individual's behaviour, but something we impute to her as a way of characterising her action. The difference between the two individuals is not some further thing (viz. the occurrence of a specific inner process), but the fact that, as their actions show, one understood correctly, while the other did not.

Taking these points into account, Wittgenstein summarises his conclusions and in doing so uncovers the real source of his difficulties. He begins by noting that the experience of meaning is irrelevant to linguistic communication and on this basis argues that if one compares 'the coming of meaning into one's mind to a dream, then our talk is ordinarily dreamless' (*RPP1*, para. 232). According to this approach, the meaning-blind man would be someone who always talked dreamlessly (ibid.) and, by implication, he would be missing out on little or nothing. However, this conclusion is not quite right. In fact, 'the use of the word "dream" here is useful, but only if one sees that it still contains an error itself' (*RPP1*, para. 234). The 'error' lies in a failure to distinguish between meaning and the experience of meaning, for, while the second need not accompany speech, the first must. Take the parallel example of understanding.

I thought the whole time that you were talking about. . . .' – Only how *was* it? Surely not otherwise, than if he really had

been speaking of that man. My later realization that I understood him wrong does not alter anything about what happened as I was understanding the words. –

If, then, the sentence 'At that point I believed that you
meant . . .' is the report of a 'dream', that means that I *always*
dream when I understand a sentence. (*RPP1*, para. 235)

Although the experience of meaning is irrelevant ('a dream'), the
idea that we understood a sentence in a particular way *at the time
it was uttered* is not. The explanation may come later, but it is an
explanation of what we understood at the time. If therefore we
compare our inclination to offer such explanations with our
inclination to report dreams, then such 'dreams' must be seen as
occurring continuously whenever we are engaged in intelligent
conversation. In this respect, therefore, the notion of a dream is
misleading; what matters is that we are continuously able to offer
an explanation, and there is no need for us to be having any
particular experience for this to be the case. The key here is to
distinguish meaning from the experience of meaning. The
meaning of an individual's words relates to the intention she had
when uttering them and this does not consist in an experience or
in any other occurrence at the time of speaking. By contrast, the
experience of meaning does relate to an experience and, if it has
any significance, it must be in a quite different field.[2]

Having made these points, we can see that confusion between
the experience of meaning and the language-game of meaning
also lies behind Wittgenstein's difficulty in thinking through the
concept of the meaning-blind man. Wittgenstein's basic idea is
that the meaning-blind man is someone who lacks the experience
of meaning. However, he links this issue with the problem of the
lightning speed of thought and takes the phrase 'I meant' to refer
to an experience at the time of speaking. He then treats the
meaning-blind man, first, as someone who has this experience in
a more determinate form then we do, and, second, as someone
who doesn't have the experience and so makes no reference to the
past at all. However, both approaches are unsuccessful for, in
seeking to eliminate the lightning speed of thought, they undermine the idea of the meaning-blind man as a conscious being. If
he is seen as only having an intention when he experiences an
image or says something to himself, his consciousness and

intentionality lose their continuity. Similarly, if he is only allowed to express intentions in the present tense, his past appears as something alien to him, something he is no better placed to interpret than those around.

The solution to these difficulties is to recognise that intentionality and the phenomenon of the lightning speed of thought have nothing to do with any experiences. In the case of meaning, therefore, we need to distinguish between the experience of meaning and the normal language game of meaning.

> What is important is that we intend something when we utter a word. For example, I say 'Bank!' and want thereby to remind someone to go to the bank, and intend the word 'bank' in the one meaning and not in the other. (*RPP2*, para. 243)

However, this intention is not an experience, for it has no content; 'the contents (e.g. images) which often go hand in hand with it, are not the intention itself' (ibid., para. 244). By contrast, the experience of meaning is indeed an experience, but one whose significance lies in a completely different field.

> That it is possible after all to utter the word in isolation, far removed from any intention, 'now with one meaning, now with another', is a phenomenon which has no bearing on the nature of meaning. . . . We are dealing so to speak with an outgrowth of the concept. (*RPP2*, para. 245)

Recognition of this point leads Wittgenstein to a final definition of the meaning-blind man and this time he makes clear that the difference between him and us has nothing to do with intentionality or with his capacity for meaningful communication.

> The man I shall call meaning-blind will understand the instruction 'Tell him he is to go to the bank – and I mean the river bank', but not 'Say the word bank and mean the bank of a river'.
>
> He will also not be able to report that he almost succeeded, but that then the word slipped into the wrong meaning. It does not occur to him that the word has something in it which positively fixes the meaning, as a spelling may; nor does its spelling seem to him to be a picture of the meaning, as it were.
>
> If for you spelling is just a practical question, the feeling

you are lacking is not unlike the one that a 'meaning-blind' man would lack. (*RPP2*, para. 571-2)

The distinction between meaning and the experience of meaning enables us to resolve the problem of the lightning speed of thought, for the source of difficulty is our inclination to treat thinking as a succession of experiences. This makes it seem magical, a process which sometimes occurs instantly and on other occasions runs ahead of itself so that it is complete even before it starts. But this approach misrepresents the relation between the thinker and her thinking, for it encourages us to treat the latter simply as something that goes on inside the former. The key is to recognise that thinking is not a process or a succession of experiences, but an aspect of the lives of conscious beings. What corresponds to the lightning speed of thought is the individual's ability at any point to explain what she is doing or saying. To say, as William James does, that the individual must somehow complete her sentence before she begins it presents this as a mystery. The point, however, is that 'the *intention* of uttering the thought may already exist before the first word has been said. For if you ask someone: "Do you know what you intend to say?" he will often say yes' (*RPP1*, para. 575). Similarly, what makes our use of language meaningful is not the continuous occurrence of special experiences, but the fact that we can explain what we are saying. Nothing that happens at the time of speaking constitutes the meaning; rather our words have meaning as the utterances of an intentional agent – 'conversation, the application and further interpretation of words, flows on and only in this current does a word have its meaning' (*RPP1*, para. 240).

If we recognise that thinking is not a process, the phenomenon of the lightning speed of thought suddenly seems much less mysterious. When we have a flash of insight this is not because the normal thinking process is magically speeded up; rather it reflects the fact that thinking has a different kind of duration than a process or activity. This is true not only in the case of a flash of insight but in other cases as well. For example, if someone says to herself 'I must go to the bank today', it would make no sense to view her thinking as something that accompanied the sentence word by word, for this would suggest that during the course of the thought the individual has no idea how it was going to end. But having a thought is neither like watching a telegram message gradually come through nor like laboriously stringing pearls on a necklace. No one can think half a thought or be three-quarters of the way through the process of thinking it. On the contrary, whether the expression of the thought is a word, a sentence or an image, the thought itself is always there in its entirety. If someone thinks 'I must go to the bank', it would make just as little sense to talk of the beginning of the thinking process as to claim that the process took place at a particular moment.

> Or, if one calls the beginning and the end of the sentence the beginning and end of the thought, then it is not clear whether one should say of the experience of thinking that it is uniform during this time, or whether it is a process like speaking the sentence itself. (*RPP2*, para. 257)

Since the concept of thinking is not the concept of an experience, the notion of duration does not apply to it in the normal way. Although we can measure how long an individual takes to express a particular thought and can describe her as being half-way through expressing it, the thought itself cannot be divided in temporal terms. If someone has only half thought out an idea, the problem is that she has not considered all its implications and it is only in this sense that her thought is incomplete. Thus, while considering an idea from various angles and working out its implications might be called a process, having an idea is not. The phenomenon of a flash of insight does not show that thought can sometimes take mysterious forms; rather it underlines the grammatical point that the concept of thinking is the concept neither of a process nor of an experience.

So where does all this leave the notion of a germ? This idea reflects our desire to reduce all aspects of the Inner to experiences, but it is misleading because, whatever the past experience may be, the idea that it contains the later explanation makes no sense. Suppose, for example, that someone is sitting lost in thought and suddenly smiles. When we ask her why she smiled, she explains 'I was just thinking how good my friends have been to me'. If we ask her what happened when she had this thought or what she experienced, she may have no particular answer other than what she has already said. On the other hand, even if she does have an answer, it would impossible to read the thought off from this. If, for example, she says that she had an image of all her friends gathered together, this image would not contain the thought, for on its own it could mean anything or nothing. Intrinsically, it is not a germ.

> Nor does something become a germ because of the later development. What remains then is that the image of the germ forces itself upon us. (Quite naturally so; for we want to see the kernel of the matter in the experience.) (*LW1*, para. 94)

What leads us to treat the experience or image as a germ is philosophical prejudice, our insistence that the later explanation can only be correct if it is contained in an event which occurred at the moment it refers to. But this involves a misunderstanding of how our psychological concepts work. The individual's account of what she thought has the same grammar as her account of what she intended and of what she meant. What we are interested in is the account of the past she is inclined to give, and the assumption that she will be able to give an account is part of what is involved in seeing her as conscious.[3]

The other aspect of the lightning speed of thought – the ability of thought to run ahead of itself – reflects a similar point, for unless we assume that the individual knows what she is about to say or do, we undermine the idea that she is the author of her own words and deeds. Without this assumption, the individual would be transformed into a passive observer and interpreter of her own words. It would be as if someone else were speaking through her, for she would have no special claim to understand the meaning of her past words, and in the present would potentially be as surprised at what 'she' was saying as anyone else. By contrast, treating the individual as a normal person involves giving her a privileged position in the language-game. The notion that she is a conscious being structures our relationship to her and presupposes that she will be able to do certain things, e.g. offer an account of what she was thinking at a certain moment or explain why she acted in a certain way, etc. Similarly the idea that she knows what she wants to say before she says it reflects the assumption that her speech is intentional. No images or experiences are necessary for this to be the case, and even where there is an image, the individual still has a special role as the person who explains what the image means. As Wittgenstein notes,

> whoever answers 'Yes' to the question, 'Do you know yet what you want to say?' may have some mental image or other, but if this could be heard or seen objectively, then there would generally not be any way of deriving what he had intended from it with certainty. (*RPP2*, para. 576)

Despite these points, the example of the flash of insight may still seem mysterious, for here the idea of a special experience seems hard to avoid. Surely, we want to argue, the individual must have a basis for saying 'Now I can do it!' and whatever serves as that basis must therefore contain the answer. But compare the use of this phrase with the schoolroom practice of a child raising her hand when she thinks she knows the answer. The child does not use this signal on the basis of having being taught to locate within herself some special experience, the occurrence of which magically guarantees that she has the right answer. On the contrary, she is simply taught to raise her hand when she thinks she knows the answer. If one asks what has to happen inside her to justify her raising her hand, the answer is nothing. The child uses a signal, but she is not told that she must do such-and-such within herself before raising her hand or that such-and-such must happen within her. Rather what matters is that after raising her hand she can generally give an answer. The key is not a special feeling, but the child's ability to master the use of the signal, and of a child that has done this, we shall say that she knew the answer from the moment she raised her hand. Similar points apply in the case of a flash of insight, for phrases such as 'Now I've got it!' get their point from the fact that subsequently the individual can indeed give an answer. Someone who claimed to have flashes of insight but could never explain what they were would thereby show that she had not mastered the use of the signal. Whatever interest her feelings of illumination might have, they would not have the same significance as a flash of insight. Wittgenstein does not deny that a problem may become clear to someone in an instant, but the justification for saying this lies in what comes later, i.e. her ability to state the solution. We are interested in the utterance 'Now I've got it' not because it expresses a particular experience but because it is a signal of understanding.

Here we can return to one of the phrases with which we started, for the exclamation 'the word is on the tip of my tongue' also functions like a signal. We are not taught it on the basis of a particular feeling, but use it spontaneously and what makes it interesting is that it is indeed often followed by our finding a word and characterising it as the one we were looking for. If we did not, the inclination we sometimes have to say that a word is on the tip of our tongue would lose its interest. The point is not that we experience a 'word-shaped gap', a hole which only one word will fill. Rather we say that we can't find the right word and later find one which does satisfy us. To say the word is already mysteriously present before the individual finds it is misleading, for the claim that she was looking for a particular word is only justified by the fact that she can usually later say what it was. As with the phrase 'Now I can do it' and the hand-raising signal, if the individual could never specify the word, the utterance would lose its interest. In all three cases, what is important is the privileged position of the speaker-agent. As with the Inner in general, what matters is what the individual says, for we treat that as offering an authoritative insight into what she meant, thought and felt at the time.

In conclusion, we can see that the real significance of the lightning speed of thought is what it shows about the nature of thinking. In particular, it brings out the special role of the individual in stating her thoughts. The individual does not report on hidden processes going on inside her; rather her statements are utterances, and her account of what goes on inside her is only of interest because she can explain and apply it. The dynamic quality of thought is not the magical attribute of a special process but reflects the special set of abilities which underlie our treatment of someone as conscious. What matters is not what goes on inside her, but that she is able to do certain things, e.g. offer an account of why she did X or what she meant by saying Y, etc. The main source of resistance to this is the idea that images are the essence of thoughts. As we have seen, however, whatever occurs – be it a mental image or a piece of inner speech – is in itself lifeless, empty; what gives it life is the thinking agent and her account of what it means. Even in the case of imagining, it is what the individual says about her image that connects it to the outer world. For example, if someone is imagining one of a pair of twins doing something, it is her statement, not the image itself, which will tell us which twin she is imagining behaving in this way. As with the lightning speed of thought, we want somehow to build the explanation into the experience, but all this does is create mystification and confusion. We say that someone thought, imagined or meant such-and-such not because particular processes occurred inside her, but because she acts in certain kinds of ways and is able to offer certain kinds of explanation. Furthermore, it is the individual's possession of these abilities that lies behind our treatment of her as someone who possesses consciousness and the ability to think.

So far our main concern has been to emphasise that thinking is not a process, and we have argued that recognition of this dissolves the apparent mystery of the lightning speed of thought. However, this approach may seem unduly negative. In particular, it may seem to leave unanswered the fundamental question as to what actually happens when we think. In an important sense, however, there is no answer to this question. To illustrate this point, it is worth considering some rather different examples of thinking, for an undue emphasis on reflective as opposed to practical thinking can easily obstruct the attempt to understand this concept. Take the case of someone making something.

> Every now and then there is the problem 'Should I use *this* bit?' – The bit is rejected, another is tried. Bits are tentatively put together, then dismantled he looks for one that fits etc., etc. I now imagine that this whole procedure is filmed. The worker perhaps also produces sound-effects like 'Hm' or 'Ha!'. As it were sounds of hesitation, sudden finding, decision, satisfaction, dissatisfaction. But he does not utter a single word. Those sound-effects may be included in the film. I have the film shown me, and now I invent a soliloquy for the worker, things that fit his manner of work, its rhythm, his play of expression, his gestures and spontaneous noises; they correspond to all this. So I sometimes make him say 'No, that

bit is too long, perhaps another'll fit better'. – Or 'What am I to do now?' – 'Got it!' – Or 'That's not bad', etc.

(*RPP2*, para. 183)

Here the soliloquy captures the worker's thoughts despite the fact that she has not said anything. However, it does not point to a separate process. On the contrary, the idea that she is working in an intelligent manner is not separable from what she actually does. If one asks 'What her thinking consists in?', there is no answer; her 'thinking' cannot be separated from her activity, for it is not something that *accompanies* her work (*RPP2*, para. 184). When we say that she thinks as she works, we are not pointing to a special process, but distinguishing her activity from purely mechanical action.

The above example shows that thinking is not something that runs concurrently with the individual's actions, but rather something that characterises them as actions of a certain kind. As Wittgenstein admits, however, there do seem to be counter-examples. Take the case of reading a difficult passage. Here it is tempting to argue that reading the text and making sure one understands it are two separate but parallel processes. But are they really separate? According to Wittgenstein, 'what accompanies the words is like a series of small secondary movements. It is like being led along a street, but casting glances right and left into all the side streets' (*RPP2*, para. 208). This captures what we are inclined to say about attentive reading, but it does not describe a specific process. The 'process of thinking' consists in checking that one has in fact understood what one has read, but what this involves is undetermined. If we tell someone to read and understand a passage, there is no special activity she has to perform apart from the reading; rather what matters is that having read the passage, she can explain it, assess its claims, etc. The interest of saying she thought about the passage while reading it is not that this points to some special inner process, but that it distinguishes between two ways of carrying out this activity; what is important is what the individual is able to do having read the passage.

To illustrate this point further, consider the example of giving someone a list of errands. Here it may be enough to give a fairly vague indication of what each errand involves. The other person may say she has understood, but 'we do not prescribe what the other has to do if he is to understand the list; and whether he really understood is determined from what he does later, or from the explanation we might ask him to give' (*RPP2*, para. 209). However, if thinking does not involve doing anything specific, why should it involve doing anything at all? If someone who checks that she has understood moves in thought along part of the path she is later to follow, why shouldn't she be able to see that she knows the way without going along it even partially? (ibid., para. 210). If the task is obvious, the individual may simply say 'yes' and the fact that she did not do anything does not show that her answer was mechanical. On the contrary, the instant response may be a sign of intelligence. The test of whether she was thinking about what was being said is not what goes on inside her, but what she later does; only if she is able to carry out the instructions accurately, will we say that she was paying attention to what she was being told to do.

Against this, it is tempting to argue that only introspection can really tell us what thinking or paying attention consists in. But, even if introspection did show us something, how could we be sure that this is *the* characteristic process of attention? (*RPP2*, para. 236). Furthermore, how would we know that the same process goes on in others? In fact, when we ask someone to read attentively, what matters is not that some process goes in inside her, but that she takes careful note of the passage being read and is able, for example, to give an accurate account of it. A description of the images she had while reading it would have a different interest; even if we could always give an account of these images when we read attentively but not when we read inattentively, this would not mean that having images constituted attention (ibid., para. 237). When we say someone has read a passage attentively, we are not interested in the colourfulness of her experience but in what she can now do. Conversely, the significance of saying she read the passage without thinking about it is that this implies that she was distracted, that the passage made no impression on her or that she won't be able to discuss it, etc. In all these cases, the idea of thinking as a mysterious inner process is irrelevant. What matters is how the person acts and the type of possibility for interaction with her that this creates. For this reason, it would make no sense if somebody who had had an animated conversation with me were thereafter to assure me that he had spoken entirely without thinking. But this is not because it contradicts all experience that a person who can speak in this way should do so without thought processes accompanying his speech. Rather, it is because it comes out here that the accompanying processes are of no interest whatsoever to us, and do not constitute thinking. We don't give a damn about his accompanying processes when he engages in a normal conversation with us. (*RPP2*, para. 238)

If, therefore, we abandon the idea of thinking as a process, what are we left with? Consider a case when we would say that a thought had occurred to someone, for example, the case of someone making a decision.

He says 'I want to go out now', then suddenly says 'No', and does something else. As he said 'No', it suddenly occurred to him that he wanted first of all to. . . . – He said 'No', but did he also *think* 'No'? Didn't he just think about that other thing? One can say he was thinking about it. But to do that he didn't have to pronounce a thought, either silently or out loud. To be sure, he could later clothe the intention in a sentence. When his intentions changed maybe a picture was in his mind, or he didn't just say 'No', but some *one* word, the equivalent of a picture. For example, if he wanted to close the cupboard then maybe he said 'The cupboard!'; if he wanted to wash his hands he might have looked at them and made a face. 'But is that thinking?' – I don't know. Don't we say in such cases that someone has 'thought something over', has changed his mind?
(*RPP2*, para. 6)

The point about thinking is that we do not apply it in relation to a specific process but use it in the context of the individual behaving in certain kinds of ways. The concept does not describe the behaviour but characterises it as the action of a thinking being and hence as the manifestation of a particular thought or intention. Here it is worth noting that we might extend the concept to an animal if it behaved in a similar way to the individual described above. If, for example, the animal had been trained to fetch an object from one place and take it to another and it started walking towards the goal without the object and then turned back, we might say that it had changed its mind. Here we know nothing about what went on inside the animal and, since it does not possess language, its thinking certainly cannot consist in its saying anything to itself; rather what justifies applying the concept is a certain complexity and purposiveness in its behaviour. Similarly, someone who is making something will be said to be thinking while she works, but this does not mean some special activity accompanied her work; rather it distinguishes this action from one of a very different sort (*RPP2*, para. 7).

As these examples show, the concept thinking does not apply to a particular process but highlights certain aspects of human activity. The best way therefore to describe thinking is to describe the difference between someone who is feeble-minded and a normal child who is beginning to think (*RPP2*, para. 11). To do this is not to embrace a form of behaviourism, for as Wittgenstein points out 'if one wanted to indicate the activity which the normal person learns and which the feeble-minded cannot learn, one couldn't derive it from their behaviour' (ibid.). The person who can think does not do something the feeble-minded cannot do; rather her whole activity has a different character and this is what our use of the concept thinking picks out. So how can that character be defined? The answer is it can't. If we do try to define it, the first problem we encounter is that anything we point to as an example of thinking only functions as such against a wider background. Furthermore, the only way of explaining the concept is in terms of examples from our own lives. The paradigm of someone who thinks is the normal human being and it is only on this basis that the concept can be extended and applied elsewhere. Although the ability to express thought in language is central to the concept of thinking, we might nonetheless extend the concept to non-language-users if their way of acting was similar enough to our own.

> If we were to see creatures at work whose *rhythm* of work, play of expression, etc., was like our own, but for their not *speaking*, perhaps in that case we should say that they thought, considered, made decisions. That is: in such a case there would be a *great deal* which is similar to the action of

ordinary human beings. And it isn't clear *how much* has to be similar for us to have a right to apply to them also the concept of 'thinking', which has its home in our life.

(*RPP2*, para. 186)

But what would be the importance of saying these people thought? Well, it might be crucial in determining our attitude to them, and in purely practical terms it will make a big difference to us whether the creatures can only learn 'mechanically' or can develop new ways of doing things themselves by trial and comparison. Here again, however, 'what should be called "making trials" and "comparisons" can in turn be explained only by giving examples, and these examples will be taken from our life or from a life that is like ours' (*RPP2*, para. 187).

To illustrate these points, Wittgenstein considers a simple experiment drawn from the psychologist Koehler. In the experiment, a monkey is trying to get a banana from the ceiling of a room, but can't reach it except by putting two sticks together and getting hold of it in that way. What, Wittgenstein asks, must go on inside the monkey for us to call this an act of thought? One answer might be that 'unless he acted through chance or instinct, the monkey must have seen the process before his mental eye' (*RPP2*, para. 224). But this is misleading. On the one hand, it would be too much (one could have the thought without having the image), and on the other, too little (we should not call it thinking if the monkey simply acted out a chance mental image). What is important is that the monkey must have reflected – catching hold of the stick must be something he gets hold of 'inwardly'. But what does this involve? Well, we'll look for signs of reflections, signs perhaps that the monkey explores other ways of getting the banana before finding the right one. We shall also look at how he learns from his experience. Suppose, for example, that to begin with it just is a happy accident. How must the monkey now act for us to say he can think?

He says to himself, as it were, 'That's how!', and then he does it with signs of full consciousness. – If he has made some combination in play, and he now uses it as a method for doing this and that, we shall say he thinks. – In *considering* he would mentally review ways and means. But to do this he must already have some in stock. Thinking gives him the possibility of *perfecting* his methods. Or rather: he 'thinks' when, in a definite kind of way, he perfects the method he has.

(*RPP2*, para. 224)

Here what is important is that we say he thinks not because we discover a particular process in him, but because he acts in a certain way. To put the idea of inner activity first gets things the wrong way round, for it is only because he acts 'intelligently' that we say thinking takes place within him.

Having made these points, it may still seem strange that we cannot define 'thinking', but the point is that we do not learn the word through a definition.

One learns the word 'think', i.e. its use, under certain circumstances, which, however, one does not learn to describe. We learn to say it perhaps only of human beings, we learn to assert or deny it of them. The question 'Do fishes think?' does not exist among our applications of language, *it is not raised.*

(*RPP2*, paras 200–1)

This may seem to undermine our earlier discussion of when we would say that a monkey would think. The point of that discussion, however, was to cast light on our concept of thinking by investigating the considerations which might lead us to apply it outside its usual context. The aim was to show that, as Wittgenstein puts it, 'there is such a thing as "primitive thinking" which is to be described via primitive *behaviour*' (*RPP2*, para. 205). Thus there are ways of acting which can (and do) lead us to describe non-humans as thinking at least in a primitive way. In doing this, we underline a similarity between their lives and ours. It is not that we detect outer signs of an inner process; rather we impute a notional inner process on the basis of the animal acting in certain types of ways. But the pattern of the concept, the notion of thinking as a mental activity, is only complete when the individual can express her thought, i.e. when she applies the concept in the first person by saying 'I think'. It would be wrong therefore to call thinking a phenomenon, for it is not a particular process nor something that can simply be derived from observation. What unites the concept is our interest in certain aspects of human life. Although there are phenomena (manifestations) of thinking (e.g. 'the thoughtful expression, the

expression of the idiot. The frown of reflection, of attention'
(*RPP2*, para. 223)), what brings them together is not some
external similarity but the concept of thinking itself.

We started this chapter seeking to pin down the specific
process which constitutes thought; as we have seen, however,
thinking is a widely ramified concept and has a variety of
applications, all of which we treat as related. We say that
someone who is talking is expressing thoughts, but we also say
that someone is thinking if she is working in a purposeful way,
e.g. making something. Furthermore, we also speak of thinking
when a person is sitting silently and apparently doing nothing
but is later able to give the answer to a problem, etc. In the face of
this variety, Wittgenstein points out that it would be possible to
have different words for the various things we call thinking:

> one for 'thinking out loud'; one for thinking as one talks in
> the imagination; one for a pause during which something or
> other floats before the mind (or doesn't) after which, however,
> we are able to give a confident answer. (*RPP2*, para. 215)

As these examples show, our concept 'thinking' is 'like a ramified
traffic network which connects many out-of-the-way places'
(*RPP2*, para. 216). What holds the concept together is the picture
of an inner process, for 'in all of these cases, we say that the mind
is not idle, that something is going on inside it; and we thereby
distinguish these cases from a state of stupor, from mechanical
actions' (ibid., para. 217). Although someone working intelligently may intersperse her work with auxiliary activities, e.g.
comparing or measuring the materials she is working on, trying
various ways of putting them together, etc., these activities are
not what we mean by thinking. Rather

> the concept 'thinking' is formed on the model of a kind of
> imaginary auxiliary activity . . . one imagines thinking as that
> which must be flowing under the surface of these expedients
> (the observable auxiliary activities), if they are not after all to
> be mere mechanical processes. (*RPP2*, paras 226–8)

What then is thinking? On the one hand, there is no answer to
this question. On the other, the answer is that it is a fundamental
characteristic of human activity and human life. The idea that
the individual thinks, has intentions, etc. is at the heart of the

notion of a person and in that sense underlies all our interaction with each other.

> If somebody tells me of some incident, or asks me an everyday question (e.g. what time is it), I'm not going to ask him whether he was thinking while he was telling me or asking me. Or again: it would not be immediately clear in what circumstances one might have said that he did this without thinking – even though one can imagine such circumstances.
>
> (*RPP2*, para. 222)

The concept of thinking does not refer to a process or to anything that happens. Rather it lies at the heart of the notion of the Inner and as such belongs to the special network of concepts which provide the framework for our understanding of human life. We use the concept to pick out one aspect of our lives and express this in terms of the metaphor of an invisible inner process. The picture expresses the fundamental distinction between the beings we treat as conscious and those we don't, and the basis for the distinction is the way members of each group behave and what they are able to do. If we are to treat someone as a conscious agent, she must, for example, be able to offer a continuous account of her waking activity and of the thoughts and intentions lying behind it. What matters is that she is able to do certain things. The notion of consciousness does not refer to a strange phenomenon occurring inside us; rather it expresses the fundamental difference between ourselves and other kinds of being.

4

THE MUSICALITY OF LANGUAGE

What we call 'understanding a sentence' has, in many cases, a much greater similarity to understanding a musical theme than we might be inclined to think. But I don't mean that understanding a musical theme is more like the picture which one tends to make oneself of understanding a sentence; but rather that this picture is wrong, and that understanding a sentence is much more like what really happens when we understand a tune than at first sight appears. (*BB*, p. 167)

In our discussions of sense-impressions and of thinking, we have criticised the idea that psychological concepts describe inner events; making this point, however, raises fundamental questions about how language operates in relation to the Inner. The idea that utterances such 'I am in pain' function as signals is already a major break with the traditional approach to concepts of the Inner, but it only forms the beginning of the radically new approach Wittgenstein advocates. To appreciate his argument, however, we must first recognise the very real problem from which it proceeds. The fact that we continually use language to express our experiences, emotions, feelings, etc. blinds us to the question as to how this is possible, and yet it is far from clear how we manage to put the Inner into language. How do we connect words with our experiences? How do we cast what is most personal into a generally accessible form? Wittgenstein's notion of an utterance only partially answers these questions, for many of the utterances we use are not learnt but spontaneous, and it is therefore rather mysterious how we come to use them in the first place. To take an example from Chapter 1, why do we suddenly talk of 'calculating in the head' when the original use of the word calculating is to describe a public activity? Similarly what makes someone suddenly say 'I feel as if everything is unreal' when the word 'unreal' wasn't originally introduced as relating to something a person might one day feel? Here language seems to operate in a vacuum and yet, despite the absence of rules and justification, it still seems to function. Someone says 'I suddenly felt as if I was being watched' and instead of treating her as if she was ill, we say 'Yes, I know what you mean'. Although strictly speaking our utterances are nonsensical, they still seem to say something, indeed, something which can often be very important. The puzzle about our experience is not that it is private, but that it is expressible; the real mystery of the Inner is the mystery of how it finds expression in language.

The problem of language is, of course, at the heart of both Wittgenstein's early and his later philosophy. In the *Tractatus*, he argues that language is a way of picturing states of affairs and that it is able to represent the world because of the isomorphism between its elements and those of reality. In his later work, Wittgenstein launches a radical attack on this account, but the true scope of this attack only really becomes apparent in his writings on the philosophy of psychology. The best way to approach the issue, however, is to return to the experience of meaning discussed in the preceding chapter. The classic instantiation of this phenomenon is the experience we have when we repeat a word in isolation and feel that it gradually loses its meaning. As we saw, this experience has nothing to do with meaning in the normal sense, and to understand it we have to view it against the background of various other strange things we say about language. For example, just as we say that words may become empty of meaning, so too we sometimes say that they are brimming with it. On such occasions, a word seems intrinsically meaningful, a picture as it were of its own meaning. Similarly, one might talk of each word having its own 'face' or atmosphere, so that the non-standard word 'knoif' has a different atmosphere from the word 'knife' (*LW1*, para. 726). This point can be generalised, for if some words have faces, presumably they all do. One might argue therefore that 'even the word "state" has a face, for at any rate "the State" has a *different* face; and so "state" would also have to feel somehow or other!' (*RPP1*, para. 328).

This sort of argument led William James to try to explain meaning in terms of special feelings associated with particular words, e.g. an 'if-feeling' associated with the word 'if'. As we saw, this account won't do as an explanation of meaning, but it does seem to capture an aspect of our experience. At this stage, however, a new problem arises, for it becomes clear that defining these feelings is no easy matter. The obvious suggestion is that the if-feeling is a feeling that accompanies the use of the word 'if', but this can't be right, for in that case the feeling might also occur on its own or as the accompaniment to something else (*LW1*, para. 369). The connection with the word 'if' must be more intimate than one of accompaniment, but it is not clear what this might be. Like its close cousin the experience of meaning, the if-feeling seems a peculiar phenomenon, a curiosity whose significance is hard to place.

The best way of clarifying these phenomena is to reconsider the question as to what someone who did not have the experience of meaning would be like. This time, however, we shall keep the question of the experience of meaning quite separate from the issue of the lightning speed of thought. In fact, we shall take our previous investigation of aspect-blindness as a guide for, as Wittgenstein notes, the two concepts are closely related. For example, one way of describing certain types of seeing as would be to say that it involves seeing a meaning. Conversely, in experiencing a meaning we might be said to hear the word as itself an embodiment of what it refers to. So what did Wittgenstein's investigation of aspect-blindness establish? The main result was to bring out the particular nature of our relation to pictures. Although a picture might be defined as a representation according to certain rules, that is not how we relate to them. Rather than decoding a picture, we see it directly as the object it depicts. As we saw,[1] this can be illustrated in terms of two types of possible reaction to the picture of a cavalry charge. On the one hand, the individual may simply recognise what such a picture depicts and deduce various things from it, e.g. how many cavalrymen charged, how compact their line was, etc. On the other hand, she may respond directly to the picture, so that it is as if she actually experiences the massed onslaught of the cavalrymen. For this type of person, the picture does not simply represent a state of affairs; rather, as the fine shades of her reaction show, the picture conjures up the event itself. The individual treats the picture in some ways as the object it depicts; she may, for example, recoil as if the cavalrymen might at any moment burst through into the room. For her, the picture is not just a sign used to convey information; rather it has its own value and may be a source of delight in itself. By contrast, the aspect-blind relate to pictures simply as representations with a particular use. The only question for them is whether a picture is accurate according to a given set of rules of representation, not whether it is convincing or lifeless, moving or flat, noble or contrived.

The implication of this for meaning-blindness is that here too what is at issue is our relation to the medium in question, in this case, language. Just as the aspect-blind can see, so too the meaning-blind would be able to communicate; the difference between us and them would be that for them words would only have meaning as part of an agreed symbolism. Unlike us, the meaning-blind would not say that a word seemed to lose its meaning if repeated many times nor would they say that every word had a particular face or atmosphere. Their relation to language would be purely functional; words would simply be symbols used to convey information by depicting particular states of affairs. For us, however, language is more than an arbitrary symbolism. Words (both spoken and written) seem to have a value of their own and to embody their meanings. Certain words (e.g. 'love' or even 'philosophy') are put on a pedestal or conferred like a badge of merit on what we consider most important (*RPP1*, para. 116). Others are treated as tainted or unutterable. Similarly, words may be hard to say or may, on the contrary, be brimming over with joyful meaning. As these examples show, words are anything but arbitrary symbols, indeed, they are so important to us that we even get quite worked up over their spelling. Thus 'if for you spelling is just a practical question, the feeling you are lacking is not unlike the one that a "meaning-blind" man would lack' (*Z*, para. 184).

The importance of the concept of meaning-blindness is to highlight the fact that there might be people who did not have our attachment to words, people to whom the familiar physiognomy of a word, the feeling that it had taken up its meaning into itself, that it was an actual likeness of its meaning, was alien (*PI*, p. 218). One crucial difference between us and such people would be the way we choose and value words.

> Without doubt it is sometimes as if I were comparing [words] by fine differences of smell: *That* is too . . ., *that* is too . . ., – *this* is the right one. – But I do not always have to make such judgements, give explanations; often I might only say: 'It simply isn't right yet.' I am dissatisfied, I go on looking. At last a word comes: *That's* it!' *Sometimes* I can say why. This is simply what searching, this is what finding is like here. (ibid.)

Here one might object that the difficulty of finding the right word is simply the difficulty of finding the correct technical term to describe a particular situation or occurrence. On this view, all we are doing in such cases is using a highly specialised symbol to represent a specific situation and therefore there is no reason why the meaning-blind should not do the same. If this were so, however, we should in principle be able to say why one word is correct and another wrong. In fact, we are not always able to do this. Furthermore, on certain occasions one word may seem appropriate and another with a very similar meaning, completely wrong. Similarly, it is significant that we sometimes treat a particular phrase or exclamation as unique or unparaphrasable. This suggests, first, that there are differences of meaning which cannot be explained in the normal way, and, second, that there is a level of grasping a sentence which goes beyond recognising its informational content. Both of these ideas are captured in Wittgenstein's claim that understanding a sentence is like understanding a piece of music; however, if we are to appreciate the point of this claim, we must first consider what it means to say that we understand music.

The history of aesthetics offers a range of accounts as to how we should understand our relation to music; for our purposes, however, we can distinguish two basic contrasting views. One holds that the aim of music is to create pleasurable sensations, experiences, etc. in the listener. The other accepts that we understand music and argues that appreciation consists in decoding the message enshrined in it. Wittgenstein, however, rejects both views. As far as the first is concerned, he argues that it fails to do justice to the nature of our response to music. In particular, the reference to sensations is inappropriate, for even when music does give us pleasure, this is not because it gives us particularly pleasant sensations (we don't say 'Put the record on again, it gave me a lovely sensation at the back of my neck'). Furthermore, even the stress on pleasure is misleading, for the whole point of music (and the other arts) is that our response takes a much more complex form than simply the expression of varying degrees of delight. The alternative suggestion that music contains a message is just as misleading, for if the point of the music lies in the decoded message, why bother to encode it in the first place? If the composer had something to say, why didn't she simply say it? While the first view treats music as a kind of drug, the second presents it as an elaborate riddle, a kind of aural crossword puzzle. In both cases, the music itself is treated as irrelevant, simply a means to some external end.

In an attempt to avoid these reductive accounts, Wittgenstein begins by asking when we would say of someone that she had listened to a piece of music with understanding. We do not say this just because the person shows signs of enjoyment, any more than we would say of a dog that wagged its tail during a performance of Beethoven's Ninth that it understood the music. Rather the individual's response must have a certain complexity and it is the reaction as a whole which justifies talk of understanding.

> Understanding music has a certain *expression* in listening, playing and at other times too. Sometimes gestures form part of this expression, but sometimes it will just be a matter of how a man plays, or hums, the piece, also now and again of the comparisons he draws and the images with which he as it were illustrates the music. Someone who understands music will listen differently (e.g. with a different expression on his face), he will talk differently, from someone who does not. But he will show that he understands a particular theme not just in manifestations that accompany his hearing or playing that theme but in his understanding for music in general.
>
> (*CV*, p. 70)

The notion of understanding is underlined by the explanations the individual may give, for example, she may seek to bring out the significance of a passage by comparing it with others or by linking it up with certain thoughts or experiences. However, these explanations are no substitute for the music itself, and they only make sense against the background of our shared response to music. Here communication presupposes kinship. If music means nothing to someone, our explanations will get nowhere. The same is true of expressive playing. Although we can show our understanding of a piece by playing it expressively, we can't explain why one way of playing it is 'right' and another 'wrong'. Furthermore, we could not teach anyone rules for playing expressively.

> How can it be explained what 'expressive playing' is? Certainly not by anything that accompanies the playing. – What is needed for the explanation? One might say: a culture. – If someone is brought up in a particular culture – and then reacts to music in such-and-such a way, you can teach him the use of the phrase 'expressive playing'. (*RPP2*, para. 468)

Understanding music involves responding to it in a certain way, but the basis of that response cannot be explicitly or systematically learnt. We are not taught rules for understanding music; rather we come to respond to it and in a way which, although spontaneous, is still often shared.[2]

Here one might object that Wittgenstein has yet to say anything about the actual experience of understanding the music. It's all very well, one might say, to talk about how that understanding subsequently manifests itself, but what about at the actual time of listening? 'If I hear a tune with understanding, doesn't something special go on in me – which does not go on if I hear it without understanding?' (*Z*, para. 162). The answer, of course, is yes, but, as with understanding in general,[3] it is a mistake to treat what goes on inside the individual as an independently-definable process. The notion of an inner process distinguishes between two types of reaction, but in saying that something different went on inside the two individuals, we are underlining this difference, not pointing to some mysterious third entity. The difference we are interested in is that between someone who is 'left cold' by the music and someone for whom it has an immediate impact. Furthermore, that response must have a certain complexity. If we are to talk of understanding, the music must not simply excite the individual; her response must be tied to the music itself and must be something other than simple delight.

In what sense, however, is there something to understand in music? Since it consists purely of musical relationship, how can it point outside itself? The answer is that our reaction to music connects it with the non-musical. Thus a particular theme

> makes an impression on me which is connected with things in its surroundings – e.g. with our language and its intonations; and hence with the whole field of our language-games.
>
> If I say for example: Here it's as if a conclusion were being drawn, here as if something were being confirmed, *this* is like an answer to what is said before, – then my understanding presupposes a familiarity with inferences, with confirmation, with answers. (Z, para. 175)

What is important here is the directness of our relation to the music, for we do not have to learn a system of correlations between the music and our lives, rather our response takes that form immediately. We listen and make connections even though there is no system of rules to justify those connections. Furthermore, we apply to the music a whole range of concepts originally used to describe human action. We say the music is meretricious, sentimental or heroic, or we describe the recurrence of a particular theme as being like a seed of hope which keeps welling up only to be submerged by doubt. Understanding the piece of music involves making sense of these connections and coming to appreciate why the piece of music makes such an impression upon us. This impression, however, only makes sense against a wider background. Although when we listen to a short phrase, we may think 'What a lot it's got in it', this is in one sense an optical illusion, for it is only in relation to the rest of the piece, and indeed in relation to the rest of our musical culture and our lives, that it has this significance (*RPP2*, para. 504).

One difficulty here is understanding how music can communicate in the absence of explicit rules – how can there be a language, where there are no definitions and no universally agreed explanations of meaning? Despite this point, we seem to have no difficulty applying the vocabulary of meaning to music. When discussing a piece of music, we say that a certain way of playing it makes no sense or we describe the recurrence of the theme at a certain point as necessary. So what is the paradigm for this necessity? In one sense,

> there just *is* no paradigm apart from the theme itself. And yet again there *is* a paradigm apart from the theme: namely, the rhythm of our language, of our thinking and feeling. And the theme, moreover, is a *new* part of our language; it becomes incorporated into it; we learn a new *gesture*.
> The theme interacts with language. (*CV*, p. 52)

The key notion here is that of a gesture, for a gesture can mean something to us even when it is not part of an established convention. Furthermore, even a conventional gesture outgrows its established meaning, for it may take on a slightly different significance from one situation to another. The V-for-victory sign may express unthinking self-congratulation or a commitment to keep on struggling, it may be a gesture of individualism or a symbol of solidarity. Our response to the gesture, and our understanding of it in a particular context, goes beyond any fixed meaning and is independent of any rules. It is not just a question of recognizing a prearranged signal. On the contrary, what underlies the language of gestures is kinship, not agreement. Understanding involves a direct response to the gesture itself and it is the directness of this response which makes communication possible. Take the related example of a facial expression such as a smile. To us, a smile may signify many things and in a particular situation its precise meaning may be very important. However, we would not necessarily be able to teach the 'language' of smiles to a Martian; a human smile may convey nothing to her or at best she may be able to learn to see a smile as some sort of sign of pleasure without being able to distinguish further as to its precise meaning. As this example shows, there can be communication without rules and this communication is not just a vague second-best. On the contrary, it can in a sense be even more specific than language, so that if we try to translate one into the other it is the language of words that comes to seem clumsy and inadequate.

Here it may seem somewhat suspect that the supposed communication cannot be put into words, but the whole point of this sort of communication is that it works on a a different level to rule-based language. The reason there are no rules in this context is because the medium and the message are indistinguishable: the person who smiles is not simply using a recognized signal designed for use in a wide variety of contexts. Rather her smile is a gesture and what it says may be unique and only possible in the particular context in which it occurred. What is needed to understand the smile is not a set of rules but an understanding of people and possibly some knowledge of the individual concerned. However, the fact that the gesture may have a unique, untranslatable meaning does not imply it cannot be explained at all. For example, we might characterise a smile as being a mixture of love and pity or as expressing hope and an awareness of the absurdity of the situation. These descriptions may roughly express what the smile meant, but only very crudely – perhaps the only way really to understand the smile would have been to see it and even then its meaning might only be apparent to someone who knew the person concerned really well.

As the above example suggests, we do not interpret gestures by reference to pre-established canons of right or wrong, and this may seem to suggest that the whole process is entirely subjective. In that case, however, what justification is there for talking of understanding? Well, we certainly do talk of understanding another person's smile and that understanding may be confirmed by our ability to predict and interpret her actions. Often, however, prediction is not the key thing; rather what matters is our ability to respond to the other person, our ability to 'find our feet' with her. The other person smiles or says something and we know what she means – her gesture makes sense to us and that we have indeed understood her is something she herself may confirm. Similarly, what matters with music is our relation to it, the particular way in which we respond to it. The mystery of music is that we find it not just enjoyable, but meaningful. Somehow an array of sounds can seem to express our deepest feelings about life and the world we live in, and a brief musical phrase can capture the very essence of a feeling or experience. What justifies the notion of understanding is the complexity of our response and the fact that, while it is spontaneous, it is also often shared. Furthermore, even if we cannot explain the significance of the music, we can still give some indication of what it means to us.

I say to myself: 'What is this? What does this phrase say? Just what does it express?' – I feel as if there must still be a much clearer understanding of it than the one I have. And this understanding would be reached by saying a great deal about the surrounding of the phrase. As if one were trying to understand an expressive gesture in a ceremony. And in order to explain it I should need as it were to analyse the ceremony. E.g., to alter it and show what influence that would have on the role of the gesture.

I might also say: I feel as if there must be parallels to this musical expression in other fields.

The question is really: are these notes not the expression for what is expressed here? Presumably. But that does not mean that they aren't to be explained by working on their surroundings. (*RPP1*, paras 34–6)

The phrase says something, but something which cannot be paraphrased – it says itself. It makes a unique gesture, but the significance of that gesture can be explored by relating it to the network of possibilities against which it has its meaning.

According to Wittgenstein, therefore, we do understand music but not because it contains a message which could just as easily have been put in words. On the contrary, we understand music as we understand gestures, and the nature of the understanding is different from that involved in understanding a prearranged signal. Here 'learning the language' does not consist in learning definitions, but in coming to respond directly to the gestures which constitute the language. Furthermore, it may be impossible to state explicitly what the gesture or the musical phrase means. 'When a theme, a phrase, suddenly means something to you, you don't have to be able to explain it to yourself. Suddenly *this* gesture too is accessible to you' (*RPP1*, para. 660). This does not mean, however, that all explanation of what the theme means is impossible. We may be able to say roughly why we find it so moving, and it may even be possible to find a gesture in another medium which corresponds to it. However, what is at stake is not the substitution of one general sign for another; rather it involves finding a link between two incommensurate realms, both of which get their importance from their relation to human life and feeling.

The peculiar feeling that the recurrence of a refrain gives us. I should like to make a gesture. But the gesture isn't really at all characteristic precisely of the recurrence of a refrain. Perhaps I might find that a phrase characterizes the situation better; but it too would fail to explain why the refrain strikes one as a joke, why its recurrence elicits a laugh or a grin from me. If I could dance to the music, that would be the best way of expressing just how the refrain moves me. (*RPP1*, para. 90)

The piece of music says something, but not because it contains some form of encoded message. Rather it speaks a language of its own and one which cannot be taught by rules, but which presupposes that the individual responds directly to what she hears and so finds meaning in an apparently arbitrary pattern of resemblances and differences.

The example of music shows how there can be communication and understanding without a prearranged symbolism: music says something to us even though it is not based on a system of agreed meanings. The natural inclination is to contrast this 'language' with the language of words, where clear rules and definitions exist. The existence of poetry, however, already calls this dichotomy into question, for as Wittgenstein notes, 'a poem, even though it is composed in the language of information, is not used in the language-game of information' (*RPP1*, para. 160). In fact, a poem can make the same sort of impression upon us as a piece of music, for here too we are inclined to say that reading or listening to it involves special experiences.

'I experience something different' – 'And what kind of thing?' – I can give no satisfactory answer. For what I could mention is not what is most important. – 'But didn't you enjoy it *during* the reading?' Of course – for the opposite answer would mean: I enjoyed it later or earlier, and I don't want to say that.

But now, you surely do remember sensations and images as you read, and they are such as to connect up with the enjoyment, with the impression. – But they got their significance only from the surroundings: through the reading of this poem, from my familiarity with its language, with its metre and with innumerable associations. (*RPP1*, para. 170)

111

A prose translation of the poem would not have the same impact and insofar as this is the case, this shows that language too does not operate exclusively on the level of explicit or paraphrasable meaning. As in music, metre and rhythm contribute to the gesture the poem makes, as does the particular choice of words, for replacing a word in a poetry with a synonym may undermine the poem's force and alter its significance.

The example of poetry underlines the musical element in language but that element is not restricted to poetry. Indeed, if the poet's words can pierce us, this is only possible because of the particular relation to language we have, because we are at home in language (Z, para. 155). The words of our language strike us as expressive in their own right, pictures as it were of their meaning, and from each a host of paths leads off in every direction so that our thoughts roam up and down in the familiar surroundings of the words. It is important to recognize, however, that this is not the only relation to language that is conceivable:

> There could also be a language in whose use the impression made on us by the signs played no part; in which there was no such thing as understanding, in the sense of such an impression. The signs are, e.g. written and transmitted to us, and we are able to *take notice of them*. (That is to say, the only impression that comes in here is the pattern of the sign.) If the sign is an order, we translate it into action by means of rules, tables. It does not get as far as an impression, like that of a picture; nor are stories written in this language. (Z, para. 145)

Here language would be a mere symbolism, an arbitrary set of prearranged signs and all talk of meaning would simply reflect the publicly-defined rules. Our relation to language, however, is not of this kind, as is clear in our reaction to invented languages. 'Esperanto. The feeling of disgust we get if we utter an invented word with *invented* derivative syllables. The word is cold, lacking in associations, and yet it plays at being "language" ' (CV, p. 52). Wittgenstein's reaction may seem extreme, but it reflects a fundamental point, for the words of our own language strike us as meaningful quite independently of their ability to convey information. Suppose, for example, we invented a language in which 'abcde' mean 'the weather is fine'. Despite having the same meaning, the two sentences have a quite different feel: whereas the one is cold and empty, the other contains a myriad of possibilities. The difference does not simply lie in the unfamiliarity of the new language, rather

> the major difference between the two cases is that in the one I can't move. It is as if one of my joints were in splints, and I were not yet familiar with the possible movements, so that I as it were keep on bumping into things. (*RPP2*, para. 259)

The metaphor Wittgenstein uses brings out our closeness to language, the fact that it becomes a second nature to us. Here the choice of words ceases to be a matter of simply choosing the right sign to represent a particular state of affairs. On the contrary, through the unique network of similarities and differences that relate it to other words, each word comes to have a unique value. Here the sound of the word, its associations and its history can all play a role. The words 'friend', 'comrade', 'mate', 'pal' and 'buddy' have the same basic meaning, but in a particular context the choice of one as opposed to others may be charged with significance. In this way, the word itself becomes a gesture, a point underlined by the significance of how a word is said. For example, in the case of the invented language, if we were told that 'abcde' was a polite thing to say, this would already give us a better understanding of the signs (ibid., para. 260). Now we would have a better idea of how to utter the sentence and a better feel for what we are doing in uttering it. This brings us back to the relation to music, for what we say operates on various levels, not just the informational. 'There is a strongly musical element in verbal language. (A sigh, the intonation of voice in a question, in announcement, in longing; all the innumerable *gestures* made with the voice)' (*Z*, para. 161).

The point therefore of Wittgenstein's comparison of language and music is to show that language involves various types of understanding. Normally we concentrate on language as a means of conveying information, but this neglects the much more varied role it actually plays.

> Understanding a piece of music – understanding a sentence.
> I am said not to understand a form of speech like a native if, while I do know its sense, I yet don't know, e.g. what class of people would employ it. In such a case one says that I am not

acquainted with the precise shade of meaning. But if one were now to think that one has a different sensation in pronouncing the word if one knows this shade of meaning, this would again be incorrect. But there are, e.g., innumerable transitions which I can make and the other can't. (*RPP1*, para. 1078)

The choice of one word or phrase as opposed to another determines the gesture we are making, the position we are adopting in relation to the other person, and in this context there may be differences of meaning which cannot be explained. The particular relations of a word or phrase to others give it a unique value or force and only familiarity with the language can allow one to appreciate the gesture that the word makes. Thus, like a theme, a phrase can contain a world of meaning, the phrase can bring together and sum up a complex network of thought and feeling. This may happen in very personal situations, for instance, when a whole relationship or a crisis in it seems to crystallise in a brief exchange. It also often happens in literature.

> The words 'Gottlob! Noch etwas Weniges hat man gefluechtet – vor den Fingern der Kroaten'[4] and the tone and glance that go with them seem indeed to carry within themselves every last *nuance* of the meaning they have. But only because we know them as part of a particular scene. It would, however, be possible to construct an entirely different scene around these words so as to show that the special spirit they have resides in the story in which they come. (*Z*, para. 176)

Doing this would be like placing a musical theme in a new context and thereby giving it a new character. In both cases, however, what is important is the ability of the words or the sounds to take on this character. A whole world of meaning comes to be encapsulated in a few words or in a musical phrase, and, although there are no rules for interpreting the gesture, we respond to it as expressing something unique and non-paraphrasable.

The force of Wittgenstein's comparison of language and music is to challenge our conventional approach to language, and it is certainly a far cry from his earlier work in the *Tractatus*. Interestingly, one claim it undermines is the idea that music (and other art-forms) can express what language cannot. This idea has a strong appeal, but only because of our tendency to take a one-sided view of language. One forgets that poetry too is language, indeed, one might almost be tempted to claim that what is expressed in poetry cannot be put into words! The paralogism here seems to have escaped the notice of the early Wittgenstein who, while criticising those who wanted to use language to express anything beyond the factual, still thought poetry could achieve this. Thus in a letter to Paul Engelmann, he praised a poem by Uhland, noting that 'if only you do not try to utter what is unutterable then nothing gets lost. On the contrary, the unutterable will be – unutterably – contained in what has been uttered!' (*LLW*, p. 7). Here Wittgenstein expresses in mystical terms what he later recognised more clearly. *Pace* the early Wittgenstein, language is not simply a vehicle for the representation of facts; on the contrary, sometimes it is like music and operates quite outside the sphere of the purely informational.

To appreciate how language can operate in this way, we need to reconsider the whole question of our relation to language, and one way of doing that is to resume our exploration of the if-feeling. As we noted earlier, the if-feeling cannot be something that accompanies the word 'if', for in that case it might also occur independently of it. This suggests that the word 'if' is itself part of the if-feeling; indeed, according to Wittgenstein, we might talk of an if-gesture and 'part of the if-gesture is the sound of the word "if" itself' (*LW1*, para. 371). To illuminate this point, he again turns to music, for he argues that 'the if-feeling would have to be compared with the special "feeling" which a musical phrase gives us. (Someone might want to speak of a "half-cadence *feeling*")' (*Z*, para. 373). Here, although it is possible to hear the musical phrase without having the special feeling, the feeling cannot be separated from the musical phrase itself, for it is the phrase which gives it its identity.

> We say this passage gives us a quite special feeling. We sing it to ourselves, and make a certain movement, and also perhaps have some special sensation. But in a different context we should not recognize these accompaniments – the movement,

115

the sensation – at all. They are quite empty except just when we are singing the musical phrase. (*LW*, para. 379)

The idea of a special feeling or atmosphere reflects the strong impression the phrase makes on us, our sense of it having a quite specific significance. To describe the feeling, we would have to find some way of bringing out what the passage means to us. One way of doing this would be to tell a story. Consider, for example, the 'quite particular expression' of the Mona Lisa.

> When we speak of the enigmatic smile of the Mona Lisa, that may well mean we ask ourselves: in what situation, in what story, might one smile like that? And so it would be conceivable for someone to find a solution: he tells a story and we say to ourselves 'Yes, *that* is the expression which *this* character would have assumed here'. (*RPP1*, para. 381)

The reason the picture seems special is because it seems to express something highly specific. Understanding our response to it does not consist in discovering the right general term for the woman's expression; rather it lies in finding the right way of bringing out its uniqueness. Similarly, if a musical phrase 'gives us a special feeling', the significance of the feeling cannot be separated from the music; what matters is the music itself and the path to understanding the feeling lies in exploring the music.

So what implication does all this have for the if-feeling? First, it underlines the point that the sound of the word 'if' is itself part of the if-feeling. More fundamentally, it illustrates the way a word (and particularly, its sound) can come to have an intrinsic value or meaning. From being a mere sign, the word 'if' acquires an atmosphere or feeling of its own; it's as if the meaning had seeped into the sign itself, so that the word becomes a picture of its own meaning, a gesture of if-ness. The if-feeling is not a feeling which happens to accompany the word 'if' but reflects the nature of our relation to language and the fact that the words we use come to seem meaningful in their own right. As with its cousin the experience of meaning, the significance of the if-feeling does not lie in its role in communication, for it is conceivable that people should use language without having an inclination to talk of such feelings. For us, however, words absorb their meanings – the word 'if' seems tentative, the word 'but' stubbornly argumentative. Here the word ceases to be a mere vehicle for its meaning and instead comes to have value in its own right. In this way, the use of a particular word conveys more than its bare informational content, the word itself becomes a gesture.

A good way to illustrate this phenomenon is to consider names, for a famous or very familiar name can itself come to seem imbued with the personality of the individual concerned. The name is not merely a label but a statement in its own right. For example, the composer Schubert used to say 'My name is Schubert, I *am* Schubert'. For us too, a famous name like Schubert can seem an embodiment of its bearer – the name seems somehow to fit the individual and his works, and it seems hard to imagine that the composer of this music could have been called anything else. Here one might object that it's just a matter of associations; however, the point is not that the name causes us to think of its bearer, but that the name itself seems redolent of the bearer's personality. One way this expresses itself is in our saying that the name fits the bearer, but what does this actually mean? It certainly isn't part of the ordinary meaning of the word 'fit': one can't say 'Many different types of things fit each other, for example, the name fits its bearer'. Nor can we call this use an addition to the concept of 'fitting'.

> An addition, after all, would be an extension; and an extension is just what is *not* found here. For one doesn't say that something is a 'fit' if *actually* it is no fit at all. As if one were merely expanding the concept. Rather we are dealing here more or less with an illusion, a mirage. We think we see something that isn't there. But this is true only *more or less.* – We know very well that the name 'Schubert' does not stand in a relationship of fitting to its bearer and to Schubert's works: and yet we are under a compulsion to express ourselves in this way. (*LW1*, para. 69)

So what should we make of this compulsion? On the one hand, it is clear that the word 'fit' is not being used in its usual sense, and for this reason 'the sentence "The name . . . fits . . ." doesn't tell us anything about the name or its bearer. It is a pathological statement about the speaker' (*LW1*, para. 72). On the other hand, although we may also use other words (e.g. say there is 'kinship' between the name and its bearer), it is not as if 'fit' was not exactly the right word. Here again one might try to explain the phenomenon by arguing that two things that are always associated eventually come to seem as if they fitted each other. However, this explanation misses the point, for our talk of fitting cannot be dismissed as an oversight or an easily explicable blunder. We don't apply the word where strictly speaking it isn't appropriate; rather we apply it where is completely inappropriate. What is strange, and interesting, is that we use this word, this picture, in what would seem to be a totally inappropriate context.

So what does it mean to say the name fits its bearer? How does our sense of the fit express itself? One way is that, while we could imagine a picture of Beethoven as he wrote his Ninth Symphony, we could not imagine a painting of how Goethe would have looked writing it (*RPP1*, para. 338). In other words, the works, the face and the name come to have a common identity – the face seems infused with the same spirit as the music and, more strangely still, so does the name. Even the word 'Beethoven' seems to possess a certain Beethovenian grandeur.

> It is as if the name together with these works formed a solid whole. If we see the name, the works come to mind, and if we think of the works, so does the name. We utter the name with reverence.
>
> The name turns into a gesture; into an architectonic form.
> (*RPP1*, para. 341)

What this phenomenon underlines therefore is the nature of our relation to words, the fact that we assimilate language so that certain sounds and symbols come to seem intrinsically meaningful, embodiments of that to which they refer. Unlike the meaning-blind man, we do not view words as signs with attached meanings, but as themselves containing meaning. We say 'Farewell' and sadness and resignation seem to fill every syllable of our utterance, indeed, the word itself can seem to contain a world of pain (*CV*, p. 52). On another occasion, the words may fall empty from our mouths and, although on one level we have said goodbye, we know in truth that the words were meaningless sounds, an empty and hypocritical gesture.

As these examples show, the *Tractatus* was wrong not just in its detailed account of how language operates, but also in its exclusive stress on the representational aspect of language. In fact, language is much closer to us than that; it is as it were our second nature. For example, it is not merely a medium into which we translate our thoughts, it is the medium in which those thoughts are formed. As Wittgenstein puts it, 'I may make a plan not merely so as to make myself understood but also in order to get clear about the matter myself. (i.e. language is not merely a means of communication)' (*Z*, para. 329). Furthermore, formulating an idea (i.e. casting it into language) may itself be treated as a deed. Thus we may be ashamed simply for thinking a certain thought. Here our shame would make no sense if we treated the imagined thought as simply the pronouncing of an arbitrary set of symbols in our mind. Rather the act of putting the thought into words is treated in itself as an action, a doing of the deed in thought. We are ashamed not because we have pronounced a certain sentence in our imagination, but because we view the use of language as itself a form of action, as itself an expression of our personality; 'the thing is, language has a multiple root: it has, not a single root, but roots' (*RPP1*, para. 891).

Language is not just the spoken equivalent of a written symbolism, the pronunciation of a prearranged code, it is also a development of instinctive sounds and reactions. It does not just represent, it also expresses. A sentence may be used not just to convey a complicated message, but also to express a world of pain or despair; as well as containing a paraphrasable meaning, words may constitute a non-phrasable gesture.

> Just think of the words exchanged by lovers! They're 'loaded' with feeling. And surely you can't just agree to substitute for them any other sounds you please, as you can with technical terms. Isn't this because they are *gestures*? And a gesture doesn't have to be innate; it is instilled, and yet *assimilated.* – But isn't that a myth!? No. For the signs of assimilation are that I want to use *this* word, that I prefer to use none at all to using one that is forced on me, and similar reactions.
>
> (*LW1*, para. 712)

As this example illustrates, language is not a foreign medium into which our thoughts and feelings have to be translated.

119

Rather we might be said to inhabit language. For us, words are not mere arbitrary signs in a system of representation, but have value in their own right and can assume many different types of significance. They can take on a ceremonial function as in promises or vows, or the very act of naming can itself become the focus of a ceremony as in baptism. Similarly, it is no coincidence that words figure so prominently in magic and religion. Indeed, even the fact that we laugh at puns illustrates the way we assimilate language, for one might expect irritation rather than amusement at such demonstrations of the 'deficiencies' in our system of representation. Thus one way of making the point about our relation to language is to note that ' "if you didn't *experience* the meaning of the words, then how could you laugh at puns?" . . . We do laugh at such puns: and to that extent we could say (for instance) that we experience their meaning' (*LW1*, para. 711).

Against the background of the above points, it becomes much more understandable that we should talk of a sentence as being brimful of meaning. But how do we come to use the word 'meaning' in this way? What exactly do we mean here? When we teach someone the meaning of the word 'meaning', we do so in connection with understanding and being able to explain a sentence. However, when we talk of a sentence being full of meaning, something rather different is at stake. This suggests that we should perhaps use a completely different word; however, this would get us nowhere, for the whole point of saying that a sentence is brimming with meaning arises from the original meaning the word 'meaning' has.

> It isn't as if we were obstinately referring to two things with the same word and then were asked: Why are you doing this, if *in reality* they are different? – The new use consists in applying the old expression in a new situation; it is not to designate something new. (*LW1*, para. 61)

As with the earlier example of the word 'fitting', use of this expression is pathological – what is interesting and important is what it shows about the individual, for she wants to use the word despite the fact that, in terms of its original meaning, it is not appropriate. An even better example of this is the way many people will assign colours to the different vowels, they may, for example, say that '*e*' is yellow. This may appear to be a strange form of madness and yet it is a reaction which many people agree in. The claim that '*e*' is yellow clearly does not use the word 'yellow' in its normal sense, and yet 'if I say "For me the vowel *e* is yellow" I do not mean: "yellow" in a metaphorical sense, – for I could not express what I want to say in any other way than by means of the idea "yellow" ' (*PI*, p. 216).

Dissecting this phenomenon, Wittgenstein distinguishes between the primary and the secondary meaning of a word, the secondary meaning consisting in using the word with its primary meaning in a totally new context. The point, however, is that someone can use a word in its secondary sense only if she can already use the word in its primary sense (ibid.). For example, someone who is familiar with the normal meaning of 'fat' and 'lean' can be asked whether she would be more inclined to say that Wednesday was fat and Tuesday lean or vice versa. Clearly the words 'fat' and 'lean' are not being used in their normal sense; on the other hand, one could not replace them by other words, for the phenomenon is that the individual wants to use these words with their familiar meanings here. 'Asked "What do you really mean here by 'fat' and 'lean'?" – I could only explain the meanings in the usual way. I could not point to the examples of Wednesday and Tuesday' (*PI*, p. 216). From a philosophical point of view, the fact that we may be able to explain these utterances (for example, in terms of childhood associations) is irrelevant; what is important is what this phenomenon shows about our relation to language. What is interesting is the way we give a word a completely new use and yet one dependent on its old meaning.

So how does the secondary meaning arise? What, for example, leads us to say that a sentence is brimming with meaning? Clearly this is not literally the case and so it seems that it must be a metaphor. However, with a real metaphor we would be able to explain why use of the word was appropriate, and yet this is precisely what we can't do in this case. Furthermore, unlike a metaphor, our use of the phrase is not arbitrary, one possibility among others; rather 'the picture *forced* itself *upon me. I want to say*: the word was filled with meaning' (*RPP1*, para. 1060). Only this phrase can express what the individual wishes to say, even though in a literal sense it is nonsense. For this to occur, therefore, the phrase must have taken on a significance beyond its literal meaning. The individual needs to have assimilated the primary meaning of the word, for if she viewed the word simply as a symbol with a particular use, how would it even occur to her to apply it independently of that use? Thus the use of words in a secondary sense further illustrates the nature of our relation to language, for it shows how we can come to have a feeling for a word, on the basis of which we then use the word in a totally new way.

The examples already given (our inclination to say '*e*' is yellow, or 'Wednesday is fat') may seem to imply that this phenomenon is relatively unimportant; however, the example of meaning already suggests that it has a more widespread significance, and this significance becomes much clearer when we relate this phenomenon to the question of the Inner. Consider the following example.

> I go for a walk in the environs of a city with a friend. As we talk it comes out that I am imagining the city to lie on our right. Not only have I *no* conscious reason for this assumption, but some quite simple consideration was enough to make me realize that the city lay rather to the left ahead of us. I can at first give no answer to the question *why* I imagine the city in *this* direction. I had *no reason* to think it. But though I see no reason still I seem to see certain psychological causes for it. In particular, certain associations and memories. For example, we walked along a canal, and once before in similar circumstances I had followed a canal and that time the city lay on our right. – I might try as it were psychoanalytically to discover the causes of my unfounded conviction. (*PI*, p. 215)

As before, what is important here is not that we may be able to explain this phenomenon, but what it shows about our relation to language. We take a proposition ('the city lies on our right') and suddenly and inexplicably talk of a feeling that corresponds to it. Our doing this, however, does not involve connecting up a feeling with the phrase; rather our use of the phrase is itself the basis for saying that we have the feeling. Here the role of language is not to represent but to express; the use of a particular phrase does not involve the application of a general rule but is itself our criterion for saying that the individual is having a particular experience.

The above example underlines the importance of language to the Inner. In fact, one of the main reasons for Wittgenstein's attack on the representational view of language is that it leads us to misunderstand the Inner. The idea that words have meaning in virtue of being correlated with an object encourages the idea of private inner objects. With regard to the Inner, however, language does not describe an independently existing entity; rather it is the basis of our talking about inner states in the first place. Furthermore, the development of a complex and sophisticated Inner is only possible because of our relation to language; only because we assimilate language and use it in a spontaneous, non-rule-governed way can our inner lives have the range and complexity they do. A good example here is the case of seeing aspects, for the key criterion for saying that someone is seeing an aspect is what the individual says and yet the utterances she makes appear on one level to be nonsense. Imagine the aspect-blind man's bewilderment when he comes across someone who looks at an unchanged picture and says 'Now it's a duck, now it's a rabbit'. Like us, the aspect-blind man has mastered the use of the word 'see', but in mastering the concept nothing prepared him for the idea of seeing as. In our case, however, we learn the concept see and then spontaneously extend it: we do not simply say we can see a picture that could be used to represent either a duck or a rabbit, rather we claim to see the picture now one way, now another. Here our utterances are not based on rules we have previously learnt and yet they become the criteria for talk of a particular experience. What happens is that we take the vocabulary of a way of understanding the drawing and use it to express an experience (*RPP1*, para. 1128). Our utterances are the criteria for the inner state, and thus a way of speaking is responsible for an experience.

Here it may seem strange that our use of language is non-rule-governed and yet still comprehensible: what is it that stops these apparently nonsensical utterances from being nonsense? To answer this, we need to go back to the idea of a gesture, for understanding gestures does not involve learning rules but directly responding to the gesture itself. The other person's gesture says something to us insofar as it is a gesture we too might make. Here people are in touch with each other but the possibility of communication rests on their self-expression taking the same form. For this reason, there is no guarantee of understanding: the gestures of one person may be transparent to us, while those of another are completely opaque. Similarly, the utterances we make might be completely incomprehensible to each other, but the point is that often they are not. One person says 'I feel as though the city lies over there' and the other person, rather than treating this as an outbreak of insanity, agrees, or at least can relate this to similar utterances she herself may be inclined to make. Similarly, when someone says that *'e'* is yellow or that Schubert's name seems to fit his works and his face, other people will often agree or at least find the utterance interesting.

So far the examples we have considered may seem trivial, but the use of language we are pointing to covers the full range of the Inner. Take the feeling that everything is unreal. As with our earlier examples, the claim that everything is unreal seems an abuse of language; despite this, many people insist that it expresses exactly what they are feeling, and, even to those who have had no such experience themselves, the statement may still convey something.

> The feeling of the unreality of one's surroundings. This feeling I have had once, and many have it before the onset of mental illness. Everything seems somehow not *real*; but not as if one *saw* things unclear or blurred; everything looks quite as usual. And how do I know that another has felt what I have? Because he uses the same words as I find appropriate.
>
> But why do I choose precisely the word 'unreality' to express it? Surely not because of its sound. (A word of very like sound but different meaning would not do.) I choose it because of its meaning. (*RPP1*, para. 125)

We do not originally learn to use the word to mean a feeling; rather we learn its primary meaning and then go on to use it in a new way, 'I choose *that* meaning as a simile for my feeling' (ibid.).

The notion of secondary sense brings out the crucial role of language in the expression of the Inner. It also undermines the idea that language always serves as a symbolism for the representation of facts. Rather, in connection with the Inner, language has an expressive function, the individual's words constituting part (or the whole) of the criteria for saying she is in a particular state. Our ability to use language in this way reflects the particular nature of our relation to language, for what we learn in the context of particular rules we then go on to apply quite independently of those rules. This may involve taking a factual proposition and using it as a component in the expression of a feeling ('I feel as if someone was watching me') or may be more specifically tied to the force of a particular word or image ('I feel abandoned, utterly abandoned'). In both cases, the individual's utterance is important not because it describes an independent state but because it is the criterion for that state. Furthermore, while the individual's use of a particular word or phrase cannot be justified in terms of a rule, it is nonetheless crucial because a different utterance would be the expression of a different state.

As we have seen, Wittgenstein's emphasis on the idea that understanding language is like understanding music is closely linked to his attempt to make us rethink the Inner. In part, however, this involves rethinking the standard Wittgensteinian view of the Inner, for Wittgenstein himself initially failed to stress sufficiently the role of language in the Inner. Take the key concept of an utterance. The standard Wittgensteinian view is to say that we learn these as the replacement and extension of pre-verbal behaviour. This is correct as far as it goes, but it ignores the fact that in relation to the Inner our use of language generates its own momentum as it were. Take the case of pain. As a child learns pain utterances, her pain behaviour (crying, holding the painful area, etc.) is gradually replaced by linguistic behaviour. However, the child does not simply learn to replace certain pieces of behaviour with pre-agreed verbal signals ('I am in pain', etc.). Rather the acquisition of language creates new possibilities and gives her pain-behaviour a new complexity. Now she no longer simply signals pain, but may 'describe' it, i.e. find words to characterise not just its location and degree but also its quality. For example, she may speak of a stabbing or a throbbing pain or she may use a more elaborate phrase, e.g. say that it's as if her head was going to explode or as if a band was being pulled ever tighter around her temples. To make sense, these expressions must tie in with other aspects of her pain-behaviour, for example, 'Argh' is not the expression of a dull ache. However, this should not be allowed to hide the fundamental point that the precise nature of the pain is characterised by its verbal expression rather than its other manifestations. Furthermore, the phrases we use to express our pain are not taught as pain expressions – the original use of the word 'throbbing' is not to describe pain nor is the word 'explode' taught in connection with a feeling we might one day have. Thus, although some utterances (*Aeusserungen*) are explicitly taught, others are spontaneous and involve taking words learnt in one way and giving them a completely new use as expressions of the Inner.

The fact that the Inner can develop in this way is dependent on the nature of our relation to language, and it is quite conceivable that there might be people who could be taught basic *Aesserungen* ('I am in pain', etc.), but who would never go on spontaneously to develop new possibilities. People who regarded words simply as pre-agreed signals or symbols and did not go on to use words spontaneously, giving a completely new use to a word with a particular meaning, would have a completely different inner life from ours, for the possibilities of their inner life would be laid down in advance. By contrast, in our case the Inner is as limitless as language itself. When Kafka says his life is a hesitation before birth, we can understand his words without having explicitly being prepared for them and without necessarily being able to paraphrase them. In our case, what happens is that we assimilate language and 'find each other' in utterances which are in a sense nonsensical. This, indeed, is the real significance of experiencing meaning, for not only does this phenomenon involve using the word 'meaning' in a secondary sense, but it also points to a wider aspect of our relation to language by illustrating the way we use language in a spontaneously expressive way.

Why should the experience of meaning be important? He says the word, says he said it now in this meaning; then, in that one. *I* say the same. This obviously has nothing to do with the ordinary and important use of the expression '*That's* what I meant by this word'. So what is the remarkable thing? That we say something of that sort? Naturally that is of interest. But the interest here does not depend on the concept of the 'meaning' of a word, but on the range of similar psychological phenomena which in general have nothing to do with word-meaning. (*RPP1*, para. 358)

The basis of our self-expression, and hence of the Inner itself, is our ability to find each other in language. This ability reflects, on the one hand, our relation to language and, on the other, the underlying kinship which manifests itself in the fact that one person's spontaneous reactions are shared by others or at least comprehensible to them. When one person says 'Everything feels unreal to me', another may remember feeling exactly the same thing and others who have not had the experience may still have a sense of what it involves. Conversely, in Wittgenstein's famous phrase, 'if a lion could talk we could not understand him' (*LW1*, para. 190). The spontaneous reactions of a being with which we had no kinship would mean nothing to us, its poetic or expressive use of language would seem a strange kind of nonsense.

This account of the Inner runs counter to some of our deepest philosophical prejudices, for we want to treat the Inner as an internalised Outer, that is to say, as a world of objects which language represents according to a system of rules. Wittgenstein's private language argument undermines this picture by showing, first, that there is no such thing as a private inner object and, second, that the language of the Inner cannot operate via description. The positive consequences of this argument, however, are less widely recognised, for by implication we must recognise that the Inner involves a fundamentally different type of concept from the Outer and that language operates here in a quite different way. Wittgenstein himself had difficulty making this step as he admits when considering the case of the feeling that something is 'eerie'.

We teach someone the meaning of the word 'eerie' [*unheimlich*] by bringing it into connexion with a certain behaviour in certain situations (through the *behaviour* is not called that). In such situations he now says it feels eerie to him; and even the word 'ghost' has something eerie about it. – How far was the word 'eerie' to start with the name of a feeling? If someone shrinks back from entering a dark room, why should I call this or the like the expression of a feeling? For 'feeling' certainly makes us think of sensation and sense-impression, and these in turn are the objects immediately before our minds. (I am trying to make a logical step here, one that comes hard to me.) (*RPP1*, para. 1088)

Here the word is initially used to describe a particular aspect of certain situations, and already in her ability to recognise this aspect, the person learning the word shows a kinship to us. The existence of this kinship is underlined by the way the individual then uses the word to express her own feelings. Furthermore, in making this transition the individual demonstrates the nature of her relation to language, for the meaning of the word 'eerie' seeps into the very word itself so that the word shifts from describing something Outer to expressing something Inner. Finally, just as the word 'eerie' itself comes to have something eerie about it, so too do related words such as 'ghost'.

The use of language in this way is typical of the Inner, for most utterances involve using language in a spontaneous or non-rule-governed way. In the case of a phrase like 'it feels eerie to me', there is no direct clash between the old and the new usage. We simply take a phrase used to describe a situation and use it to express a feeling. In other cases, however, the utterances may strictly speaking be nonsense, and the only way of understanding them philosophically is to accept that language is not external to our inner life but the very medium in which it occurs. Think, for example, of the great poetic expressions of emotion.

'Black is the beauty of the brightest day' – Can one say 'Well, it *seems* as if it were black?' Have we then an hallucination of something black? – So what makes these words *apt*? – 'We understand them.' We say, e.g. 'Yes, I know exactly what that's like!' and now we can describe our feelings and behaviour.

(*RPP1*, para. 377)

If one considers expressions of this kind, one is less likely to think of the Inner as something pre-given which then has to be forced into language. Furthermore, such examples underline the point that the complexity and structure of the Inner reflects the network of relations embedded in language.

It is important, however, that there are all these paraphrases! That one can describe care [*Sorge*] with the words 'Black is the beauty of the brightest day'. I have perhaps never sufficiently stressed the importance of this paraphrasing.

Joy is represented by a countenance bathed in light, by rays streaming from it. Naturally that does not mean that joy and light *resemble* one another; but joy – *it does not matter why* – is associated with light. To be sure, it might be that it is no more *natural* than the sound of the words themselves – enough that it exists. ('Beethoven' and Beethoven's works.)

(RPP1, para. 853)

We say that the world of sorrow is a grey world, but not because we believe that sorrow affects an individual's eyesight. Furthermore, the connection between sorrow and a lead-grey sky is not something a Martian could deduce from studying either the sky or our behaviour when sorrowful. Rather it is a connection we spontaneously make or come to feel is apt. Through such connections and other similar talk, we communicate our feelings to one another; indeed, it is only because our relation to language makes this sort of talk possible that our inner worlds can have the complexity they do. In this sense, one might almost say that language is the Inner, for it is within language that the individual's possibilities of self-expression develop, and the limits of her linguistic expression are the limits of her inner life. It is important to note, however, that this point concerns the complexity, not the quality, of someone's inner life. Although it is possible for a child to experience deep and powerful emotions, its feelings cannot have the same complexity as those of an adult. Unlike Ivan Karamazov, a child could not feel that its soul was torn between the glories of Schiller and an abyss of sensuality.

The interaction of language and experience is also evident in the way certain pictures get embedded in our lives, for what may at first seem a mere turn of phrase can gain a unique expressive value and so come to be the only way of expressing the experience we are having. If, for example, someone says 'As you said it, in my heart I understood', she means the gesture (*RPP1*, para. 345), she is not simply using a picture; rather those particular words are the only way of expressing what she feels. Here language is not simply a vehicle for our feelings, but structures and characterises our experience itself.

> Doesn't it matter that I want to say that? Isn't it important? Is it not important that for me hope lives in the *breast*? Isn't this a picture of one or another important bit of human behaviour? Why does a human being believe a thought comes into his head? Or, more correctly, he does not *believe* it; he lives it. For he clutches at his head; he shuts his eyes in order to be alone with himself in his head. He tilts his head back and makes a movement as a sign that nothing should disturb the process in his head. – Now are these not important kinds of behaviour?
> (*RPP1*, para. 278)

The supreme example of a picture or metaphor that has become embedded in our lives is in fact the picture of the Inner itself. Although what we observe is something Outer, our reaction to it can only be captured in terms of the Inner.

> Observing an animal, e.g. an ape that investigates an object and tears it to pieces, one may say: 'You see that something is going on in him.' How remarkable that is! But not more remarkable than that we say: love, conviction, are in our hearts. (*RPP1*, para. 347)

The picture of the Inner is not simply a metaphor but expresses our sense of what is unique about intelligent animals. If we want to characterise our reaction and our relation to such beings, there is no better way of doing this than in terms of the picture itself.

Against Wittgenstein's account, one might object that we do sometimes have difficulty in putting our feelings into words and that therefore feelings can on occasion pre-exist their expression. However, this misses the point, for it confuses a logical and a temporal relationship. There are indeed times when we struggle to express what we feel, but even on these occasions it only makes sense to talk of feeling something if that something might come in some form or other to be expressed. To say 'I feel an inexpressible something' says nothing, or rather since it is itself an expression, it tells the other person that the individual is in one of those frustrating situations where whatever she says seems an inadequate expression of what she feels. Sometimes she may subsequently find the right words for her experience and in such cases all this shows is that the language-game of expressing the Inner is not an easy one. Even on those occasions where we can find a way expressing our feelings, we may nonetheless be unable to explain why one particular gesture or phrase is uniquely appropriate. Here the attempt to express our feeling in general terms may seem to trivialise it, so that in different ways language seems both clumsy and profoundly expressive. Like a poem, the right utterance seems to capture what defies words – abandoning the rules on which language is based, it reaches out to others in a spontaneous but shared gesture.

As these examples show, language is not external to the Inner but constitutes the very element in which it exists. However, this is only possible because language is more to us than a system of representation. The idea that a sentence may brim with meaning is irrelevant to the normal game of communication, but is important insofar as it illustrates the way we assimilate language. Although we tend to concentrate on language as a system of rules, the role it plays in our lives is more complex than that, for it has an important non-representational role. In relation to the Inner, what matters is not the correct application of linguistic rules, but the rule-free use of language; people communicate not because they share rules, but because what one is inclined to say strikes a chord in another.

> 'The sentence "If only he would come" may be laden with our longing.' – What was it laden with there? It is as if a weight were loaded on to it from our spirit. I should indeed like to say all of that. And doesn't it matter, that I want to say that?
> *(RPP1*, para. 277)

Here our utterances do not convey information but function as a gesture and, like a gesture, they may convey a unique meaning – all we hope and feel about his arrival may be crystallised in the utterance itself. That we can express ourselves in this way is itself striking, but even more so is the fact that others can understand us. We say something which even we cannot explain and yet another person may hear us and understand exactly what we mean. The point, however, is that in these cases we understand language not via rules but in the same way we understand a facial expression or a gesture.

To sum up, language plays a very different role in our lives from that of simply representing facts. The *Tractatus* treatment of language as soulless symbolism for representing states of affairs ignores the value we place on words and what they can mean to us. Ironically, Wittgenstein later suggested that the book itself is a counterexample to the view of language it presents. Thus its incantatory style ('The world is everything that is the case. The world is the totality of facts, not of things. The world is determined by the facts and by these being *all* the facts', etc.) might itself be seen as a form of word-magic. As Wittgenstein puts it, 'When I began in my earlier book to talk about the world (and not about this tree or that table) was I trying to do anything except conjure up something higher by my words?' (*MS 110*, p. 178). The aim of this chapter has been to outline Wittgenstein's later views which provide a perspective from which such a use of words is much more readily comprehensible. In place of the idea of language as purely informational, we have stressed the musical element in language, the gestures formed both by how we say what we say and by the particular words we choose. For us, particular words can come to have a unique force – the word comes to seem meaningful in itself and have a unique value in terms of the limitless network of ideas and associations which link the sound and meaning of one word with those of others. Finally, we have tried to show how this relation to language plays a crucial role in the development of the Inner, for expression of the Inner is based on spontaneous, ruleless use of language.

5

THE COMPLEXITY OF THE INNER

Suppose we were observing the movement of a point (for example, a point of light on a screen). It might be possible to draw important consequences of the most various kinds from the behaviour of this point. And what a variety of observations can be made here! – The path of the point and certain of its characteristic measures (amplitude and wave-length for instance), or the velocity and the law according to which it varies, or the number or position of the places at which it changes discontinuously, or the curvature of the path at these places, and innumerable other things. – Any of these features of its behaviour might be the only one to interest us. We might, for example, be indifferent to everything about its movements except for the number of loops it makes in a certain time. – And if we were interested, not in just *one* such feature, but in several, each might yield us special information, different in kind from all the rest. This is how it is with the behaviour of man; with different characteristic features which we observe in his behaviour. (*PI*, p. 179)

In the previous chapters, we have often used the term 'the Inner' as a convenient way of referring to our psychological concepts in general. However, the term contains a danger, for it fosters the temptation to see the various elements of the Inner as essentially alike, different components of a homogeneous whole. In fact, our psychological concepts fall into various categories and, within these groups, there are differences as well as similarities. To understand these differences, we must explore the grammar of the concepts, for it is not enough simply to note that our experiences take a variety of forms. The complexity of the Inner reflects not differences of degree, but differences of concept.

> If I now say that the experience of remembering and the experience of pain are different in kind, that is misleading: for 'experiences of different kinds' makes one think perhaps of a difference like that between a pain, a tickle, and a feeling of familiarity. Whereas the difference of which we are speaking is comparable, rather, to that between the numbers 1 and $\sqrt{-1}$
>
> (*RPP1*, para. 108)

As this quotation suggests, there is a strong temptation to underestimate the complexity of the Inner, and this is reinforced by the inclination to treat all differences as simply experiential. In most cases, however, 'intrinsic' differences are grammatical differences in disguise. The essential difference between pain and intention, for example, is not that they have different contents, but that they are radically different types of concept. Conversely, if anxiety and sorrow are similar, this is not because they 'feel' the same, but because there are similarities in their grammar. If someone said her experience of anxiety was similar to joy rather than sorrow, we would say not that she experienced the emotion differently from us but that she can't mean by 'anxiety' what we do. The aim of this chapter therefore is to explore the complexity of the Inner and provide a rough map of the relations between our various psychological concepts. In doing this, it will also seek to reinforce Wittgenstein's account of the Inner by underlining the different ways in which the various psychological concepts work.

In tracing the grammar of psychological concepts, one crucial feature is how the concepts relate Outer and Inner. In every case, the Outer provides the criteria in terms of which the Inner is characterised, but the particular relation of Inner and Outer differs from case to case. Take the case of love. Here the temptation is to focus exclusively on the content of the experience. For example, one might define love as a uniquely intense experience which the individual cannot misidentify if she is indeed experiencing it. Such a definition seems prosaic and by the same token uncontroversial. But, in fact, it significantly misrepresents the way we use this concept. As Wittgenstein points out, love is something that can be put to the test (*RPP1*, para. 959) and hence, in contrast to pain, it might be said not to be a feeling at all. Although the intensity of the individual's feeling is important, it is not the only thing that matters; rather we distinguish real love from infatuation and take the individual's future actions as a guide to how her experience should be classified.

> 'If it passes, then it was not true love.' Why was it not in that case? Is it our experience, that only this feeling and not that endures? Or are we using a picture: we test love for its *inner* character, which the immediate feeling does not discover.
>
> > (*RPP1*, para. 115)

The grammar of love is not the grammar of an intense feeling. If the individual says or does certain things, we say that she cannot really have been in love; in other words, we give an important weight to manifestations of the experience other than simply the individual's claims about its intensity. It is also interesting to note that in this case our classification of experience, the particular way we define love, will reflect our general outlook on life and human psychology. As this suggests, the Inner is not a brute given, but something structured by the particular concepts we adopt. Furthermore, in a case of this sort the concept is like a badge of honour – 'we have this word "love" and now we give this title to the most important thing' (ibid.).

The example of love illustrates one way in which a psychological concept connects up Inner and Outer, but it is important to recognise that other concepts make this connection in a variety of different ways. Although there must be some link between the experience and its possible manifestations, that link takes a different form from one case to another. Wittgenstein's dictum 'Inner states stand in need of outer criteria' is not a recipe for uniformity, but an exhortation to recognise the complexity of the Inner.

> How do we compare the behaviour of anger, joy, hope, expectation, belief, love and understanding? – Act like an angry person! That's easy. Like a joyful one – here it would depend on what the joy was about. The joy of seeing someone again, or the joy of listening to a piece of music . . .? – Hope?

That would be hard. Why? There are no gestures of hope.

(*LW1*, para. 357)

These differences provide the key to understanding our psychological concepts. For example, the above remarks indicate why it is easy to imagine an animal angry, frightened or unhappy, but not hopeful. The problem in the last case is that the animal's behaviour lacks the necessary articulations: to express hope the animal would have to be able to speak. Furthermore, it is not just the behaviour in the narrow sense which is important. If, for example, we are to talk of sorrowful behaviour, this must include not just how the individual acts but also the occasion and context of her action. Thus, in comparing the various psychological concepts, one must interpret the word 'behaviour' in the broadest of senses.

> Take the various psychological phenomena: thinking, pain, anger, joy, wish fear, intention, memory, etc., – and compare the behaviour corresponding to each. – But what does behaviour include here? Only the play of facial expression and the gestures? Or also the surrounding, so to speak the occasion of this expression? And if one does include the surrounding as well, – how is the behaviour to be compared in the case of anger and in that of memory, for example? (*RPP1*, para. 129)

The key point is the complexity of the Inner: even talk of comparing different types of behaviour understates the extent of the differences, for it is as if one were to talk of the different states of water and mean by this its temperature, the speed with which it is flowing, its colour, etc. (*RPP1*, para. 130).

One way of bringing out the differences between the various psychological concepts is by considering the inner content of each. This may seem strange, since we earlier criticised the idea that our psychological concepts are differentiated by their content. The point, however, is to explore the different ways in which the notion of content relates to the different types of concept. The discussion of content is therefore simply one way of bringing out other wider differences. As we saw in Chapter 2,[1] the notion of inner content has its clearest application in relation to sense-experience, for we tend to think of the content of an experience as 'the private object, the sense-datum, the object that I grasp immediately with the mental eye, ear, etc. The inner picture' (*RPP1*, para. 109). But what does talk of a content express? As we have seen, one advantage of the notion of the inner picture is that it captures the subjectivity of sense experience, i.e. it allows us to make a distinction between the individual's account of her visual experience and an account of what actually happened. Furthermore, the notion of a content corresponds to the possibility of the individual offering a continuous account of what she is seeing. This brings out the importance of duration, for one reason the concept seeing can be said to have a content is that the individual can coherently offer a second-by-second account of it. By contrast, knowing does not have genuine duration and so would not normally be said to have an inner content. Although time concepts can be applied to it, they apply in a quite different way. An individual can learn something and later forget it, but knowing something is not an experience she can describe second by second. Furthermore, unlike seeing, it is not interrupted by a break in consciousness (e.g. sleep) or by a shift of attention. Similarly, while the individual is aware of her changing sense-experiences and can signal when a particular change occurs (e.g. when she can no longer see such-and-such a thing or no longer distinguish such-and-such a sound), she cannot do the same with respect to her knowledge, for in this case there is no continuous process to be monitored.

To mark these differences, Wittgenstein suggests that one might call seeing, hearing, etc. 'states of consciousness' and knowing, believing, intending, etc. 'dispositions' (*RPP2*, para. 45). The general difference between the two is that one does not need to do a spot-check to determine whether the former are continuing, indeed, if one needed to do a spot-check, this itself would show that the state had been interrupted. While we can check that we still know pi to ten places by saying what the digits are, we do not have to check whether we are still hearing or seeing anything. Furthermore, since sense-impressions have genuine duration, we could time each one with a stop watch. By contrast, the duration of knowledge, an ability or understanding could not be measured in this way (ibid., para. 51). Such tests may seem to focus on a fine distinction, where the real one is enormous. But to this, Wittgenstein replies:

> this enormous distinction (I would always say) consists in the fact that the two concepts are embedded quite differently in our language-games. And the difference to which I called attention was merely a reference to this pervasive distinction.
>
> (*RPP2*, para. 54)

The temptation is simply to treat seeing and knowing as different experiences; what is important, however, is to explore their different grammars, and one way of doing this is to note that seeing has a content in quite a different sense from knowing.

Seeing, hearing, tasting, etc. are not the only components of the Inner which have genuine duration and hence it is not surprising that there are other concepts where the notion of content is naturally at home. If what we perceive belongs to the content of experience, so too does what we imagine and also what we feel. In general, therefore, one might define the 'content' of experience as: 'what changes, what goes, in space and time. If, e.g. one talks to oneself, then it would be the imagined sounds (and perhaps the feeling in the larynx or something like that)' (*RPP1*, para. 733). However, once it is applied more generally, the notion of a content itself becomes fragmented, assuming a slightly different meaning in the different cases. In the case of vision, one could describe the experience-content as 'what can be produced in a picture in its subjective meaning, when its purport is: "*This* I see – whatever the object may be that produces the impression" ' (*RPP1*, para. 694). Similarly, a picture can be used to show what the individual is imagining. But what about the other types of sense-impression? With hearing, there is a possibility of representation, though not a visual one, but with taste, touch and smell even this is impossible. In these cases, the only way the individual can describe the content of her exper- ience is through language, through a verbal account of the succeeding experiences. In this respect, the latter senses are similar to sensations and feelings, for here too the only means of access to the content of the experience is via language. What brings all these groups together, however, is the common feature of genuine duration; the key grammatical similarity is that in each case the individual can give a second-by-second account specifying the content of her experience.

Wittgenstein labels psychological concepts which involve genuine duration concepts of 'undergoings' (*Erfahrungen*), and he treats them as a subset of the wider category, concepts of experience (*RPP1*, para. 836). As we have seen, both images and impressions are undergoings, as are sensations or feelings. But what about emotions such as sadness, joy, grief and delight? The temptation here is to argue that these too must be undergoings if they are real. Surely, one wants to say, grief is something one feels, an experience one undergoes. However, to place it in the same category as sense-impressions and sensations would be misleading. One reason for this is that, while sensations are primarily expressed through utterances (the individual's account of what she is feeling), the emotions are characterised by particular ways of acting. There are, for example, joyful, sad and angry ways of behaving. What each of these concepts does is to pick out a particular pattern in human life and for this reason it characterises the individual's state in a wider sense than the attribution of a particular sensation or feeling. For example, sadness typically manifests itself over a period of time, not just in a moment. By contrast, there is nothing unusual in a momentary sensation. Of course, a particular emotion may bring with it certain sensations, e.g. the queasy feel of fear, but even when this occurs, the sensation is not the emotion. Although the emotion may involve experiences or 'undergoings', the emotion itself is not an 'undergoing'.

To illustrate these points consider the example of grief or sadness. If we try to treat this as a sensation, the first problem that arises is the question of why it makes no sense to suggest that someone might have this experience every other minute or for five minutes in every hour. With a sensation, there is no reason why its duration should not be brief or why it should not alternate with sensations of a very different kind, so why not in this case? The concept of sadness, however, involves a wider reference than to what the individual is feeling at a particular moment. Sadness has a reason, a history – it is part of a world of thought and feeling. Furthermore, unlike a sensation, it manifests itself in the way the individual acts – be it in obvious ways such as crying or in more subtle ways such as taciturnity in place of talkativeness or indeed talkativeness in place of customary reserve. To make these points is not to deny the existence of experiences which often accompany sadness. Indeed, insofar as emotions are linked with particular ways of acting, these themselves may produce characteristic sensations, e.g. the tension in the neck of the literally downcast individual. In many cases, however, even these experiences only gain their significance from the emotion itself. Consider, for example, the characteristic sad feeling expressed in the words 'It brings a lump to my throat'. Why is it we do not get this sensation in contexts other than those of sadness? Well, what if someone did? The problem here lies in the question of how we judge the sameness – what gives the sensation its particular character is precisely its context. If someone who was in good spirits claimed to have it, we might question whether she was referring to the same sensation as us. Here there is a similarity with the experiences we get when listening to music; for, as we noted,[2] the particular feeling the music gives us only gains its significance from its relation to the music and through that to other things.

In terms of the above account, pain fills a somewhat unusual position, for, unlike other sensations, it is not expressed primarily through language but is characterised by particular types of behaviour. As Wittgenstein notes, this makes it akin to emotions such as joy and sorrow (*RPP2*, para. 63). On the other hand, it is the classic example of a sensation and hence of an 'undergoing'. To resolve this apparent tension and to underline the differences between sensations and emotions, it is worth contrasting pain with sorrow. The first and most obvious difference is that pain is localised in a particular part of the body, whereas sorrow is not. If someone insists that sorrow must have a location, one response would be to say that, while pain is located in the body, sorrow is located in the soul. Similarly, what corresponds to the part of the body which has the pain is the object which causes us the sorrow. We feel pain in some part of the body, but sorrow at or over something. As this point suggests, pain and sorrow have quite different types of cause and, in the latter case, the cause is also the object of the emotion (*RPP2*, para. 148). These differences show why it would not make sense to suggest that someone might experience sorrow in situations where we experience pain: the essential difference between them is not that they correspond to different inner processes, but that they relate to different types of pattern in human life. As Wittgenstein puts it,

> The concept of pain just is embedded in our life in a certain way. It is characterized by very definite connections. . . .
>
> Only surrounded by certain normal manifestations of life, is there such a thing as an expression of pain. Only surrounded by even more far-reaching manifestations of life, such a thing as the expression of sorrow or affection. (*RPP2*, paras 150–1)

Sorrow is a more sophisticated concept than pain; not only does it require a more complicated background, but its meaning is more complex. While it is easy to apply the concept pain to animals, it is less easy to do so with the concept sorrow (and even harder with concepts such as melancholy or remorse).

One way of underlining the different dimensions in which pain and sorrow operate is to note that, while sorrow can colour our thoughts, pain cannot.[3] Another way of contrasting pain and sorrow is to note that while it is possible to feel a sudden, momentary stab of pain, it would not make sense to talk of feeling sorrow for just a few seconds. Rather part of the pattern of sorrow is that it has a course and that course presupposes a certain amount of time. Sorrow, one might say, has an object and a history, pain simply a cause. By the same token, pain and sorrow have a different type of duration. Compare, for instance, the meaning of uninterrupted pain and uninterrupted sorrow. The former could be measured with a stop-watch, and might stop unexpectedly and then start again equally abruptly; the latter, on the other hand, could not be timed in the same way, since neither its start nor its finish need be so clearcut. Someone may gradually become sad, but she cannot gradually come to be in pain. Similarly, while it might be possible to create a scale of painfulness, one could hardly begin to do this for sorrow; to say one pain was twice as painful as another would make sense, but not that one sorrow was twice as deep as another.[4]

These grammatical points underline the conceptual differences between sensations and emotions, but they also provoke questions, for some may see them as calling into doubt the reality of emotions. To deny that sorrow is a sensation or feeling is, one might argue, tantamount to denying the existence of sorrow altogether. Wittgenstein's point, however, is not that we do not in some sense feel sorrow but that here the word 'feel' has a very different meaning from its use in connection with sensations. Here the problem is that the idea of a sensation dominates our approach to the Inner, so that the attempt to distinguish emotions from sensations makes the former seem odd. Far from simply clarifying, Wittgenstein's account may seem to create a new mythology of the mind, for it avoids the question of where we feel emotions and so gives rise to unease. 'Here the thought is: "After all, you feel sadness – so you must feel it somewhere; otherwise it would be a chimera" ' (Z, para. 510). One response to this difficulty is to argue, as William James did, that the emotions are in fact conglomerates or congeries of bodily sensations. Take the case of depression. Surely when one is depressed one feels something? To this, Wittgenstein answers that it depends what you call 'feeling' it.

> If I direct my attention to my bodily feelings, I notice a very slight headache, a slight discomfort in the region of the stomach, perhaps a certain tiredness. But do I mean that, when I say I am severely depressed? (RPP1, para. 133)

Although all these sensations may be present, they do not constitute depression, indeed, talk of bodily sensations might be said to trivialise the emotion. The physical aspects of depression are not what upsets the individual and, if she can express what she feels, it is much more likely to take the form of a statement such as 'I feel locked in a prison from which I can never escape' or 'I feel a burden weighing on my soul' (ibid.) and these are hardly what we would normally call descriptions of sensations. This point is underlined by the fact that we do not learn the expression 'I am depressed' in circumstances characteristic of a particular bodily feeling. Rather the individual behaves in a certain way and on this basis we say she is depressed and teach her to say it of herself. Although the depressed individual may report that she has certain bodily feelings, depression does not consist in having those feelings, nor do those feelings have to be present for it to be correct to say that someone is depressed.

Despite these points, objections may continue, for other emotions seem to offer harder cases. For example, there may still be a temptation to argue that grief and joy are specific feelings or at least sets of feelings. Once again, however, it is interesting to ask where these feelings are located, for the most obvious location for grief and joy is in the mind and that already puts them in a quite different category from any sensation. An alternative answer but one which also brings out the distinctiveness of emotions would involve invoking the pictures we mentioned in Chapter 4, e.g. locating joy in the heart and grief in the stomach. As we saw,[5] however, these pictures are not intended to be literally true – although joy is located in the heart, it is not a pleasurable version of heartburn, nor is grief a bit like having an upset stomach. These pictures will therefore be of little interest to the rigorous physicalist. Instead she may want to argue that the experiences of grief and joy are somehow composite and distributed throughout the body (*RPP1*, para. 449). Perhaps, as James believed, closer analysis will show that grief and joy are made up of a complicated set of feelings. The problem with this supposition, however, is that it clashes with the grammar of these concepts. We do not say someone is grief-stricken on the basis of knowing that she is having such-and-such feelings, indeed, we may recognize that someone is grief-stricken without her having said a word to us about her bodily feelings. Similarly, someone who says 'I feel sad' does not do so because she has noted a certain feeling or set of feelings within herself. Rather the utterance is itself part of the pattern of behaviour of someone who is sad. Far from being its constituents, the bodily feelings associated with an emotion may even be a distraction from it. As Wittgenstein notes,

> if I am scared stiff over somebody's illness and say 'this fear is terrible', the stomach disturbance and constriction in the chest and so on are not what is almost unbearable. I have endured worse bodily upsets than these. One might even treat the bodily symptoms as a distraction from the emotion.
>
> (*LPP*, p. 70)

Here one might also note that emotions have a different type of duration from sensations. Fear wells up and subsides, but typically it does not simply start and stop as a bodily sensation may. Similarly someone may be said to be sad for days, but we would not normally say she had a particular bodily feeling for days because in this case the experience is only continuous if the individual is continually aware of it. Thus it is not just depression but the other emotions as well that belong to a different category from feelings.

The obvious objection to this account is that it separates emotions and bodily sensations too drastically. For example, it seems to ignore the way in which adopting a particular expression can conjure up the corresponding emotion.

> How does it come about that – as James says – I have a feeling of joy if I merely make a joyful face; a feeling of sadness, if I make a sad one? That, therefore, I can produce these feelings by imitating their expression? Does that show that muscular sensations are sadness, or part of sadness? (*RPP1*, para. 451)

The first point here is that these sensations certainly play a large part when the philosopher sits in her study and seeks to pinpoint the nature of the emotions by introspection.

> If someone imitates grief for himself in his study, he will indeed readily be conscious of the tensions on his face. But really grieve, or follow a sorrowful action in a film, and ask yourself if you were conscious of your face. (*RPP1*, para. 925)

A further point is that when we try to make a sad or a joyful face, we usually do not use a mirror to do this. So how do we do it? Isn't it by imagining ourselves sad, by conjuring up sad thoughts and adopting an appropriate expression? Thus in a sense the feeling of sadness is the basis for thinking we have made a sad face rather than the product of our assuming that expression.

To make these points, however, is not to deny that adopting a certain expression or posture may affect the way we feel (we do, after all, say such things as 'Chin up'). Insofar as this is true, however, it is of empirical not conceptual interest; it may help us avoid or curb depression, but it casts no light on its nature. Here it is important to distinguish between the cause of an emotion and its object. Generally the two will be the same, but in logical terms the cause is distinct from its object. Even it were discovered that posture caused depression, the feelings caused by poor posture would not be what we get depressed about (being out of work is depressing, but having an uncomfortable feeling in the back is not). Similarly, even if a change of posture puts us in better spirits, we would not normally cite this as an explanation of our new mood. We don't say 'Now I feel much better: the feeling in my facial muscles and round about the corners of my mouth is good' (*RPP1*, para. 454). Thus, even if it was discovered that the glands of a sad person secrete differently from those of a cheerful person and that this was a or the cause of sadness, it would not follow from this that sadness was a sensation caused by the secretion (*RPP1*, para. 803). Any causal stories we may develop are irrelevant to questions of the content of our experience. The nature of an emotion is revealed not by experiments to discover its causes, but by what an individual who is in the emotional state says and does. Furthermore, her use of the expression 'I am sad' is not based on discovering a particular set of sensations within herself. Indeed, anything that could only be established through looking is not what we mean by joy, sorrow, etc., for the words simply aren't used that way (*RPP1*, para. 456).

All this does not mean that sensations are never associated with particular emotions. Indeed, certain links are obvious. For example, catching one's breath is a characteristic reaction of surprise and therefore it is natural that surprise should often be accompanied by the sensation of catching one's breath (*RPP2*, para. 1). More generally, since there are often physiological phenomena which accompany particular emotions, this itself implies certain characteristic sensations.

> We assume, of course, that certain accompanying physiological phenomena occur in someone who expresses fear, for after all he is supposed to be human. A rapid pulse, laboured breathing, higher blood pressure, perhaps, and a series of neurological phenomena which are more difficult to observe; all this is in turn accompanied by certain characteristic feelings. If someone breaks into a cold sweat then he has the sensations of sweating. (*LW1*, para. 413)

However, this does not undermine the point that these accompanying phenomena and feelings do not constitute fear. We would not say someone was afraid if all of these occurred, but the person's other reactions were not those of fear. Similarly, if it were showed that inducing these phenomena could cause fear, this would demonstrate an empirical connection between conceptually distinct occurrences, not that fear consisted in these feelings.

Having made these points, it is worth returning to our original question and asking what the content of an emotion is. As we saw, in the case of a visual or aural sense-impression the content is given by the individual's representation of what she perceived. With the other senses and with sensations or feelings, the content is given by the utterances which give it expression. But what about emotions? The difficulty of specifying a content itself underlines the fact that emotions belong to a different category from sense-impressions or sensations and feelings. One way, however, of characterising their content is in terms of the pictures we mentioned in the last chapter. For example, one might talk of the darkness of depression or of the flames of anger (*RPP2*, para. 148). Such pictures can also be used to characterise the intensities of different emotions, for example, one might contrast the blackness of despair with the greyness of depression. A particular occurrence of an emotion might also be captured in a more specific picture of this kind, as, for instance, Faust's despair is conveyed in the phrase 'Perpetual cloud descends'. Furthermore, since the notion of content is looser, it could be drawn from almost any field of human expression. The despairing individual may feel just like the individual in Munch's *The Scream* or she may find that the best expression of what she feels is a piece of music or sculpture. As all examples suggest, the content of the experience is not some mysterious private entity; rather we can only talk of a content in relation to some possible manifestation of the experience. If the world looks grey to a grief-stricken individual, what 'stands before her mind', what she experiences, is not an inner state – grief – but a grey world, the cause of her grief (*RPP1*, para. 441).

At this stage, it is worth considering what is involved in imagining or remembering an emotion. The inclination is to say that both consist in having a mental image or picture of the emotion, and

> one thinks that one has already done everything by speaking of a picture, for longing just is a content of consciousness, and its picture is something that is (very) like it, even if it is less clear than the original. (*RPP1*, para. 726)

But what does this really mean? The notion of an image similar to the original says very little. In fact, if we want to imagine fear, we do not conjure up the picture of a feeling, but imagine being afraid. This may involve mental images insofar as it involves imagining a frightening situation, but if we want an image of fear itself, the best picture would be that of someone who is actually afraid. Ironically it is the Outer that turns out to offer the best picture of the Inner. If we want to 'show' someone what fear is like, the best way to do so won't be to teach her recherché forms of introspection but to show her fear portrayed on the stage. In this case, the actor might be said to have a picture of the emotion, but only in the sense that the concept of this emotion unifies and gives sense to her proceedings. The picture is not an explanation of her proceedings but part of their description (*RPP1*, para. 726).

As this example suggests, one way of capturing the content and course of an emotion is to portray it in a series of actions and the same could even be done in a series of facial expressions. Of course, someone may have an emotion and not display it but this does not undermine the fact that it is the typical manifestations of an emotion that give it its specific character. Here it is also interesting to note that, even when the emotion is hidden, its expression can still in a sense be used to characterise it. Take the example of longing or a wish.

> 'Wish is a state of mind that relates to an object.' In order to make this more intelligible, one thinks perhaps of yearning, and of the object of our yearning's being before our eyes and that we look at it longingly. If it is not there in front of us, perhaps its picture goes proxy for it, and if there is no picture there, then an image. And so the wish is a stance of the soul towards an image. But one really always thinks of the stance of a body towards an object. The stance of the soul to the image is just what one represents in a picture: the man's soul, as it leans with gestures of longing towards the picture (an actual picture) of the object. (*RPP1*, para. 275)

A wish normally expresses itself in a statement, i.e. in language, but if we want an image of its content, of the individual's state, the natural way to do this is in terms of the Outer. Similarly, when the individual hides her desires, it is the picture of unconcealed desire that provides their image. There may be no longing or fear written on the individual's face, instead they may as it were be written on her soul.

So far we have contrasted sensations and feelings with emotions, but many concepts of the Inner fall into none of these categories. One group among these is what might be called aspects of the intellect – concepts such as understanding and remembering, thinking and intending or knowing and believing. These have completely different characteristics from both sensations and emotions, and themselves fall into several categories. The first and most important point is that they have a different kind of duration from either sensations or emotions. Although we may know something for a certain amount of time, it would be strange to treat knowing as a particular process which endures throughout that period. Similarly, although deciding what to do may be a process, intending itself is not – its start, finish and course is not something the individual might monitor. Rather she decides to act in a certain way and will be said to have that intention until she either carries it out or changes her mind. As for thinking itself, we saw in Chapter 3 that this is not a process and hence not something to which the notion of duration applies straightforwardly. It would make little sense, for example, to try literally to give a second-by-second account of someone's thoughts. If someone thinks 'the solution lies in always taking the shortest route', it would be wrong to treat her thought as occurring over a particular stretch of time, for she did not think it bit by bit. On the other hand, it would be strange (and inaccurate) to represent her thinking as a vacuum enlivened by occasional bursts of instantaneous thought. Here it is also interesting to note that thinking differs from genuine inner states such as pain or sadness in that there is no utterance corresponding to 'I am in pain' or 'I am sad'.

> We don't say 'I think' as the expression of a mental state. At most we say 'I'm thinking'. 'Leave me alone, I'm thinking about. . . .' And of course one doesn't mean by this: 'Leave me alone, I am now behaving in such and such a way.'
>
> (*RPP2*, para. 12)

To explore the intellectual concepts, let us begin by considering remembering. The natural inclination is simply to treat this phenomenon as a mental process with its own specific experiential content. However, the notion of content is difficult to flesh out and we are therefore tempted to treat it as yet another ineffable experience. Wittgenstein, however, points out that if we consider a particular case of remembering, there is no sign either of an experience or of a process. 'If someone asks me what I have been doing in the last two hours, I answer him straight off and I don't read the answer off from an experience I am having' (*RPP1*, para. 105). The implication is that remembering is not an experience at all and this may seem paradoxical, but imagine if someone did treat it as an experience. Suppose someone said 'Now I know what remembering is like!' or 'I shall never forget the experience I just had, namely, remembering'. Neither of these utterances makes sense and this shows that it is not just for us that remembering is not experience, but that in others too it could not be one. The point of the concept is its relation to a particular ability. Someone is said to remember when she can accurately say what happened in the past, and what experiences she does (or does not) have in the course of doing this are irrelevant to the use of the concept.

But, if remembering is not an experience, why are we so inclined to think of it as an inner process? One reason is that we tend to treat it as a kind of perception, a looking into the past. Here the notion of an inner process captures the possibility of error, for just as the individual can misperceive, so too she can misremember. What can also confuse us is the fact that there is a process of trying to remember just as there are cases of remembering which do indeed involve experiences. For example, in seeking an exact account of a particular incident, we may as it were do a mental reconstruction of what happened, visualising one by one the events which comprised the incident we are trying to remember. This activity might be said to involve a process and, unlike the first case we mentioned, may take a particular time to complete. Here remembering is in some ways similar to imagining, and this differentiates it from those cases where we simply give an account of the past without as it were having to think about it.

When I say 'Memories of that day rose up in me' it looks

different. Here I am inclined to speak of a content of the experience, and I imagine something like words and pictures which rise up before my mind. (*RPP1*, para. 111)

Here there may indeed be a process, for the memories may become clearer or fade or one memory picture may give way to another. However, there is nothing ineffable about the process, for here as in general it only makes sense to speak of a content where that content can be specified.

The test 'Does it make sense to say "Now I know what it's like to X" ' is an important one and can be used not only to underline the nature of remembering but generally to bring out differences between various concepts of the Inner. Take the case of a sensation or feeling. Here

when someone says 'Now I know what a tingle is', we know that he knows through his 'expression of the sensation'; he jerks, makes a particular noise, says what we too say in this case, finds the same description apt as we do.

(*RPP1*, para. 113)

The sensation case differs therefore from the normal case of memory where the expression of remembering is not the expression of an experience, but simply involves saying what happened in the past. As we have seen, however, there can be memory-experiences and in the same way one can speak of memory-feelings, for example, the feeling that an event in the distant past belongs to a different world. In this sort of case, someone might well say 'Now I know what it's like to feel that something happened a long, long time ago'. Thus 'we might actually speak of a feeling "Long, long ago" and these words are an expression of the feeling, but not these: "I remember that I often met him" ' (ibid., para. 114).

How then do sense-impressions compare to remembering in this respect? Would it make sense for someone to say 'Now I know what it's like to see?' At first glance, this seems perfectly in order, but what *is* it like to see? The difficulty here is that there seems to be nothing to describe apart from what one actually sees. The reason we find this confusing is because we want to treat seeing like a sensation. In fact, seeing is better compared to an ability than an experience. The key change in someone who could not see and now can is not that she has a new set of experiences, but that she can now do things she previously couldn't. Her experience may be said to have a new dimension, but what characterises that dimension, and hence what constitutes its content, is not an account of sensations, but an account of what she can see. Against this, one might point to the exhilaration of a blind person who is suddenly able to see, but, if there are experiences of joy and wonder here, these are certainly not a feature of our normal visual experience. If there are particular visual experiences, these are things like being dazzled or being unable to focus. There may also be experiences which are only accessible to the sighted. For example, the feeling of isolation created by being surrounded on all sides by the sea or the sense of power on looking down from a great height. Here it would make sense to say 'Now I know what that experience is like' and its content can be described. Seeing itself, however, is not an experience in the sense that a sensation or a feeling is. There is no explaining what it is like – not because language is inadequate, but because it does not belong to that kind of category.

What about emotions though? What would we make of someone who said 'Now I know what it's like to fear'? This seems to make better sense than someone saying she knows what it's like to remember, and yet it is not like the sensation case, for there is no particular experience the individual can point to which constitutes her fear. In fact, the key difference between us and someone who had never known fear would be that she did not share an aspect of our lives. Her ignorance of fear could not be compared with never having had a headache or not having experienced the 'pins and needles' sensation. Rather the fact that she had not known fear would mark her out as a different type of person, not simply someone who had not had the same experiences as the rest of us. If she were to 'experience' fear, the change would bring her closer to us and would be more akin to a change in her attitude or approach to things rather than simply the acquisition of a new experience. To illustrate this, consider a more unusual emotion and one which it is quite conceivable that not everyone should have had, namely, despair. Here people often say that it is impossible to know what this experience is like unless one has experienced it. But it is not like having a particularly unusual sensation. What matters is not just how the individual describes her experience, but also how she later acts, e.g. her later attitude and relation to others. If despair changes her, this is not because the experience just happens to have certain consequences. Rather part of the measure of what she experienced is the degree and way in which it affects her subsequent behaviour. The expression of her new 'experience' is that she understands differently, sees things in a new light; what before seemed foolish or reprehensible may now seem comprehensible, where she once felt contempt she may now feel sympathy, and what she once took for granted may now be a source of delight.

Returning to the concepts of the intellect, we can see that understanding is similar to remembering, for it would make no sense to say 'Now I know what it is like to understand'. As this suggests, understanding is neither an experience nor a feeling, although it may involve these. Unlike an emotion, it does not have a characteristic expression in behaviour but is akin to an ability. Someone who comes to understand something learns to do something new and this does not necessarily involve having an experience or an image, although it may do so. For example, when the individual suddenly understands how to continue a sequence, she may see a formula in her head, but even here the image does not constitute her understanding. The understanding lies in the application of the image and, if someone can continue the sequence but has no image, she will still be said to understand. There are certainly experiences which can be associated with understanding (the joyful feeling of 'Now I can go on') and even certain bodily sensations (a loosening in the chest maybe or a feeling of lightness in the head). However, these do not constitute understanding. Nor should understanding be thought of as a further, specific but non-describable mental process. As we saw in Chapter 3, if a soldier turns left on being ordered to turn right, her understanding of the command is not separable from her action. The action itself justifies us in saying she understood the order wrongly. The notion of a further undescribable process explains nothing. Although it may take some time to understand something, there is no specific mental process which must occur before we can talk of understanding. Furthermore, like thought in general, understanding does not have duration in the way a process would and sense-impressions and sensations do. Someone may understand gradually or in a flash, but even in the former case, it would be impossible to plot the growth of understanding on a second-by-second basis.

A further key grammatical point about understanding is that, unlike a sense-impression or sensation, it is not interrupted by a break in consciousness. This point also holds for other concepts of the intellect such as believing, knowing and intending. Provisionally (and slightly misleadingly),[6] Wittgenstein calls these concepts 'dispositions', and he notes that

> an important difference between dispositions and states of consciousness consists in the fact that a disposition is not interrupted by a break in consciousness or a shift in attention. . . . Really one hardly ever says that one has believed or understood something 'uninterruptedly' since yesterday. An interruption of belief would be a period of unbelief, not, e.g. the withdrawal of attention from what one believes, or, e.g. sleep. (*RPP2*, para. 45)

For these reasons, it would make no sense for someone to try to monitor such dispositions continuously. While an individual might signal the continuance of a sensation by holding her hand in the air, it would be ridiculous to ask her to do the same for an intention (*LPP*, pp. 301–2). An intention is not something which starts, continues, then stops; rather an individual is said to be intending to do something from the moment she decides to do it until such time as she does it or changes her intention. All that is necessary for her still to be intending to do something is that she has neither forgotten her intention nor changed it. This makes the duration of an intention quite different from the duration of a sensation. The content is also different, for here the content is a decision. For this reason, intensity words do not apply to it – although we say 'I firmly intend', 'I fully believe', etc., these statements indicate what would be needed to change our minds, not the intensity of a particular mental state. The individual does not notice a fading or a growing intention; rather she commits herself to a particular way of acting and may wish to underline the degree of that commitment. A pain or a desire may flare up, but not an intention.

The suggestion that intention and belief, etc. are dispositions creates a problem, for it raises questions about how the individual knows that she is disposed in a certain way. With others, the problem does not arise, for the individual can observe the other person and infer from this how she is disposed. But what is she supposed to do in her own case? Traditionally, philosophers have argued that we know our own beliefs directly and those of others indirectly. But how does one know one's own beliefs? What does the state of belief look like 'from inside'? Iconoclastically, Wittgenstein argues that it is misleading to talk of the individual knowing her own beliefs, and he denies that she discovers them introspectively. But this account too runs into problems, for, if belief is a disposition we recognise in others, why can't we observe it in ourselves? Furthermore, how can the concept belief be made up of such disparate elements? For, according to Wittgenstein, the first person uses of it are non-observation-based utterances, while the third person uses are reports based on observation. This gives the verb a peculiar asymmetry as is illustrated by the case of mistaken belief for, while it makes sense to say 'He believes it's raining and it isn't' or 'Suppose I believed it was raining and it wasn't' or even 'I believed it was raining and it wasn't', it makes no sense to say 'I believe it is raining and it isn't'. So does this mean that the first person present says something different from the third person uses and the first person uses in the past and the hypothetical mode? The answer would seem to be 'yes', and yet such a conclusion would be highly paradoxical.

The general issue at the heart of the problem here is the question of whether the individual can observe her own dispositions.

A belief, a wish, a fear, a hope, a fondness; each can be called a state of man; we can count on this state in our behaviour towards this man, we can infer his reactions from his state.

And if someone says: 'All this time I had the belief. . .', 'All my life I have wished. . .', etc.; he is simply reporting a state, an attitude. – But if he says 'I believe he's coming' (or simply 'Here he comes') or 'I wish you'd come' (or 'Please come'), then he is acting according to that condition, not reporting that he is in it.

But if that were right, then there ought to be a present form of that report, and hence, on the one hand, the *utterance* 'I believe. . .' and, on the other hand, the *report* 'I am in the state of belief. . .'. And similarly for wish, intention, fear etc.

(*RPP1*, para. 832)

However, the attempt to construe 'I believe' as the report 'I'm in a state of belief' runs straight into what Wittgenstein called Moore's paradox: if the individual reports her belief, why should she not report that she believes it is raining and that it isn't? After all, people often hold mistaken beliefs, so the report might be correct, and yet for some reason the individual herself can never make it.

The key to clarifying this paradox is to note that the individual's description of her own state of mind is also indirectly the description of a state of affairs. In other words, someone who says she believes P is thereby committed to asserting P itself. Describing one's state of belief might be likened to describing a photograph in order to describe what the photograph depicts; the problem of Moore's paradox is 'that I should further be able to say that this photograph (the impression on the mind) is trustworthy. So I should be able to say: "I believe that it's raining, and my belief is trustworthy, so I trust it" ' (*RPP1*, para. 482). However, while the individual can trust or distrust her senses, she cannot trust or distrust her belief. The reason for this becomes clear if one considers what it would be like if someone did append a statement about her state of belief to all her assertions. If, for example, a station announcer said 'The train at platform 4 is for London and personally I believe it', the second part of her statement would add nothing to the first. By contrast, if she said 'The train at platform 4 is for London, but I don't believe it', we should not know what to make of her statement since the second part cancels the first. The reason therefore that the individual cannot observe her belief is that by adopting a neutral or evaluatory stance towards it, she undermines it. Someone who said 'I believe it's raining, but it isn't' would thereby show that she didn't believe it was raining and thus undermine her own assertion. As Wittgenstein notes, there

155

can be no first-person equivalent of the third-person use of the verb for the same reason that a verb meaning to believe falsely would lack a first-person present indicative (*LW1*, para. 141).

One implication of this is that no proposition about a state can be logically equivalent to the utterance 'I believe . . .'. This can be illustrated by trying to recast Moore's paradox in terms of brain states, for, if the utterance did say something about the individual's state, this should be reproducible in terms of the brain instead of the mind. However, any statement about someone's brain is logically independent of any statement about the outside world, so no statement of the form 'My brain is in state A and the world is in state Z' would ever be a contradiction. For this reason, 'no assertion about the state of my (or anyone else's) brain is equivalent to the assertion that I believe – for example, "He will come" ' (*RPP1*, para. 591). As this shows, the problem with Moore's paradox is that it ignores the relationship between the subject and her utterances. An assertion (whether or not prefixed by the words 'I believe') is an expression of belief, not a report on it, and the individual undermines her role as a subject if she tries to adopt the same relation to her belief as to that of others. While the supposition that she believes something may be expressed as two unrelated propositions, viz. that a certain mental state pertains in her and a particular state of affairs outside her, this is not true of the assertion. There the two propositions are not independent, for 'the *assertion* that *this* is going on *inside* me asserts: this is going on outside me' (*RPP1*, para. 490). The concept of belief is based around the privileged first-person use, where the individual expresses her belief rather than reports on it. If she does try to assess it, the result is nonsense, or rather it is as if two people were speaking through the same mouth, one of them expressing the belief, the other confirming or denying it.

This may explain why Moore's paradox arises, but it still leaves it unclear why the individual cannot adopt the same relation to herself as she adopts towards others:

> How is it that I cannot gather that I believe it's going to rain from my own statement 'It's going to rain'? Can I then draw no interesting conclusions from the fact that I said this? If

someone else says it, I conclude perhaps that he will take an umbrella with him. Why not in my own case?

(*RPP1*, para. 704)

The natural suggestion is that the individual does not need to draw conclusions from her own words because she is directly acquainted with the mental state which is their source. But this misses the point, for it suggests that what the individual knows is of the same kind as what others know; in the classic formulation, the individual knows her state directly, others know it indirectly. However, this idea of knowledge (and observation) reduces the individual to a nonsensical passivity in relation to herself. The point is not that the individual has more information on which to base hypotheses about how she shall act, but that it is she who decides how to act and so has no need of hypotheses at all. As Wittgenstein puts it,

> What would be the point of my drawing conclusions from my own words to my behaviour, when in any case I know what I believe? And what is the manifestation of my knowing what I believe? Is it not manifested precisely in this, that I do not infer my behaviour from my words? That is the fact.
>
> (*RPP1*, para. 744)

The fundamental point is that the individual's relation to herself is not one of observation. The individual does not have to infer her intentions from her acts; rather as an agent she forms intentions. The same point can be illustrated with respect to conviction, for there too what we say of others contrasts with what we say of ourselves. For example, we say 'I noticed in her tone of voice that she does not believe what she says', but we don't apply this to ourselves (*RPP1*, para. 737). The individual will of course be said to feel or know her own conviction and therefore not need to infer it from her own actions or words. But what does this actually mean? How does the individual find out what her convictions are? The answer is that she doesn't find out; rather her 'knowledge' of her convictions is expressed precisely in the fact that she has no doubt what they are (*RPP1*, para. 745). The individual's privileged place in the language-game (and the different basis of the first and of the third-person uses of psychological concepts) reflects the idea of the individual as subject and agent. Although we may treat belief, intention, etc. as the principles lying behind an individual's actions, it makes no sense to do the same thing in relation to ourselves. The individual does not need to make hypotheses about the principles lying behind her deeds, instead she simply acts.[7]

So far we have dealt with the basic form of our various psychological concepts, but we also play more sophisticated games. Utterances such as 'I believe' or 'I intend' are not based on observation, but even these concepts can on occasion be used in a different way. In fact, it is not even true that all first-person uses of psychological concepts are utterances (*Aeusserungen*). For example, there are what Wittgenstein calls 'functional states' (*RPP1*, para. 61). Here the individual does observe herself and may note that she is reacting in a particular way, for example, that she is irritable or liable to switch from one mood to another at the slightest excuse. Such reports contrast with utterances, e.g. pain expressions, in that they are not manifestations of the state involved. There are also concepts which include both an utterance and a report. For example, while 'I'm furious' is generally an expression of anger, 'I'm angry' is rarely one (*RPP1*, para. 127). The difference here is that 'I'm furious' is not an expression of self-observation; it is a direct expression of the anger itself, the anger as it were bubbles over into the exclamation itself (*LW1*, para. 13). By contrast, 'I'm angry' may be said in a tone of surprise by someone who suddenly notices that she has become quite worked up about something that does not merit it. There are also psychological concepts which, unlike belief, do refer to dispositions the individual might notice in herself, e.g. jealousy (*RPP1*, para. 178).

The example of anger underlines the complexity of psychological concepts, for it shows that, while the individual generally manifests the state she is in rather than reporting on it, it is also possible for her to take a different relation to herself and her own actions. One consequence of this is that psychological concepts can have a variety of meanings, depending on how the concept is being used. Consider the case of hope. At first glance, this seems straightforward: the words 'I hope' are an utterance – they are not based on observation, but express a particular state.

As Wittgenstein points out, however, the real situation is more complicated.

> I say to myself 'I still keep on and on hoping, although . . .' and in saying it I as it were shake my head over myself. That means something quite other than simply 'I hope!' (The difference in English between 'I am hoping' and 'I hope'.)
>
> (*RPP1*, para. 465)

The point here is that, while 'I hope you'll come' is an expression of hope, 'I'm still hoping you'll come' might not be. In the first case, the expression is clearly an utterance; in the second, however, the expression may be a report in which the individual treats herself as if she were an outside observer. Here the individual really does treat her hope as a state in which she finds herself; she might, for example, note that while she knows something won't happen, she still catches herself hoping that it will. The difference between the two uses of the concept hope comes out in the fact that it makes sense to say 'I believe I still hope you'll come' but not to say 'I believe I hope you'll come' (*RPP1*, para. 4). In the first case hope is something the individual is describing in herself, whereas in the second case it is something she is voicing.

The idea of description reflects the nature of the relation the individual takes up to herself, but it also affects the content of what she says. For example, in noting that she is in a state of hope, she might report various things, e.g. that she often imagines the fulfilment of her hope, that every day she says to herself such-and-such or sighs, that she frequently does such-and-such in the hope that . . ., etc. (*RPP1*, para. 466). Each of these things may be part of the individual's description of her state of mind at a particular time, and this contrasts with the usual case of the individual remembering what she hoped (ibid., para. 468). Generally in remembering what she hoped, the individual does not have to recall her behaviour at the time or even her thoughts. Rather she simply says that she hoped, and this utterance has the same status in relation to the past as the utterance 'I hope' in the present. The difference can be underlined by considering the case of forgiveness, for the phrase 'I forgive you' is an expression of forgiveness and does not mean 'I am engaged in a particular process, namely, that of forgiving you'. On the other hand, someone might say 'Gradually I'm coming to forgive her' or 'I'm trying to forgive her' and here one really might talk of a process and so of description and observation.

These examples show that the normal language-game can be modified so that in some contexts the individual can take up the same relation to herself as a third party might. This can even happen in the case of belief. For example, someone might note that she believes bad news too easily, and this possibility could even be taken to provide a use for the paradoxical statement 'I believe what you say, but don't trust my belief'. The possibility of taking up this unusual relation to oneself can also produce other paradoxical utterances. For example, someone might say 'I know it is true, but I can't believe it' and mean by this that she can't take to heart and act on what, in her more reflective moments, she knows to be the case. As we saw in the earlier case of hope, in some of these contexts the individual can be said to be describing her state of mind. However, this again raises problems, for why should 'I still hope he'll come' be a description of a state of mind, while 'I believe' is not? Furthermore, doesn't this all conflict with what we said in Chapter 1? There we emphasised that, according to Wittgenstein, first person psychological concepts are not descriptions.

The first point to note is that in a sense all psychological utterances might be said to say something about the individual's state of mind, for each can be used as the basis for inferences about how the individual is likely to act. Even a request such as 'Give me an apple' could be said to indicate something about the individual's state, for it shows that she desires an apple. However, we certainly wouldn't call this request a description of her state (*RPP1*, para. 463), so why should we do so in the case of 'I want an apple'? Since the two utterances have roughly the same sense, it would seem strange to call one a description of a state and the other not. The fact that one mentions the subject and the other doesn't should not be allowed to confuse us. The propositions 'I believe it's raining', 'the sentence "It is raining" is true' and 'It is the case that it's raining' all say the same thing despite one referring to an individual, one to a sentence and one to a state of affairs. So, if reference to the subject is not enough to make an utterance a description of a state of mind, what is? If 'I believe' is not a description of a mental state, what utterances are? Wittgenstein offers a number of examples: 'I am sad' or 'I am in a good mood' or perhaps 'I am in pain' (*RPP1*, para. 470). One characteristic of these utterances is that unlike expressions of belief, their purpose is to tell others how the individual is feeling. Furthermore, the states they refer to all have genuine duration, unlike knowledge claims or beliefs. By contrast, the statement 'I can speak Eskimo and know the dates of all the Kings and Queens of England' would not be called a description of the individual's state of mind nor would the statement 'I believe the world is flat'.

This contrast brings out an important point, for one mark of genuine descriptions of inner states is that the state has a characteristic expression in behaviour. If someone says 'I am sad', we shall expect her to act in certain ways for as long as that state continues. On the other hand, if she says 'I believe it's raining', this may affect decisions she will make, but there is no specific way of acting that corresponds to it. As this suggests, we only call something a state of mind if it has genuine duration and shapes an individual's conduct on a continuous basis; indeed, it is because it has genuine duration that a description of the changing state is possible. In the case of hope, when the concept is used to describe the individual's state, it has genuine duration, but when it is simply used to express a hope, it does not. For example, if someone says 'I hope you'll come', it would be strange to reply 'How long have you been hoping that?' To this, the appropriate answer might be 'For as long as I've been saying so' and this would simply underline the fact that the question is irrelevant (*RPP2*, para. 722). By contrast, if someone says 'I'm still hoping he'll come', it may be of real interest to know how long she has been hoping this. Furthermore, the answer to the question may involve describing the various emotions the individual has about this subject, and these descriptions will in turn relate to her behaviour for, as we have seen, one characteristic of emotions is that there are typical ways in which they manifest themselves.

Thus one reason for calling fear and hope states of mind is that unlike knowledge, they have duration and characteristic expression in behaviour. A characteristic description of a state of mind would be the alternation of fear and hope, e.g. 'In the morning I was full of hope, and then . . .'. Anyone would call that a description. But it is characteristic of it that this description could run parallel to a description of my behaviour. (*RPP1*, para. 596)

Since belief and intention generally do not have this type of expression, they would not normally be called descriptions of a state of mind. However, even with these concepts there are circumstances where they might almost be said to describe a state of mind. Compare, for example, the two utterances: 'The whole time I believed in the law of gravity' and 'The whole time, I believed I heard a low whisper'.

In the first case 'believe' is used similarly to 'Know'. ('*Had* anyone asked me, I *would have* said. . . .') In the second case we have activity, surmising, listening, doubt, etc. And even if 'believe' does not *designate* these activities, still they are surely what makes us say that here we are describing a state of mind or mental activity. We may also put it like this: we form a picture of the man who believes the whole time that he is hearing a low rustle. But not of the man who believes in the correctness of the law of gravity. (*RPP1*, para. 597)

Similarly, although 'I intend to X' is not normally a description, the statement 'my intention grew stronger every hour' might well be called one. Why? Because it is part of a network of thoughts and feelings, part of an inner struggle which could be described.

To round off this discussion, let us consider a final example, the concept fear. The basis for this language-game is the cry of fear. As with other psychological concepts, a state of mind can be inferred from the cry, but this does not mean the cry is a description of a state of mind. As Wittgenstein notes, 'we don't shout "Help" because we observe our own state of fear' (*RPP2*, para. 724). If a cry is not a description, there is no reason for saying that the utterance which replaces it is one. However, there are applications of the concept of fear which are descriptions, e.g. 'I'm less afraid of her now than I used to be' or 'For years, the very mention of airplanes filled me with fear'. What makes these statements descriptions is the fact that the individual observes and assesses her own reactions. Generally, she can support them by offering illustrations of her state of mind and descriptions of

162

how she acted and what she said. So what, one might ask, does 'I am frightened' really mean? The answer is not to be found via introspection. In fact, the real question is 'In what context does the utterance occur?' and the answer is 'Many different types of context'. The words 'I'm frightened' may be a cry of terror, a shameful confession of fear, a critical self-judgement or a wry self-observation. In each case, the individual takes up a different attitude to herself; the key difference, however, is between cases where the words function as a direct expression of the state and those where they are based on self-observation. On one level, these two types of cases are distinguished by the tone and manner in which the words are uttered. For example, in contrast with a cry of fear, the self-mocking 'I'm afraid' may be said light-heartedly and even with a smile. More profoundly, what distinguishes the different types of statement is their purpose. Someone who is describing her mental state has a different intention from someone who simply gives expression to that state and this difference will manifest itself both in the manner of statement and its context. For example, in contrast with expression, describing involves 'observing, considering, remembering behaviour, a striving for accuracy, the ability to correct oneself, comparing' (*LW1*, para. 51). Thus describing a mental state is a very specific language-game, something that gets done in a very particular context (*LW1*, para. 27).

As this example shows, within the basic asymmetry of psychological concepts, there is also room for variation. The language-game has a certain basis and structure, but in particular contexts it can be given a new, slightly paradoxical twist. This affects the first person rather than the third for, while 'He is afraid' is always a description, 'I'm afraid' may or may not be. As Wittgenstein puts it, 'a cry is not a description. But there are transitions. And the words "I am afraid" may approximate more, or less, to being a cry. They may come close to this and also be far removed from it' (*LW1*, para. 51). This raises a final problem, for if the utterance 'I'm afraid' can belong to two different types of game, is it always clear to which game it belongs? As we saw, a key difference between the games is the purpose of the utterance, for this indicates the individual's relation to her fear; however, not everything we say is said with a definite purpose and so the exact status of an expression may be unclear. On many occasions, this may not actually matter and, if it does, we can ask the individual to clarify her purpose, so that the status of the expression is fixed by what comes after it.

> I say 'I am afraid . . .', someone else asks me 'What did you want to say when you said that? Was it like an exclamation; or were you alluding to your state within the past few hours; did you simply want to tell me something?' Can I always give him a clear answer? Can I never give him one? – Sometimes I shall have to say: 'I was thinking about how I spent the day today and I shook my head, vexed with myself, as it were': – but other times: 'It meant: Oh God! If I just wasn't so afraid!' – Or: 'It was just a cry of fear!' – Or: 'I wanted you to know how I feel.' Sometimes the utterance is really followed by such explanations. But they can't *always* be given.
>
> (*LW1*, para. 17)

The expression 'I'm afraid' is a complex tool, something that can appear in a variety of games. Indeed, it is possible to imagine people who as it were thought much more definitely than we and so had many words where we have one. For example, 'I tend to fear her' might mean many things (*RPP2*, para. 734). It could mean that I am often afraid when I meet her or that in her presence I tend to be subdued or that without consciously feeling any fear of her, her judgements and re-actions weigh more heavily with me than would normally be the case.

The case of fear shows how complex even one of our psychological concepts can be. The aim of this chapter as a whole, however, has been to bring out the complexity of the Inner itself. As we have seen, our psychological concepts can be grouped in rough families (sensations, emotions, dispositions, etc.), but even then there are often considerable differences within families or analogies which hold between some members of one group and some of another. The Inner is neither a homogeneous series of private experiences nor a hotchpotch of ineffable states; rather it comprises a variety of concepts, each of which relates the Outer and Inner in a slightly different way. To plot this complexity, Wittgenstein drew up several plans for the treatment of psychological concepts, and the best way to summarise the chapter is to quote one of them.

> Ought I to call the whole field of the psychological that of 'experience' [*Erlebens*]? And so all psychological verbs 'verbs of experience'. ('Concepts of experience.') Their characteristic is this, that their third person but not their first person is stated on grounds of observation. That observation is observation of behaviour. A subclass of concepts of experience is formed by the 'concepts of undergoing' [*Erfahrungs begriffe*]. 'Undergoings' have duration and a course; they may run on uniformly or non-uniformly. They have intensity. They are not characters of thought. Images are undergoings. A subclass of 'undergoings' are 'impressions'. Impressions have spatial and temporal relations to one another. There are blend-impressions. E.g. blends of smells, colours, sounds. 'Emotions' are 'experiences' but not 'undergoings'. (Examples: sadness, joy, grief, delight.) And one might distinguish between 'directed emotions' and 'undirected emotions'.[8] An emotion has duration; it has characteristic 'undergoings' and thoughts; it has a characteristic expression which one would use in *miming* it. Talking under certain circumstances and whatever else corresponds to that, is thinking. Emotions colour thoughts. One subclass of 'experiences' is the forms of 'conviction'. (Belief, certainty, doubt, etc.) Their expression is an expression of thought. They are not 'colourings' of thoughts. The directed emotions might also be called 'attitudes'. Surprise and fright are attitudes too, and so are admiration and enjoyment. (*RPP1*, para. 836)

This plan is neither exhaustive nor definitive, but it gives some idea of the complexity of the Inner and the sort of distinctions which structure the grammar of its various concepts. If we now ask why we are interested in the Inner, we can see that we have many types of interest in it. That someone has a particular intention has a very different interest from the fact that she has a particular sensation, while the fact that she is in pain has another type of interest altogether. However, these points still leave one fundamental issue unexplored, for why we do use the

Inner/Outer picture at all? What is the real significance of the picture which lies at the very heart of our lives? These questions are the ones we shall turn to in the next chapter.

6

THE INNER/OUTER PICTURE

The characteristic of the mental seems to be that one has to guess at it according to the Outer in others and *knows* it only in one's own case.

But when, through more careful thought, this opinion goes up in smoke, what turns out to be the case is not that the Inner is something Outer, but that 'inner' and 'outer' no longer qualify as types of evidence. 'Inner evidence' means nothing and therefore neither does 'outer evidence'. (*LW2*, pp. 61-2)

In the preceding chapters, we have criticised the conception of the Inner as a mysterious hidden entity. In particular, we have emphasised the link between the Inner and the Outer, for talk of inner states only makes sense where there are outward criteria for those states. Having made these points, several important questions remain, for, if the Inner/Outer picture is so confusing, why do we use it? The picture cannot simply be dismissed as misleading, for reference to it is part of the grammar of our psychological concepts. Thus until we can clarify its significance, our account is lacking a fundamental element. A second difficulty, related to this one, is the clash between Wittgenstein's attempt to demystify the Inner and our sense that it genuinely is mysterious. Even people we know well may suddenly act in ways which make us feel we don't really know them at all. Similarly, in the midst of everyday activity we may suddenly be struck by the 'otherness' of other people and wonder at the simple fact that there are consciousnesses other than our own. On such occasions, the idea that the Inner is hidden seems an undeniable truth. Indeed, insofar as we are often uncertain what others are thinking or feeling, we might well be said to experience the hiddenness of the Inner every day. So what should we make of this? Is the Inner hidden? And if so, in what sense?

The most obvious reason for believing the Inner to be hidden is the uncertainty that affects our judgements about the inner states of others. When, for example, someone appears to be in pain, it seems self-evident that what matters is not the complaints, but what lies behind them. The natural way of representing the situation is to say that 'there is something Inner here which can be inferred only inconclusively from the Outer. It is a picture and it is obvious what justifies this picture. The apparent certainty of the first person, the uncertainty of the third' (*LW1*, para. 951). The asymmetry here is easily presented as a metaphysical truth and, since the start of modern philosophy, the idea that the individual has privileged access to the contents of her own consciousness has been treated as self-evident. According to Wittgenstein, however, the asymmetry in our concepts is purely grammatical. The individual has no doubts about the content of her own experience because our language-game excludes any such doubt. The basis of the game is that the individual's sincere utterances about her own experience are treated as necessarily correct. To introduce doubt here would alter the language-game; in particular, it would undermine the notion of the subject. Talk of privileged access and knowledge is therefore misleading. The reason the individual cannot be wrong about her own thoughts is because within the language-game she has the role of expressing those thoughts, and hence there is no gap between what she (sincerely) says her thoughts are and what they actually are. If, for example, we are trying to guess someone's thoughts, it is that individual and not anyone else who states whether the guess is correct. As Wittgenstein puts it,

> The Inner is hidden from us means that it is hidden from us in a sense that it is not hidden from *him*. And it is not hidden from the owner in the sense that *he gives expression to it*, and we, under certain conditions, believe his expression and there error has no place. And this asymmetry in the game is expressed in the sentence that the Inner is hidden from other people. (*LW2*, p. 36)

The point is not that the individual sees something only she can see, but that we treat her as a subject and on the basis of her utterances ascribe to her particular thoughts, feelings and experiences. The asymmetry of our psychological concepts is not a metaphysical truth, but is simply the reflection of a language-game based on the notion of a subject whose utterances are treated as necessarily correct.

This may make the notion of the subject seem unduly arbitrary and one might object that the language-game must have some connection with reality. But to a certain extent Wittgenstein does not deny this. Although grammar does not express any truths, our language-games operate against a particular background and, if certain things were different, the language-game would become impossible or lose its point. With regard to the asymmetry of our concepts, Wittgenstein emphasises two points: 'One, that in general I foresee my actions with greater accuracy than anyone else; the other, that my prediction is not founded on the same evidence as someone else's, and that it allows different conclusions' (*LW1*, para. 893). Although these facts do not determine our concepts, they do provide the necessary background to it. For example, if asking another person what she intended to do rarely helped predict her actions, the nature of our language-game, and our attitude to it, would change. Similarly, if others could generally predict the individual's actions better than she could, the notion of the individual as an agent with particular intentions, etc. would be undermined. This point ties in with others, for it is not just that we able to make better predictions about one body (our own) than others. Rather our whole relation to our own body is different. Generally, the individual does not observe her own body and is not surprised by its actions. Similarly, when she expresses an intention, this has a different kind of basis from predictions about how others will act. Here she needs no evidence for her statement, but simply says what she intends to do. Her statement is not so much a prediction as a commitment to seek a certain goal. By contrast, when someone else predicts what another will do, this is a genuine prediction, based on an extrapolation either of the individual's previous behaviour or that of people in general.

These points show how our subject-based language-game requires a certain setting if it is to make sense. It would be wrong, however, to treat these background facts as determining our grammar, for it would be quite possible to construct a different grammar against the background of precisely the same facts. For example, there could be a group of people who rejected the notion of a subject and ridiculed the idea that the individual acted. Unlike us, they would treat expressions of intention as ungrounded predictions which just happened to be correct. Instead of saying 'I intend to go to the bank', the individual might simply predict that her body would shortly start moving in a bankward direction. The fact that the individual was able to predict the actions of one body but not of others would simply be treated as a quirk of nature. Such a fatalistic attitude may seem peculiar, but it is not incoherent; what makes it seem so odd is that it rejects an idea which is central to our lives. What such examples illustrate, however, is that although our language-games presuppose certain facts, those facts do not determine our grammar; against this particular background, we may find certain ideas so natural as to seem inescapable, but, despite this, it remains conceivable that other people might erect a different grammatical structure upon exactly the same facts.

As we have seen, the asymmetry in our concepts reflects the asymmetry in our relation to our own bodies and to those of other people, and that asymmetry is taken up within the language-game and expressed in terms of the notion of the subject. One difficulty, however, is that our grammar all too easily assumes a misleadingly mystical appearance. For example, the individual's grammatical role of subject when combined with the fact that others cannot predict what she is thinking or feeling may be expressed in the metaphysical claim that 'a man's thinking goes on within his consciousness in a seclusion in comparison with which any physical seclusion is a form of openness' (*LW2*, p. 21). The idea of seclusion here is misleading, for it suggests that there is some hidden entity where none in fact exists. It would be like saying that someone who talks in a language we do not understand is hiding something; certainly we cannot understand her message, but this is not because she is being secretive. Imagine there was a group of people who continually revealed their deepest thoughts, but in a language we could not understand. Here we would 'have no idea what was going on inside them' despite the fact that 'what is going on inside them' lies quite open to view (*RPP2*, para. 568). *Ex hypothesi*, the innermost thoughts of these people are clearly expressed only in a way we do not understand. They are not hidden, but are simply unknown to us. As Wittgenstein puts it, 'someone can hide his thoughts from me by expressing them in a language I don't understand. But where in this case is the mental thing which is hidden?' (*RPP2*, para. 564). In fact, nothing is hidden, and all the talk of hiding does is hinder attempts to understand the grammar of our concepts.

To clarify that grammar, consider the claim that the Inner is necessarily hidden. The natural way to support this claim is to point to cases where we genuinely don't know what someone is thinking. However, such cases are double-edged, for if the Inner is sometimes hidden, this implies that sometimes it is not. In fact, the notion of knowledge clouds the issue, for what really matters is that the individual has a different relation to her own thoughts than to someone else's. The key difference is not that the other person is uncertain where she lacks doubt, but that her thoughts are grammatically defined as hers and no amount of certainty on the other person's part will change that (*LW1*, para. 963). This point leads Wittgenstein to turn tradition on its head and claim that the individual cannot know her own thoughts, while others can.

> 'Can one know what is going on in another person in the way he himself knows it?' – How, then, does he know it? He can express his experience. A doubt in him as to whether he really has this experience – analogous to the doubt as to whether he has such-and-such a disease – does not enter into the game; and for that reason it is wrong to say that he knows what he experiences. But the other can of course doubt whether that person has this experience. So doubt enters into the game, but for that very same reason it is also possible for there to be complete certainty. (*LW2*, p. 92)

Wittgenstein's point is that knowing involves finding out and is one form of conviction as opposed to others (e.g. believing, suspecting or not knowing). But none of these concepts can be applied to the individual's relation to her own thoughts, and yet if talk of doubt is inappropriate, so too is talk of belief or knowledge. By contrast, the individual may try to discover the thoughts of another, and if, for example, she comes across that person's secret diary, this may give her grounds for saying she knows what the person is thinking. The same contrast can be underlined by noting that sincerity is enough to guarantee the correctness of the individual's utterances about her own thoughts, but is not enough with regard to the thoughts of others. However, sincerity is irrelevant with respect to knowledge claims. Thus the comparison with knowledge makes more sense with respect to the individual's relation to other people's thoughts than to her own (*LW2*, p. 23).

These points undermine the idea that the Inner is a private entity accessible only to the individual concerned. However, the existence of lying and, more generally, the possibility of pretence seems to revive the notion of the Inner as something hidden. Surely this possibility shows that the essence of a psychological state lies in the inner reality, not in the outer manifestations? Even here, however, there must be a connection between the Outer and the Inner, for if we are to distinguish between the individual lying and her telling the truth that difference must somehow manifest itself. If the difference between the real and the feigned state was something only the individual herself could know, how could we even distinguish between the two? Furthermore, how could the difference between an unknowable X and an unknowable Y matter to us? In fact, pretence does have characteristic outer manifestations. For example, if someone is pretending to be upset, she will usually stop pretending when she thinks she is alone or when it is no longer to her advantage. By contrast, someone who is genuinely upset will not act in either of these ways. Here the crucial difference between the two people is not that one has something she is hiding, while the other does not. Rather one is trying to deceive us and the other is not. What confuses us here is the basic model we are inclined to use, and yet this model is wrong in both cases: neither the truthful nor the false statement is a description of an inner reality. Rather one is a sincere utterance and the other is not.

As these points suggest, lying about the Inner belongs to a different category from lying about the Outer. To know that she is lying the individual does not have to compare her utterance with her inner state. On the contrary, that she knows when she is lying follows from the grammatical point that her sincere utterances are necessarily correct. What makes the utterance false

172

is its insincerity and hence it is impossible for her to lie without knowing that she is doing so.[1] Here there is a temptation to construe the awareness that we are lying as a special kind of experience or feeling. But this is misguided, for, if lying was a feeling, its connection with not telling the truth would be contingent, so that it might occasionally occur when we were telling the truth. In fact, the individual needs no basis to know she is lying. Furthermore, it is part of the concept of lying that it presupposes a motive and a situation. It is not like a feeling which may occur inexplicably and in various combinations. Rather it belongs to a particular pattern of human behaviour and the features of that pattern distinguish it from others. The whole point of deception and non-deception is that they have different contexts and different consequences, even if on some occasions the only difference is that the individual later confesses she was lying. The difference between lying and telling the truth is not that they involve different inner states, but that they have different manifestations. Like all other 'inner states', lying has outward criteria and, if it did not, it could be of no interest.

To underline these points, it is worth taking a closer look at the example of pain. Here again the possibility of pretence seems to make reference to an inner state indispensable. The difference, we want to say, between a genuine pain-utterance and one that is feigned is that the inner state of pain is present in the first case and not in the second. Despite Wittgenstein's claim that inner states stand in need of outer criteria, we are tempted to claim that being in pain and pretending to be in pain have the same outer manifestation but different inner characters. In his lectures, Wittgenstein recognises that the phenomenon of pretence seems to create problems, but he notes that 'if you come at this instance from the other end, lying may present no particular puzzle; i.e. none not present in "I've got a pain" ' (*WLPP*, p. 305). Our inclination is to treat the sincere utterance as a report on the individual's inner state, but, if it was simply a report on something we could never know, why should we be interested in it? In fact, what is important is that the utterance connects up with other aspects of the individual's behaviour. In this sense, the utterance is a signal and we make a crucial distinction between cases where we treat the signal as genuine and those where we say it is being abused. What is important is that the sincere utterance and the false one belong to different patterns of behaviour and so they don't in fact have the same manifestations. Although feigned pain is intended to look like the real thing, it has completely different connections and consequences. Some of the behaviour and the utterances may be the same, but the wider patterns in which they belong are fundamentally different, even if they partially overlap.

To illustrate these points, consider the case of a child starting to feign pain. The child will have been taught pain-utterances on the basis of acting in certain ways, e.g. crying and holding the painful area, etc. So when would we say that she has started to pretend? One possibility is that she starts to use the signal in inappropriate circumstances. 'A child discovers that he will get treated kindly if, when he is in pain, for instance, he screams; then he screams, so as to get treated that way. *This* is not pretence. Merely one of its roots' (*LW1*, para. 867). What is lacking at this stage is the concept of deception and the intention to deceive. Before the child can be said to be pretending, it must not only act as if in pain when not in pain, but also realize that pain signals can be used to mislead. Only then does her behaviour belong to the pattern we call pretence. The introduction of pretence makes the language game more complicated and in this sense 'an expression of pain is not related to pain and to pretence in the same way. Pretending is not as simple a concept as being in pain' (*LW2*, p. 81). For this reason, a child may so to speak be too young to pretend, for 'we only talk of pretence in a relatively complicated pattern of life' (*LW2*, p. 40). Feigned pain is not a special inner state, but a pattern within the weave of human behaviour and one which recurs in an infinite number of variations. Like the concept pain, it demands a certain background and, since it is an extension of the language-game, the context it requires is even more complicated than that of pain itself. 'A dog could not pretend to be in pain because its life is too simple for that. It does not have the joints necessary for such movements' (*LW1*, para. 862).

So does this mean Wittgenstein is denying that there is an inner difference between being in pain and pretending to be in pain? In one sense, obviously not. To say pain and feigned pain are distinguished by the fact that the inner state of pain is present in the first, but not in the second is simply one way of expressing the grammatical distinction between the two concepts. Reference to an inner state underlines the different significance of the two signals, and that is certainly something Wittgenstein doesn't want to deny. On the other hand, reference to the inner state is misleading because the reason we are interested in genuine and feigned pain utterances is that they have different contexts and different consequences. The simulated expression of pain is designed to appear the same as the genuine pain-expression, but what is important is that over the full range of the patterns the two are different. As Wittgenstein puts it, 'something proves itself to be pain or pretence. And that is essential to the concepts "pain" and "pretence", even if it doesn't happen in every one of their applications' (*LW2*, p. 57). Thus it is wrong to treat pain and pretence as inner states which can never be manifested fully or with certainty through the Outer. Rather the point is that we play a highly complicated game within which 'the Outer signs signify pain, pretence and much else in an extremely complicated way, sometimes unambiguously, sometimes in an uncertain manner' (*LW2*, p. 59).

What prevents understanding here is our tendency to oversimplify the grammar of our psychological concepts.

> The primary difficulty arises from the fact that we imagine an experience (such as pain) to be like an object, for which we naturally have a name, and the concept of which is therefore very easy to grasp.
>
> So we always want to say: We know what pain means (namely *this*), and so the difficulty therefore lies only in the fact that we simply cannot identify it with certainty in another person. We don't see that the concept 'pain' should first be investigated. The same holds for pretence. (*LW2*, p. 43)

Both concepts pull together aspects of an individual's behaviour in terms of a pattern whose unity is constituted by reference to the Inner. The idea that they represent different inner states is one way of expressing the difference between the two patterns, but, if we want to understand the inner state, we must explore the pattern itself. The difficulty with pretence is that 'it seems to render external evidence worthless, i.e. to nullify the evidence.

One wants to say: either he is in pain or he's experiencing pretence, everything external can manifest one or the other' (*LW2*, p. 42). But this is misguided because pretence does have its own particular outward signs and, if it didn't, we wouldn't want or be able to talk about it.

One way of underlining the particular nature of our language-game is to contrast it with other possibilities. The tendency is to think that our game 'corresponds to reality' and is the only possible one. In fact, it is conceivable that other people should play quite different games. For example, it would be possible for a group of people to reject the Inner/Outer picture and treat all pain-utterances as genuine.

> They say 'if it isn't true, then how can one say it?!' They have no comprehension of a lie. 'He wouldn't say that he was in pain if he wasn't! If he did say so, he would be crazy.' Now we try to make the temptation towards lying comprehensible to them, but they say: 'Yes, it would certainly be pleasant if he believed ---, but that isn't true!' They don't so much condemn lying; rather it is something they feel to be absurd and disgusting. As if one of us began to go around on all fours.
>
> (*LW2*, p. 20)

Here it is important that lying is not rejected on moral grounds; rather these people reject the very concept of lying. How then would they react if we told them that you can never trust the Outer or that one person could never know what another was feeling? The picture which to us seems so natural as to be inescapable may mean nothing to them; indeed, the idea that the Inner was always hidden might strike them as a joke or as a strange and sad form of madness. They might treat our scepticism as a form of paranoia and, if we showed them what we regard as a clear case of duplicity, they would explain it some other way or treat it as an oddity about which there is no more to be said. Even if the individual admitted she had been lying, they might reject the confession and treat the utterance itself as a form of delusion ('She contradicts what she earlier said, she must be ill'). One could also imagine the opposite example, that is to say, a group of people whose concepts allowed no room for pretence because any form of pain behaviour was itself ridiculed or punished. ' "Shamming", these people might say, "What a ridiculous concept!'' (As if one were to distinguish between a murder with one shot and one with three)' (*Z*, para. 384). For these people, complaining is already so bad that there is no room for shamming as something worse (ibid.). Like the previous group, such a people would have no use for our Inner/Outer picture. For them, pain-behaviour is not something which needs to be examined to check whether it is genuine or not. Rather it is something shameful and that is all there is to it.

As these examples show, there is nothing inevitable about our concepts of pain and pretence or about the Inner/Outer picture itself. Although we could try to teach these people our concepts, there is no guarantee we should succeed. Furthermore, even if we did succeed, this would not prove that our language-game was correct; it would be like teaching people to play chess who had only previously played draughts. Similarly, we could not say that only now did these people know what pain was, for that would imply that they had never felt pain before. It would also be wrong to suggest that they had previously overlooked something, made as it were a systematic but elementary conceptual blunder. The point is that we make a distinction where they do not, and the possibility of making a distinction does not imply that a distinction has to be made. We ourselves do not make a distinction wherever one would be logically possible; rather we make distinctions where these are important to us. If someone now says that the difference between pain and feigned pain must matter to them, this simply underlines how much the difference matters to us. In teaching them our language-game, what we are doing is teaching them a new way of looking at (and reacting to) other people's pain-expressions. The clearest way to express our teaching is not in the apparently factual statement 'it is never certain when someone is in pain', but in the prescription 'Be mistrustful in the face of other people's expressions of pain' (*RPP1*, para. 150). What our picture of the Inner and the Outer expresses is not the truth, but a particular way of understanding and relating to others. Compared to people who do not have a concept of pretence we play a more complex game, and this means that our whole way of life is different, although, as Wittgenstein notes, this does not necessarily mean it is less beautiful (*LW2*, p. 27). If our world contains the possibility of deceit, it also contains the possibility of integrity.

These points underline Wittgenstein's general claim that inner states stand in need of outer criteria, but they fail to explain why we are so wedded to the idea that the Inner is hidden. Why is it that we always want to treat the Outer as mere appearance, an obstacle to perception of the inner essence? This idea certainly doesn't correspond to our practice. Although when doing philosophy we may be tempted to claim that the Inner is necessarily hidden, we are less inclined to say this when someone is writhing on the floor after being hit on the head. Similarly, if a friend 'opens her soul' to us, we don't say 'how can I possibly know what she is feeling, when all I have to go on is something Outer?' Even the example of lying can be turned against the claim that the Inner is hidden, for, when someone tries to lie and is unsuccessful, this provides a striking illustration of the 'openness' of the Inner.

> If I lie to him, and he guesses from my face and tells me so – do I then still feel that what is within me is in no way accessible to him, that it is hidden? Don't I feel much more that he can see right through me? (*LW2*, p. 33)

Although others can sometimes be a closed book to us, this is not always the case. The Inner is therefore not hidden because it is the Inner, rather, if it is hidden, this is only in particular cases. Why then do these cases assume such importance when we reflect on the nature of the Inner? Why are we so inclined to claim that we can never really know what others are thinking and feeling?

One way of approaching this question is to compare the idea that the Inner is hidden with the idea that the future is hidden. In both cases, what seems to be a straightforward truth turns out to be something else, for, as Wittgenstein notes, the idea of something hidden arises in certain cases but not in all.

> Does the astronomer calculating an eclipse of the moon say: of course, no one can *know* the future? We express ourselves in that way when we feel uncertain about the future. The farmer says it of the weather; but the carpenter doesn't say that no one can know whether his armchair will not collapse.
>
> (*LW2*, pp. 81–2)

In both cases, the claim that we cannot know draws a line, marking a boundary which we take to be important. 'We can then ask "What is the characteristic of what we can really know?" And the answer will be: We can only *know* where there is no possibility of error, or: where there are clear rules of evidence' (*LW2*, p. 49). Thus the claim that we cannot know the Inner picks up on a feature of our language-game. In particular, it highlights the uncertainty which seems to characterise our judgements about what others are thinking, feeling and experiencing. Whether we express this in terms of the privacy of the Inner or the unreliability of the Outer makes little difference. The real question is: what creates this uncertainty? And what does it really consist in?

One suggestion is that this uncertainty reflects the possibility of pretence. As we have seen, recognition of this possibility is an important feature of our language-game. However, it would be wrong to see the possibility of pretence as the only – or even the central – source of the uncertainty inherent in our psychological concepts. In fact, the question of pretence can be a distraction, for preoccupation with it can blind us to the simple but fundamental point that 'it doesn't follow from the absence of pretence that each person knows how another is feeling' (*LW2*, p. 27). This is graphically illustrated by the fact that we may misread someone not only when she is concealing her feelings, but also when she is doing her utmost to make herself understood (ibid., p. 28). This makes the issue of uncertainty look rather different and raises new questions about how we should understand the Inner. To answer these questions, we need to take a fresh look at the rules of our language-game; and this time, rather than taking pretence as the starting point, we shall concentrate directly on the nature of those rules themselves.

Compared with other language-games, one of the most obvious features of our game with psychological concepts is the scope for disagreement. In the case of colour, for example, our judgements are generally the same, and we have specific tests for recognising those who are colour-blind. By contrast, 'there is no such agreement over the question of whether an expression of feeling is feigned or genuine' (*LW2*, p. 24). Here the scope for disagreement seems almost unlimited. As Wittgenstein notes, a painter may depict an expression of blissful joy and someone else may see it and say 'Perhaps it is only pretence' (*LW2*, p. 61). If this sort of disagreement is possible, however, it is because of the nature of our game; what lies behind it is the fact that the language-game does not involve clear rules of evidence. In our game, there are no fixed criteria which are generally recognised as conveying certainty. We do not say that anyone who acts in such-and-such a way or who adopts such-and-such an expression must be sad. On the contrary, the criteria vary and individuals may come to different judgements on the basis of exactly the same evidence. However, this does not mean that the game is totally arbitrary. There are limits to disagreement. For example, there are cases of pain-behaviour which only a mad person would treat as pretence. Similarly, the absence of criteria which, by definition, convey certainty does not mean that we are never certain; no criteria constitute proof, but there are criteria which can convince. The point is that what convinces one person may not convince another – one person may be sure someone is upset, where another person is uncertain or convinced of the opposite. Although certainty enters the game, it does not do so via proof and incontrovertible evidence.

As the above remarks indicate, the criteria on the basis of which we make psychological judgements are not rigidly defined – what one person may take as a smile of sad resignation, another may see as expressive of faintly glimmering hope. However, this suggests that it is not only the state of the person being described that enters into the judgement, but also that of the person making the judgement. The problem this creates is that it threatens to undermine the idea that a judgement is being made.

> Suppose you say: *this* person mistrusts the utterance because he is more mistrustful than someone who trusts it.
>
> The question is, how can the disposition of the person judging play an important role here, when it otherwise does not? Or again: how can such a judgement be *correct*? How can we nevertheless speak of a judgement here? (*LW2*, p. 24)

The answer is to look at what is involved in the judgement, for, although in making the judgement the individual takes up a particular position in relation to the person she is describing, her statement also involves an element of prediction. Suppose, for example, that someone hears bad news and that one person judges her to be genuinely moved by it, while another treats the signs of sadness as mere affectation. Here we have two ways of understanding the behaviour and two reactions to it – one person sympathises with what she believes to be genuine sorrow, the other is angered by what she views as hypocrisy. However, the differing judgements also have implications for how we would expect the individual to act; if she now abandons all her favourite pastimes, we may conclude that she was genuinely upset. As this example suggests, the element of prediction is only loosely defined. Just as we do not have fixed criteria for inner states, nor do we define exactly what their consequences are. However, that there are consequences is crucial: although what is to be expected is not rigidly defined, it is essential that one can in general terms say what sort of behaviour one would expect.

> We play with elastic, indeed with flexible, concepts. But that doesn't mean they could be distorted *just as you pleased* and without resistance, that they are therefore *unusable*. For if trust and mistrust had no foundation in objective reality, they would only be of pathological interest. (*LW2*, p. 24)

So far we have noted two features of our language-games with psychological concepts – first, that there are no criteria which are generally recognised as conferring certainty; and second, that what is involved in saying that someone is in a particular state is not rigidly defined. These two points lead on to a third, for the basis of our psychological judgements often cannot even be specified. For example, 'one may note an alteration in a face and describe it by saying that the face assumed a harder expression – and yet not be able to describe the alteration in spatial terms' (*RPP1*, para. 919). To capture this feature of our language-game, Wittgenstein uses the term 'imponderable evidence'. This brings together the fact that our judgements are based on the reactions of the individual (they are based on evidence) and the fact that we often cannot specify what led us to make the judgement we did (the evidence is imponderable). It also underlines the fact that it may be necessary to know the individual before we can apply psychological concepts to her, i.e. make judgements about her inner state.

This is what is important: from certain pointers and from my knowledge of the individual, I can know that he is pleased to see, etc. But I can't describe what I observe to a third person, and, if this person trusts my observations, I can't in this way convince him of the genuineness of the pleasure.

(LW2, p. 86)

The game we play is based on evidence but in a way that is far from clearcut. Not only are we often unable to specify the evidence which leads us to say that someone is in a particular state, but there can also be disputes over what the evidence indicates. We cannot say exactly what it was that made us think her feelings changed, and what one person saw as a hardening of the expression, another may have seen as a flicker of fear.

The notion of imponderable evidence brings out a further point, for it shows that playing the language-game involves a special sensitivity on the part of the observer. Only if she has a direct relation to the appearances concerned will she be able to make the kind of judgement needed, for in a game which does not involve set criteria, it would be impossible to specify rules of interpretation. For this reason, someone who did not relate to the appearances, someone who was 'all at sea with them', would be unable to apply the relevant concepts. Here we come back to seeing aspects, for it is only in terms of this phenomenon that our relation to others can accurately be captured.

> 'We *see* emotion' – As opposed to what? – We do not see facial contortions and *make the inference* that he is feeling joy, grief, boredom. We describe the face immediately as sad, radiant, bored, even when we are unable to give any other description of the features. – Grief, one would like to say, is personified in the face. This is essential to what we call 'emotion'.
>
> *(RPP2*, para. 570)

Here it is ironic that the Outer which earlier seemed irrelevant now appears as essential; indeed, it becomes clear that having a direct relation to the behaviour of human beings is a prerequisite for taking part in our practices. Consider, for example, the concept of a smile. It is significant that we are not taught this concept via a rule, but through examples. Furthermore, as we become more sophisticated, we extend the concept and make all sorts of new distinctions without having to have further guidance at every stage. We come to distinguish between different nuances of smile, so much so that some smiles (e.g. that of the Mona Lisa) may seem to contain a whole world of significance and express something which can only be explained in terms of a specific story or set of events. However, the difference between various types of smile or between a smile and a non-smile cannot be defined mathematically. We don't say 'Look, her smile is half a millimetre too wide. It can't be genuine.' Rather we react directly to the facial expression itself – she looks at us and we think 'She's smiling, but she does not really mean it'. Thus there are no rules for determining what is to count as a smile and the term can only be used on the basis of seeing and reacting to human expressions in a particular way. A sneer and a grin may be virtually indistinguishable in mathematical terms, but for us they have as different an aspect as the duck and the rabbit in the ambiguous picture.

The importance here of seeing aspects is that it captures the directness of our relation to human behaviour and expression. Contrary to our philosophical prejudices, the Outer is not a system of signs we have to decode, nor is it a set of symptoms which give rise to hypotheses about hidden causes. Rather it is something we respond to directly, seeing a particular smile as cruel even if we cannot specify what it is that makes it so. The directness of the relation – the fact that it is not mediated by rules of interpretation – brings with it a sensitivity to subtle differences, for we may react quite differently to two almost identical expressions. Here it might be objected that if we judge a particular smile to be sad, this must also be expressible in a purely visual concept. However, what cannot be captured in this way is why we judge two quite different smiles to be in this respect the same. Our judgement that the face is sad is a judgement about the structure we perceive, but it groups together appearances in a way which would seem capricious to someone who did not relate to human facial expressions directly and in the way we do. The concept of aspect perception also has the value therefore of bringing out the sense in which our language-game rests on kinship. Someone to whom a human smile meant nothing would be like the aspect-blind – she would see the changes we do, but would not understand why we now say the face looks completely different. Although she might develop rough-and-ready rules for interpreting human expressions, she would lack any real insight or sensitivity and hence would be in constant danger of mistaking one expression for its opposite.

———————

The above points throw some light on why we hesitate to use the word 'know' in relation to the Inner. The problem is not that the Inner is hidden, but that the language-game it involves is very different from those where we normally talk about knowledge. For example, if knowing someone is glad to see us involves being secure in our relation to her, e.g. being certain rather than uncertain in our own pleasure, this itself differentiates it from other kinds of knowledge. Another difference is that, when we are certain, the basis of that certainty is often unclear. Since the individual cannot prove her assertion, the claim 'I know he was pleased to see me' is equivalent for other people to the statement 'I had the definite impression he was pleased to see me'. Moreover, the statement's implications have none of the clarity we associate with knowledge. If it was submitted to a court of law,

> the case would not be the same as that of a physicist who stated that he had done an experiment and *this* was the result. . . . If I have known the other person for a long time, the court would probably also allow my statement to stand, give it weight. But my absolute certainty would not signify *knowledge*. For from knowledge the court would have to be able to draw quite definite conclusions. (*LW2*, p. 88)

If we now return to the question of the uncertainty in our language-game, this can be seen as having various components. On the one hand, it may reflect uncertainty about how the individual is likely to act. On the other hand, it may involve an inability to understand, to 'find our feet', with the individual. Here it is not a question of whether she is pretending, rather the uncertainty goes deeper. The difficulty lies not just in prediction but in our relation to the other person. To illustrate this point, Wittgenstein suggests that we look at our uncertainty about other people's pain in the light of the question as to whether an insect feels pain (*RPP2*, para. 661).

> *One* kind of uncertainty is that with which we might face an
> unfamiliar mechanism. In another we should possibly be
> recalling an occasion in our life. It might be, e.g. that someone
> who has just escaped the fear of death would shrink from
> swatting a fly, though he would otherwise do it without
> thinking twice about it. Or on the other hand that, having this
> experience in his mind's eye, he does with hesitancy what
> otherwise he does unhesitantly. (*RPP2*, para. 669)

Our uncertainty may as it were be objective or subjective; it may
stem from uncertainties about the entity being judged or from an
uncertainty about our relation to that entity. As this suggests,
judgements about what others are feeling, etc. have two aspects;
they bring together a predictive and a non-predictive element, for
'even when I "do not rest secure in my sympathy" I need not
think of uncertainty about his later behaviour' (*RPP2*,
para. 670). The question is not just how the other will behave,
but how that behaviour should be understood. We may be unsure
what judgement to make about someone's inner state not just
because we are uncertain how she will act, but also because of an
uncertainty in our relation to her, e.g. an uncertainty about
whether to call what she is experiencing sadness or self-pity.

The different aspects of our psychological concepts raise
questions about their very nature, for what do we actually know
when we know the Inner? Take the example of knowing that
someone is pleased.

> 'I know that he was pleased to see me.' What follows from
> that? What of importance? Forget that you have correctly
> represented his mental state! Can I really say that the import-
> ance of its truth lies in the fact that it has certain conse-
> quences? – It is pleasant to be with someone who is glad to see
> us, who behaves thus-and-so (if we know various things about
> his behaviour from earlier days). (*LW2*, p. 49)

Knowing that someone is in a particular inner state involves
having some idea what to expect from her, but it also involves
being able to relate to and understand her. Furthermore, the
ability to understand the individual in terms of an Inner is the
reflection of an underlying kinship between the two individuals,
for it is conceivable that we should come across a group of people

whose inner life we could form no picture of whatsoever. Indeed, Wittgenstein points out that to a certain extent this already happens. 'It is important for our study that someone may feel concerning certain people that their inner life will always be a mystery to him. That he will never understand them' (*CV*, p. 74). Conversely, where we can construct an Inner, this presupposes an ability to relate and to understand. As Wittgenstein puts it, 'that I can be someone's friend rests on the fact that he has the same *possibilities* as I myself have, or similar ones' (*LW2*, p. 72).

Kinship with other people (and the ability to relate directly to their behaviour) is therefore crucial to our mastery of psychological concepts. Making such judgements does not involve applying a fixed rule, but presupposes a sensitivity, a 'feel' for human behaviour. It is like making an aesthetic judgement.

> [A] band moves before me and at one time I say 'That is a pattern S', at another 'This is pattern V'.[2] Sometimes I don't know which it is for a while; sometimes I say at the end 'It is neither of them'.
>
> How could I be taught to recognise these patterns? I am shown a simple example, then more complicated examples of both types. It resembles the way in which I learn to distinguish between the style of two composers. (*LW2*, pp. 42–3)

If someone now asks why we use concepts with boundaries that are so hard to grasp, the answer is the importance of these boundaries in our lives (ibid.). It is the fine shades of human behaviour that interest us and dominate our relation to each other as human beings.

> It is always presupposed that the person who smiles *is* human, and not just that what smiles is a human body. Certain circumstances and the connection with other forms of behaviour are also presupposed. But, having presupposed all this, another person's smile is pleasant to me.
>
> If I ask someone the way in the street, I prefer a friendly answer to an unfriendly one. I respond directly to the behaviour of others, I presuppose the *Inner* insofar as I presuppose the *human*. (*LW2*, p. 84)

The Inner is not a brute reality, it is neither a set of private experiences nor a set of brain states; rather it is the concept which lies at the heart of all our mutual interaction and understanding.

These points underline the importance of our relation to the other person in judging the psychological state she is in. If the behaviour of others 'left us cold', we would not be able to find our way around it with the non-rigidly defined concepts we actually use. However, this point should not be allowed to obscure the other aspect of psychological judgements, for even if the evidence is imponderable, it is still evidence. Although there are no rules, it does make a difference what judgement one makes.

> 'The genuineness of an expression cannot be proved; one has to feel it.' – Very well, – but what does one go on to do with this recognition of genuineness? If someone says, 'Voilá ce que peut dire un coeur vraiment epris'[3] – and if he also brings someone else to the same mind, – what are the further consequences? Or are there none, and does the game end with one person's relishing what another does not?
>
> There are certainly consequences, but of a diffuse kind. Experience, that is varied observation, can inform us of them, and they too are incapable of general formulation; only in scattered cases can one arrive at a correct and fruitful judgement, establish a fruitful connection. And the most general remarks yield at best what looks like the fragments of a system.
>
> (*PI*, p. 228)

Our language-game does not have clear rules of evidence, so that applying psychological concepts presupposes a certain type of sensitivity on the part of the person making the judgement. Like our concepts, that sensitivity has two elements – an ability to understand and an ability to predict. Differences in understanding mean that agreement is not guaranteed and that within our game there are no recognised experts. However, application of the concepts is not arbitrary. Although there are no rules, experience can develop one's judgement and 'there are those whose judgement is "better" and those whose judgement is "worse". More accurate prognoses will generally issue from the judgements of those with better knowledge of mankind' (*PI*, p. 227).

The above sections describe some features of our language-game with psychological concepts and provide some indication of why we are inclined to say that no one can *know* what another is feeling. However, they may also make the game seem odd, for why do we use such strange, flexible concepts? Why not play a simpler game, based on clear evidence and rigid criteria? The answer is that no other game could play the same role in our lives. To illustrate this, consider what another game would be like. Is it conceivable, for instance, that we should adopt a different sort of concept, one which

> brings behaviour, occasion and experience into necessary connection? Why not? But we would then have to be so constituted that we really did always, or almost always, react similarly to similar circumstances. For if we believe his expression of feeling to be genuine, then in general we behave differently than if we believe the opposite.
>
> (*LW2*, pp. 22-3)

In reality, our reactions to others are not uniform and what one person sees as a genuine cry of pain, another may see as a manipulative attempt to gain attention. For this reason, we would not know what to do with a concept involving a necessary connection (ibid.). It would be like the idea of a rigidly-defined concept of a heap of sand. We could imagine a group of people who had the ability to tell at a glance the number of grains in a heap of sand and therefore found it useful to have strictly defined concepts of a heap, a small heap, a mound, etc. For us, however, such concepts would be highly impractical. In the case of psychological concepts, the contrast would be even greater. Suppose a group of people defined pain in terms of a particular chemical reaction in the brain and used a machine to test for this reaction. In their game, the machine's verdict and not the individual's utterances and behaviour is treated as definitive. Here it is already questionable whether we would want to call this a concept of pain and as for playing the game, it is not clear that it would be either desirable or even possible. Would we, for example, accept that an apparent malingerer was in pain if the machine said so? Or that a friend wasn't despite the spasms contorting her face? The new game with its unanimity and clarity would certainly be a far cry from the old one. Although people might play it, the very fact that they did so makes them a radically different type of people from us.

As well as allowing scope for variations in our reactions to each other, the flexibility of our concepts ties in with another important aspect of our lives, for it allows them to cope with the diversity and variation which is characteristic of human behaviour. As the notion of imponderable evidence makes clear, fine shades of behaviour play a key role in our language-game; indeed, Wittgenstein argues that irregularity and diversity are crucial in our response to something as alive and as human. If we are to imagine a language-game of fixed rules and clear criteria, we must also imagine a people whose behaviour took clear, simple patterns. The lives of such a people would be very different from our own and how we would relate to them is unclear. They would differ from us in a similar way to a people whose only concept of music was of the sort produced by mechanical music boxes. Although we might find their music enjoyable, its regularity and precision would make it very different from our own. The music would lack a dimension – the series of sounds might be pleasant but in a mechanical way, the most important thing would be missing, one might almost say it would lack a soul.

To illustrate these points, let us return to the example of facial expressions. Suppose there were a group of people whose facial movements could indeed be captured in simple, rigidly defined concepts. For example, their faces are such that they only ever snap between four expressions, each of which is always absolutely the same. What would we make of such expressions? And how would we relate to such a people? We certainly could not relate to their behaviour as we do to normal human behaviour. For example, it is doubtful whether they could be said to smile, for this is a particular expression within a play of features. A face with a limited set of expressions would make a different impression from one with an indefinite number. 'A facial expression that was completely fixed couldn't be a friendly one. Variability and irregularity are essential to a friendly expression. Irregularity is part of its physiognomy' (*RPP2*, para. 615). Once again, the importance of our relation to the other person, and to the form her behaviour takes, is underlined. Seeing something as the manifestation of an Inner involves relating to it in a particular way and this is only possible if the expression is of a certain kind. A set of geometrically-describable facial expressions would strike us as strange and mechanical and, even if one of them was similar to a smile, it is unlikely we would see it as expressive of anything, let alone of a particular feeling or emotion.

The absence of mathematical regularity in human behaviour brings us back to our idea that the Inner is hidden and cannot be known for, according to Wittgenstein, what really lies behind this claim is the unpredictability of human behaviour. If someone's behaviour was predictable in every detail, not only would the concepts of the Inner lose their importance in relation to her, but it would be hard to see her as a conscious individual. The lack of fine shades in her behaviour and its predictability would undermine our sense of it as the actions of a person as opposed to a machine. Here what is important is that we do not regard ourselves and others as complex machines. On the contrary, the concept of the Inner expresses our sense of the distinctness of a certain type of being.

> 'I don't know what's going on inside it right now!' That could be said of the complicated mechanism say of a fine clock, which triggers various external movements according to very complicated law. Looking at it one might think: if I knew what it looked like inside, what was going on right now, I would know what to expect.
>
> But with a human being, the assumption is that *it is impossible* to gain an insight into the mechanism. Thus indeterminacy is postulated. (*RPP2*, paras 664–5)

The idea that we can never know exactly what another individual is thinking and feeling reflects the nature of our relation to others, expressing our sense of them as conscious, living beings. For us, spontaneity and an absence of simple regularity are characteristic of life and, in particular, human life. The comparison of the individual's Inner with a hidden mechanism falls down, for it misses the essence of our relation to ourselves and others. As Wittgenstein notes, 'I believe unpredictability must be an essential characteristic of the Inner. As also is the endless diversity of expressions' (*LW2*, p. 65).

Here it is worth considering what is involved in ascribing to someone an Inner or a soul.[4] Take the dispute about whether animals have an Inner – what is it makes people decide one way or the other?

> Those who say that a dog has no soul base this on what he can and can't do. For if someone says that a dog can't hope, – where does he get this from? And whoever says that a dog *has* a soul can only base this on behaviour he observes in the dog.
> 'Only look at the face and the movements of a dog, and you'll see that he has a soul.' But what is it in the face? Is it only the similarity with the play of human features? Is it, at least amongst other things, the lack of rigidity? (*LW2*, p. 65)

The other way of making this point is to imagine what might lead us to say a human being lacked an Inner. Clearly it would have to be something about her behaviour and yet, as Wittgenstein notes, 'the *only* thing I can imagine here is that this human body is mechanical in its movements, and not like ordinary human bodies' (*LW2*, p. 66). In other words, what would indicate the lack of an Inner is the absence of the fine shades of behaviour which count as evidence in our language-game. Suppose, however, that the people who were like this started to give signs of pain, would this lead us to conclude that they did indeed have an Inner? That would depend. If all they did was scream and writhe, we might treat this as an automatic reaction, but 'if they pull a painful face and look as if they are suffering, then we would already have the feeling of seeing *inside them*' (ibid.). Here Wittgenstein again turns the idea of the hiddenness of the Inner on its head, for before we can speak of someone's Inner as hidden, we must be convinced that it exists and for this to happen we must be able to relate to her Outer. The soulless person would cease to strike us as soulless if her behaviour acquired the plasticity and non-predictability of our own. Only then we would have the sense of an Inner into which the fine shades of her behaviour and expression gave us an occasional insight.

The importance of unpredictabilty in our reaction to something as alive and conscious helps explain why we play the game we do. In the face of the variety of life, only flexible concepts are capable of fulfilling the function we require. Concepts governed by fixed rules would be unable to cope with the variation which for us is the essence of life. Instead of learning simple rules, we are given examples of the concept and then apply it in new contexts including some where the new case involves significant dissimilarities from the first.

> If we imagine life as a weave, then this pattern (pretence, for example) is not always complete and is varied in a multiplicity of ways. But we, in our conceptual world, keep on seeing the same, recurring with variations. That is how our concepts take it. For concepts are not for use on a *single* occasion.
>
> *(RPP2*, para. 672)

Our concepts have to function against an ever-changing background and must involve a degree of indefiniteness, otherwise they would be inapplicable in the face of irregularity (*RPP2*, para. 652). This point underlines the importance of our kinship with others, for application of our psychological concepts involves making a judgement about what is significantly the same, hence it involves a feeling or sense of the significance of the pattern being described. Someone who felt neither envy nor anger would have difficulty understanding why we place one set of actions in one class and a similar set in a completely different one.

Having examined some aspects of how our language-game works, we can return to the question of the hiddenness of the Inner. As we have seen, this idea is misleading in that there is no hidden inner entity and not every occasion when someone is not transparent to us involves an attempt at concealment on her part. In fact, it is only on the basis of a certain kinship that we can see each other as having an Inner, and in that sense what is striking is the degree to which we understand each other rather than the opposite. Insofar as our language-game is characterised by uncertainty, this is not because of metaphysics, but reflects the rules of our game. 'It is not that objective certainty does not exist *because* we do not see into another's soul. The first expression means the same as the second' (*LW2*, p. 25). Instead of saying the Inner is hidden, it would be less misleading if we said that the game we play is one where certainty is excluded. Alternatively, one might say that our relation to others is such that sometimes the other person seems transparent to us and sometimes not. The key point is that the concept of the Inner is part of our game, not its empirically-given basis. 'What I want to say, therefore, is that the Inner differs from the Outer in its *logic*. And that in any event this logic clarifies the picture of Inner and Outer, makes it comprehensible' (*LW2*, p. 62). Our concepts of the Inner and the Outer are not the expression of metaphysical truths, but part of the particular game we happen to play. If that game involves uncertainty, this is not because the Inner is private or the Outer inherently unreliable. Rather the uncertainty is built into our concepts, so that 'the uncertainty of the ascription "He's in pain" might be called a constitutional uncertainty' (*RPP1*, para. 141).

The uncertainty of our language-game is one factor which can lead us to misunderstand it, for we assume that the language-game must be simpler than it is and mistake the uncertainty for a defect. In fact, there is nothing wrong or missing from the language-game; the fact that the Outer makes the Inner probable is not a defect in the evidence, but the key to understanding its nature. What really matters is

> not that the evidence makes the feeling (and so the Inner) *merely* probable, but that we treat *this* as *evidence* for something important, that we base a judgement on this involved sort of evidence and so that such evidence has a special importance in our lives and is made prominent by a concept.
> (*Z*, para. 554)

If the possibility of acting sorrow on the stage proves the unreliability of evidence, it also proves its reality (*LW2*, p. 67). The evidence is not uncertain because it is Outer but because it is part of a particular game. The uncertainty lies in our concepts, not in the relation between the Outer and the Inner. As Wittgenstein puts it, 'the connection between evidence and that for which it is evidence is here not a fixed one. And I don't mean "the connection between the Outer and the Inner" ' (*LW2*, p. 88). On the contrary, that connection is crucial and, since the Outer constitutes the criteria for the Inner, one could say that uncertainty about the Inner is uncertainty about the Outer (ibid.), for an uncertainty about whether someone is pleased is an uncertainty about the genuineness of her smile.

One way of undermining the idea that the Outer is the source of uncertainty is to note that in a sense the Inner too may be indeterminate. Consider, for example, our earlier discussion of the difference between genuine and feigned emotion. As we saw there, pretence involves more than simply using pain expressions when not in pain; rather it presupposes a pattern of behaviour of a particular kind and one which is sufficiently complex for the concept of deceit to be at home in it. One implication of this, however, is that one cannot simply divide outer expression into the two exclusive categories – genuine and feigned. For example, someone might give signs of joy, then act in a completely unexpected way and yet not in a way that showed she was pretending but in a way which simply leaves us at a loss of what to make of her initial reaction (*LW2*, p. 90). Here it is not the Outer that it uncertain; rather the person's behaviour defies our normal categories, so there is no clear answer as to how we should represent her Inner. If we ask, 'What inner state was she in?', the question has no answer. In this sense, the foundation of our language-game (and what makes possible our use of psychological concepts) is the fact that our behaviour is sufficiently regular for us to be able to see patterns in it. On the other hand, it is not so regular as to be describable in terms of rules, so that if we do describe it in terms of patterns, these must be sufficiently flexible to encompass a degree of irregularity.

What does it mean, though, to say that our concepts have a degree of indefiniteness built into them? As we have already seen, the criteria for a particular state are not rigidly defined, but more fundamentally, what is involved in saying that someone is in that state is also not completely determined. Not only are the consequences of the inner state unspecified (or only specifiable in general terms), but it may be unclear whether or to what extent the individual's state falls into any of the general patterns we invoke. Thus

it is *not* the case that uncertainty in recognizing his annoyance, for example, is simply an uncertainty about his future behaviour. It lies much more in the uncertainty of the criteria for the concept. So sometimes he is, as it were, transparent, sometimes not. And it is misleading if one thinks of the real annoyance as, so to speak, the expression of the *inner* face, such that this facial expression is perfectly clearly defined and it is only the outer one which leaves it uncertain whether his soul really has this expression. (*LW2*, p. 70)

Here the uncertainty in the application of the concept of annoyance is nothing to do with the unreliability of the Outer; rather it reflects the loose fit between our concepts, which treat life as the recurrence of the same, and the limitless variety of that life itself. The life-pattern we refer to with the concept 'annoyance' has a limitless number of forms and, although there are certain clear or typical examples, there are others where it is less clear what is being said when we describe someone as annoyed. In such cases, it may be impossible to extract the precise meaning of the claim from the particular context in which it is being applied. Indeed, we may again feel tempted to claim that language is inadequate, that the uniqueness of the real defies the universality of language – 'she was annoyed and pleased all at once, you would have to have been there and to know her as I do, to understand what I mean'. Here the difficulty in describing the Inner reflects not its hiddenness but the limitless variety which characterises human life.

To underline this point, consider a more unusual example – the concept love. Suppose an individual is involved with two people and we are uncertain which she loves most. The first inclination is to assume that, if we do not know this, she must. To a certain extent this is correct, for if she says she loves one of them and not the other, this may be enough to settle the matter. With a sophisticated concept like love, however, the language-game allows for the possibility of self-deception and lack of self-knowledge. Furthermore, the individual herself may be genuinely uncertain which she loves, so that in that sense even she would not know her Inner. To resolve the question, we might propose various tests, for example, if she has to choose between them, we might take that as decisive. However, the tests may conflict and the normal use of the concept love does not establish any one of them as definitive. We may therefore conclude that there is no determinate answer as to whom she loves best. Here her inner state is not something that we cannot know because we cannot penetrate the veil of the Outer. Rather there is nothing determinate to know. We could specify a new test to decide what conclusion we should reach, but the point is that our existing concept is not of this nature. Like other psychological concepts, it has a degree of indeterminacy built into it. The circumstances of her later life may persuade us (and her) to view her feelings one way or another. On the other hand, we may simply accept that there is no answer – that there is no simple way of describing what she felt. Here the indeterminacy of the Inner is a feature of its very essence.

This example highlights our tendency to take the Inner for granted. We want to treat it as an object which is simply there and, if we encounter difficulties describing it, we blame these on its inaccessibility. In fact, it is better seen as a construct, a picture we use in our mutual understanding. Our ability to view each other's actions and statements as expressions of an Inner presupposes a kinship between us, for there is no guarantee that such an understanding should exist. It is conceivable, for example, that we should come across people who we were simply unable to 'find our feet with'. Their behaviour, while not random, may strike us as illogical and it may be impossible for us to relate it to the patterns that characterise our lives. The same point applies to their utterances, for, as we saw in Chapter 4, statements such as 'the vowel "*e*" is yellow' or 'Everything feels unreal to me' are literally nonsensical and yet we can find each other through them, so much so that such unique, non-paraphrasable communication can be what means most to us.

The kinship which lies behind our psychological concepts also makes itself apparent in another way, for what gives unity to these varying and irregular patterns is our sense that they group together what belongs together. In this way, we are able to treat a host of different things (e.g. a facial expression, a gesture, a piece of behaviour and some utterances) as expressions of the same inner state. There is no guarantee, however, that we should be able to understand all living beings in this way; in principle there is no reason why the linguistic and non-linguistic reactions of all beings should be the same. As Wittgenstein famously remarked, 'if a lion could talk, we could not understand him' (*LW1*, para. 190). Similarly we might come across apparently intelligent people whose actions we could make no sense of. In such a case, what should we say of their inner life? Depending on how different their lives were from ours, we might conclude

196

either that their inner life was simply different from ours or that they had no inner life at all, i.e. that they were not in fact the conscious beings they appeared to be. Here it is also interesting to consider our conception of the inner life of a mad person, for we tend to think of this as an indescribable flux and yet the incoherence of this flux is simply a symbol of the incoherence of her actions.

To sum up, we can see three related aspects of our language-game as contributing to the indeterminacy which characterises it. First, it is a game based on fine shades and one where the criteria are not fixed. The idea that talk of knowledge is inappropriate reflects the fact that 'one must be acquainted with a person to be able to judge what significance to ascribe to his expressions of feeling, and [also] that one can't describe what it is that one recognizes in them' (*LW2*, pp. 89–90). Second, the consequences of a particular inner state are not rigidly determined.

> One can't say what the essential observable consequences of an inner state are. When, for example, he really is pleased, what is then to be expected of him and what not? There are of course such characteristic consequences, but they can't be described in the same way as reactions which characterize the state of a physical object. (ibid.)

Finally, the importance of variation and the consequent flexibility of our concepts mean that there is no rigid fit between our concepts and experience, that the Inner is not always determinate.

> Genuineness and its opposite are not the only essential characteristics of an expression of feeling. One can't, for example, say whether a cat which purrs and then lashes out was pretending. It could be that a person gives signs of joy then acts in a completely unexpected manner and yet we couldn't say that the first expression was not genuine. (ibid.)

If we now ask, 'Could these uncertainties be eliminated?' there is no clear answer to the question. The 'impossibility' of knowing what someone else is feeling is in a sense both a physical and a logical impossibility. 'First of all: one can think of possible ways of gaining information about another person that don't in fact exist. So there is a physical impossibility' (*LW2*, p. 94). If, for example, we could read someone's thoughts directly from her nervous system, our current game would be undermined – why bother with uncertain utterances, one might argue, if you can read the book? On the other hand, there is a logical impossibility in that our game is characterised by the absence of more exact rules of evidence. Throwing over the game would involve a huge change in our lives and would radically change our relation to others as well as to ourselves. How would the fact that others could predict our behaviour affect our relation to ourselves? Would we still regard our deeds as our own or would we view our own lives fatalistically as the playing out of a mechanical process? The hypothesis that we could read and so predict the behaviour of others conjures up a completely new world and it is hard to follow through the hypothesis and to be sure how we might react to this world. In the end, the question of whether we would accept a different game is an open one.

> There now remains the question whether we would give up our language-game, which rests on 'imponderable evidence' and often leads to uncertainty, if we had the possibility of exchanging it for a more exact one which, on the whole, had similar consequences. We could, for example, work with a mechanical 'lie-detector', and redefine a lie as whatever produces a certain result on the lie-detector.
>
> The question, therefore, is: would we change our form of life if such-and-such were placed at our disposal? And how could I answer that? (*LW2*, p. 95)

Where then does all this leave the Inner/Outer picture? As we have seen, this picture is neither an expression of metaphysical truth nor a depiction of the facts of the matter. Rather the picture expresses certain conceptual relations which together form our concept of the human subject. Here it is worth reconsidering our earlier discussion of thinking and consciousness, for now we can set these issues in a wider context. As we noted then, thinking cannot be represented accurately either as an activity in itself or as an accompaniment of other activities. Rather the word 'thinkingly' (as opposed to 'mechanically') characterises the way an activity is carried out. One way of capturing this difference is to treat thought as if it were a continuous inner monologue. For example, 'when a man acts intelligently we may say "It's almost as though he spoke to himself" ' (*WLPP*, p. 286). In such cases, however, there is no necessity for the individual actually to talk to herself; rather the point is that there is a potential explanation of all she is doing and that if she is interrupted and asked she will be able to give it. Here the possibility of giving an explanation is pictured in terms of a continuous activity of thinking. Similarly the difference in the way the person acts (the fact that she acts thinkingly) is represented in terms of a special supplementary activity. The person who acts thinkingly does many things which someone acting mechanically does not and 'thinking is the imaginary auxiliary activity; the invisible stream which carries and connects all these kinds of actions' (*RPP2*, para. 228). Talk of the Inner is a way of representing these ideas – the world of consciousness and ceaseless flow of thoughts and experiences is a picture which captures our concept of a subject.

As well as expressing certain conceptual relations, the Inner/Outer picture captures fundamental aspects of our relation to others. Indeed, to the extent that the Inner seems irredeemably mysterious, this reflects our sense of the mystery of life. As we saw, the absence of predictability and mechanical regularity is central in our response to something as alive and more particularly as human. There is a qualitative difference between our reaction even to an animal and to a complex machine and that difference goes beyond the fact that the actions of the latter are easier to describe in mathematical terms. Watching an animal, we see it as alive, just as looking into the face of a human being we see it as conscious. Here the Inner/Outer picture connects up with our deepest feelings and reactions. As Wittgenstein notes, 'I am inclined to speak of a lifeless thing as lacking something. I see life definitely as a plus, as something added to a lifeless thing' (*Z*, para. 128). Similarly, a human face makes a unique impression upon us:

> The expression of soul in a face. One really needs to remember that a face with a soulful expression can be *painted*, in order to believe that it is merely shapes and colours that make this impression. It isn't to be believed that it is merely the *eyes* – eyeball, lids, eyelashes, etc. – of a human being, that one can

be lost in the gaze of, into which one can look with astonishment and delight. And yet human eyes just do affect one like
this. (*RPP1*, para. 267)

Such reactions are important because they illustrate the attitudes
which underlie our language-game – the notion of the Inner may
be a picture but it captures the essence of our relationship to
others (and to ourselves).

One way of underlining the special role which the Inner/
Outer picture plays in our lives is to note that talk of someone
having an Inner can hardly be called an opinion. For example,
when we look into someone's eyes with astonishment and delight
it would seem strange to say that we merely believed she has a
soul (ibid.). Here the word 'believe' goes against the grain, for it
treats something pivotal to our whole lives as on the same level as
a contingent truth. What would it be like to believe someone had
a soul/Inner and discover she didn't? It could hardly be compared to discovering that someone who we believed lived in
London actually lived in Manchester. In fact, the claim that
someone has an Inner is an expression of our relation to her as a
human being, not the statement of an empirical truth. Thus,
while we might say of someone 'I believe she is suffering', it
would be strange to add 'and I also believe she isn't an
automaton' (*LW1*, para. 321). One way of illustrating this is by
considering what it would actually mean to say that someone
wasn't an automaton. What information would this give if it was
said of another human being? None, or at the very most that this
man always behaves like a human being and not occasionally
like a machine (*LW1*, para. 322). The statement that someone is
not an automaton conveys no information because what it
expresses is a relation that precedes opinion: 'my attitude towards
her is an attitude towards a soul. I am not of the opinion that she
has a soul' (*LW1*, para. 322). 'But what is the difference between
an attitude and an opinion? I might say: Attitudes come before
opinions' (*LW2*, p. 38). In the case of the soulless tribe, what
would change if we ceased to regard them as soulless would be
our whole relation to them. In part, this might manifest itself in
changes in the way we treat them. For example, as Norman
Malcolm suggested in Wittgenstein's lectures, 'when the slaves
become useless, we shall no longer do away with them' (*WLPP*,

p. 166). However, the use of the picture itself expresses a change in our relation to them. Indeed, at the extreme one could imagine distinguishing between beings where the essential expression of the distinction was the choice of picture we used to describe their essence. Thus

> normally, if you say 'He is an automaton' you draw conse-
> quences, if you stab him [he'll not feel pain]. On the other
> hand, you may not wish to draw any such consequences, and
> this is all there is to it – except further muddles. (*LC*, p. 72)

———————————

7

THE MIND, THE BRAIN AND THE SOUL

The prejudice in favour of psycho-physical parallelism is also a fruit of the primitive conception of grammar. For if one accepts a causality between psychological phenomena that is not mediated physiologically, one is taken to have thereby admitted the existence, *alongside* the body, of a soul, a ghostly spiritual entity. (*RPP1*, para. 906)

The account of the Inner outlined in this book is likely to face two contrasting challenges. Some will complain, as Iris Murdoch has done, that Wittgenstein's approach to the Inner comes dangerously close to denying the most crucial aspect of an individual's existence. In contrast, others will argue that Wittgenstein has not gone far enough and is himself still a prisoner of the anthropocentric myth that human consciousness is somehow special. However, as we shall try to show in this chapter, both these criticisms misrepresent Wittgenstein's argument; indeed, both are founded on the very confusions he was trying to undermine. Rebutting these criticisms should further clarify the thrust of Wittgenstein's argument and illuminate the non-substantive nature of his philosophy. It will also enable us to underline the importance of distinguishing our shared notion of the Inner (and associated ideas such as the mind), on the one hand, from moral or religious concepts such as the soul and, on the other, from scientific concepts such as the brain. We shall conclude by considering Freud, whose work seems to pose a particular challenge to Wittgenstein's account, for it seems to refute our current psychological concepts and also to present a scientific but substantive view of what human life is really about.

Let us begin, however, by considering the idea that Wittgenstein is in some sense denying the existence of the Inner. Here talk of existence is already a sign of confusion, for this suggests that what is at stake is whether a particular thing or object exists, whereas the real issue is the significance of a particular concept or group of concepts. That we use the concept of the Inner (wonder what is going on inside someone's head, talk of innermost thoughts and feelings, etc.) cannot be denied, what needs to be clarified is the particular grammar of this type of concept. The exact philosophical terminology we use to clarify the Inner is not important – as Wittgenstein said elsewhere 'say what you choose, so long as it does not prevent you from seeing the facts' (*PI*, para. 79). What does matter, however, is clarity, for the difficulty is that we misinterpret our own concepts. To illustrate this point, consider a variant of tennis which Wittgenstein called inner tennis. This game is identical to ordinary tennis except that the players have to form certain images while they play. This imposes a new demand on them, and it might be objected that it is one that is too easily eluded since only the individual herself can say whether she is following the rules. Let us suppose, however, that all the players are totally honest. The important question is the status of the 'inner move':

> What sort of move is the inner move of the game, what does it consist in? In this, that – according to the rule – he forms an image of . . .? – But might it not also be said: *We do not know* what kind of inner move of the game he performs according to the rule; we only know its manifestations? The inner move of the game is an X, whose nature we do not know. Or again: here too there are only external moves of the game – the communication of the rule and what is called the 'manifestation of the inner process'. (*Z*, para. 649)

Here we have three descriptions of the move, all of which Wittgenstein accepts as possible. One person compares the inner move to a move in an ordinary sense, another stresses the differences and rejects this comparison ('there are only really external moves . . .'), while the third compares it to an action which happens in secret and which no one but the agent herself knows ('the inner move is an X'). The issue, however, is not which of these descriptions is accurate, for *ex hypothesi* they all describe the same reality. Rather what matters is that we are not misled and 'that we see the *dangers* of the expression "inner move of the game". It is dangerous because it produces confusion' (ibid.).

As this illustration shows, Wittgenstein's aim is neither to affirm nor to deny the Inner, but simply to clarify the precise nature of the concepts it involves. Despite this, one could still argue that his approach is inherently rationalistic. For example, someone might claim that the private language argument clashes with our sense that the deepest experiences are incommunicable. So doesn't Wittgenstein in this sense deny or at least distort the Inner? But what exactly are the experiences Wittgenstein is supposed to be denying? If there are private, indescribable experiences, how strange that we can talk about them and that others can know what we mean! In fact, Wittgenstein's account of language and its role in the Inner allows us to understand how words can be used not just to express common experiences we all share but also to capture the rare and the unique. The example of literature and poetry, in particular, shows how what seems inexpressible can nonetheless gain expression. Similarly, in everyday life an image or a phrase may somehow capture a complex thought or feeling which cannot be otherwise expressed or explained. Here what would be rationalistic would be to claim that all communication (and self-expression) must be on the basis of public definitions and agreed rules. Wittgenstein, however, shows how our relation to language enables us to go beyond such definitions and use language to give spontaneous expression to what we feel. Far from ruling out statements such as 'Everything I do feels somehow new to me' or 'I feel a burden on my soul which nothing can shake off', Wittgenstein presents them as important examples of how language operates when the Inner is being expressed.

Here it is interesting to contrast Wittgenstein's later position with the views he held during the period of his early philosophy, for then he held that our most profound experiences could not be captured in language. In his lecture on ethics, for example, he discussed the religious experience expressed in the utterance 'I feel as if whatever happens no harm can come to me' and concluded that such expressions were nonsensical, since the individual cannot explain what they mean. Although the individual may be safe from the threat of being struck by lightning or safe from the threat of an avalanche, she cannot be safe *tout court*. Later, however, Wittgenstein recognised that the demand for explanation is misguided. Not all language works through agreed rules; rather words can be like gestures and have a direct and unique meaning which cannot be paraphrased. Just as music can express much we cannot explain, so too can language. Acceptance that language operates on different levels and in different ways makes it possible to understand and accept the full range of human self-expression. Far from constraining the Inner in a rationalist straitjacket, Wittgenstein offers the only account which enables us to make full sense of it. His claim that inner states stand in need of outward criteria is not a limitation on the world of experience, but simply a reminder that the idea of an experience which in principle has no expression is a philosophical illusion. If someone says 'I can't describe what I feel at the moment', that too is an utterance, and it is possible that the individual may later find words to describe it. Even if she does not, her actions or her other words may give us some idea of what she is feeling or we may simply recognise that she is in that state we too sometimes experience where the power of our emotion is such that we can find no appropriate expression for it. Wittgenstein has no need or desire to deny the possibility of 'indescribable experiences', all he does is point out that these too can only play a role in our lives insofar as they manifest themselves in some way or another.

A different way of expressing the idea that Wittgenstein is denying the Inner is to claim that he reduces everything to behaviour. However, Wittgenstein's stress on the criterial link between Inner and Outer is precisely an attempt to escape such reductionism. Take the case of psychology itself. As we saw in Chapter 1, this seems a paradoxical science, for the object of its investigations (the Inner) by its nature defies observation. Should we therefore conclude that the proper object of psychology is behaviour and not human states of mind? Consider what actually happens in the laboratory:

> if someone does a psychological experiment – what will he report? – What the subject says, what he does, what has happened to him in the past and how he reacted to it. – And

not: what the subject thinks, what he sees, feels, believes, experiences? (*RPP1*, para. 287)

The opposition here is misleading, for the two accounts are different representations of the same thing. It is a bit like suggesting that describing a painting involves describing an array of colours and shapes but not what someone looking at it sees. Although the two descriptions have different forms and uses, there is no clash between them. Furthermore, it is quite clear which would normally be of more interest to us. The notion of behaviour only becomes reductive if it is construed in a narrow way. Wittgenstein, however, uses it in the widest possible sense to include all we say and do and the context of those actions. In this sense, there is nothing 'more' than behaviour. What the concepts of the Inner do, however, is underline the particular nature of our interest in 'behaviour', for we are not simply interested in it as the occurrence of a particular physical event. Rather it has interest for us as the action of a human being, as something which has to be understood as the expression of a continuous flow of thoughts, experiences, feelings, etc. Thus the dichotomy between idealism and materialism breaks down:

> When I report 'He was put out', am I reporting a behaviour or a state of mind? (When I say 'The sky looks threatening', am I talking about the present or the future?) Both. But not side by side; rather one in one sense, the other in another. But what does this mean? (Is this not a mythology? No.)
>
> (*RPP1*, para. 289)

The difficulty is the narrowness of our philosophical view, for we want to treat the Inner either as a thing (albeit a strange and ghostly thing) or as nothing. By contrast, Wittgenstein stresses that the Inner is a different kind of concept altogether. 'Am I saying something like "and the soul itself is merely something about the body"? No. (I am not that hard up for categories)' (*RPP2*, para. 690).

The idea that we are only interested in behaviour is in a sense rather ironic, for one could easily turn it on its head and say we are not interested in the individual's behaviour at all except insofar as it shows what she was thinking and feeling, etc. Thus our relation to others is not a relation to bodies which mysteriously act thus-and-so; rather it is a relation to human beings, and one way the distinctiveness of this relationship expresses itself is in terms of the concept of the Inner. We want to know not just what the other person did and said, but 'what went on inside her'. Although Wittgenstein refers to the concept of the Inner as a picture, this is certainly not intended to deny the reality of what it expresses. He is not saying that on the investigation the Inner turns out merely to be a metaphor. On the contrary, he emphasises that the picture and the concept structure our whole relation to others. If someone asks, 'what then is the Inner, if it is not "something about the body"?' the question itself contains an error, for it assumes that every substantive must refer to a thing. Rather than asking 'What is the Inner?' it is more enlightening to ask 'What difference does it make to say of someone that she has an Inner as opposed to saying that she's an automaton?' This brings out the fact that in talking of someone as having an Inner, we view her actions as those of a thinking being, that is to say, as expressing desires and feelings which make sense against a wider background of thoughts and experiences. In other words, the notion of the Inner brings into play a whole network of concepts which would otherwise have no place. In doing so, it changes our attitude and relationship to the being concerned, or rather the very fact of talking of an Inner itself expresses and embodies the special nature of our relationship to a person.

One difficulty with Wittgenstein's account is that it seems to ignore the fact that each of us has our own direct experience of being conscious. Thus someone might object that in our own case we do not simply attribute to ourselves an Inner, rather we know we have one because we constantly experience it as the essence of our lives. But what does it mean to say that we constantly experience the Inner? How can we describe or explain what it is like to be conscious? Here we seem to run into an insuperable obstacle for, although all experiences are conscious, it seems there are no specific experiences of consciousness itself. In the search for a description, words seem to fail us, the ineffable mystery of the mind defies our clumsy efforts to pin it down. To understand the difficulty here, it is worth returning to the example of seeing, for as we noted in Chapter 2 this tends to be our paradigm of conscious experience. As with consciousness, it seems impossible to describe what seeing is like; we can describe what we are seeing and we can describe particular visual experiences (e.g. being dazzled), but we cannot describe seeing itself. As we have seen, one reason for this is that seeing is not an experience in the sense that a feeling or a sensation is. Consequently, the only sense in which we can describe the content of seeing is by describing what we see. However, there is another important point, for we need to recognise that eventually the demand for explanation and description becomes senseless. At bedrock the concept can be taught, but not described. Seeing is not a phenomenon; rather it is a concept we use in relation to human beings who can play a particular game. A child, for example, is taught to describe the world and it is taught to use the concept in the first person, i.e. to say 'I can see such-and-such'. The child does not identify a particular inner event, rather it masters a particular game and those who cannot do so are called 'blind'.

To underline this point, it is worth asking what a description of seeing would be like and what purpose it would serve. This may seem an unnecessary inquiry, but the point is that requests for information only make sense within a language-game and hence, when one reaches bedrock, their meaning becomes unclear. At that stage, either the person already knows the language-game (in which case, she already 'knows' what seeing is) or she does not know it, in which case all we can do is try to teach it to her. Consider the parallel case of trying to explain what is involved in taking dictation:

> the normal person can, e.g. learn to take dictation. What is that? Well, one person speaks and the other writes down what he says. Thus, if he says, e.g. the sound a, the other writes the symbol 'a', etc. Now mustn't someone who understands this explanation either already have known the game, only perhaps not by this name, – or have learnt it from the description?
>
> (*LW2*, p. 75)

Of course, someone may understand the principle involved in a technique and contingently be unable to master it (e.g. she may understand the principle of writing but be unable to make decipherable marks or memorise the written symbols), but the key point is that there is no general description of the concept outside the language-game in which it is used. We can teach someone to use the concept 'dictation' and the individual may describe her feelings when dictating, but what dictating involves cannot be described independently of the game itself. The concept of dictation cannot be defined outside the language-game, and, within the language-game, it can only be taught, not described. In a similar way, the content of our concept seeing is given by our language-games involving the word 'to see' and hence is neither describable nor definable independently of those games.

As these remarks indicate, the reason we cannot describe seeing is not that it is ineffable or that it is a peculiarly elusive type of experience, but rather because in the appropriate sense it is not an experience at all. Furthermore, the concept cannot be explained from the outside. The attempt to describe what it is like to see misfires before it starts and, since no coherent enterprise is specified, it is not surprising that success proves elusive. The same point applies to the attempt to describe consciousness, for consciousness is not an experience. For that reason, there is no such thing as a general description of what it is like to be conscious. The only way to describe the 'world' of consciousness would be to give illustrations of our psychological concepts, and these would be of different types, for the only thing that holds together the concepts of pain, thinking and seeing, etc. is that they are all concepts we use in relation to conscious beings. To understand the concept of consciousness, we do not need to define or describe it, but to recognise what is involved in saying that someone is conscious; what is important is not a description, but an understanding of the significance of the concept.

Here someone might object that science can define seeing and so will presumably one day do the same for consciousness. However, this objection misses the point. If scientists manage to frame a concept which applies to precisely the same cases as our existing psychological concepts, this does not show that the real meaning of the concept has been discovered. Furthermore, the essence of our concept is its first-person use and this has nothing to do with any scientific definition.

If the psychologist informs us 'There are people who see', we could ask him 'And what do you call "people who see"?' The answer to that would be of the sort 'Human beings who react so-and-so, and behave so-and-so under such-and-such circumstances'. 'Seeing' would be a technical term of the psychologist, which he explains to us. Seeing is then something which he has observed in human beings. (*LW2*, p. 78)

This new concept may coincide with the old one or it may differ from it, but it does not tell us what seeing really is. While it may serve to distinguish between different groups of people, it does not teach us how to use the form of words 'I see . . .'. Instead it replaces one game with a radically different type of game and for that very reason it cannot be a rival to it. A scientific concept of 'seeing' might describe a certain pattern of behaviour (or, indeed, neurological activity), but it would not belong in the same category as our existing concept, for the essence of that concept is its use in the first person as an expression of experience.

The idea that our psychological concepts might be given a more scientific definition misrepresents their nature. These concepts describe neither 'inner phenomena' nor behaviour, rather they pick out certain patterns in human life that interest us. The concept of the Inner completes that pattern, for it is treated as the unseen thread that lies behind the outer manifestations. For Wittgenstein, therefore, psychology deals neither simply with behaviour nor with ineffable inner states. 'I would like to say: "Psychology deals with certain *aspects* of human life." Or: with certain phenomena. – But the words "thinking", "fearing", etc., etc., do *not* refer to those phenomena' (*RPP2*, para. 35). The phenomena are what can be observed, but what our concepts express is the interest which makes us link these events together. A pause during activity, a pensive look, the sudden start of inspiration, all these might be called the phenomena or manifestations of thinking, but the key element that binds these elements together is not some observed common quality but our concept of thinking and hence the language-games we play with the words 'I think . . .', 'She is thinking . . .', etc. Here it is important to recognise the distinctiveness of our psychological concepts. They are not proto-scientific concepts, nor are they doomed attempts to pin down inner mysteries; rather they express a particular interest and way of looking at human behaviour, an approach captured in the idea of the Inner, which treats that behaviour as the self-expression of a conscious being.

One implication of these points is that the concepts we use are not defined independently of their application to human beings; outside that context their use becomes uncertain (although not impossible; we do, for example, use some of our psychological concepts, or simplified versions of them, in relation to animals). The statement 'Man thinks' is not a description of a chance attribute of man; rather the concept of thinking and the concept of a normal human being are internally related.

> 'Man thinks, feels, wishes, believes, intends, wants, knows.' That sounds like a reasonable sentence, just like 'Man draws, paints and makes models', or 'Man is acquainted with string instruments, wind instruments . . .'. The first sentence is an enumeration of all those things man does with his mind. But just as one could add: 'And isn't man also acquainted with instruments made from squealing mice?' to the sentence about the instruments – and the answer would be 'No' – so there would have to be added to the enumeration of the mental activities a question of the kind 'And can't men also . . .?'
>
> (*RPP2*, para. 14)

Our psychological concepts are concepts we use in our inter-action with each other and they are not definable independently of that. If we say that animals (or for that matter computers) think, we point to a similarity between their actions and our own, rather than describe a phenomenon which has various types of manifestation. ' "Man thinks, is afraid, etc., etc.": that is the reply one might give to someone who asked what chapters a book on psychology might contain' (ibid., para. 19).

So far we have largely been arguing against the idea that Wittgenstein denies the Inner; however, the other objection takes the opposite tack and claims that his account is anthropocentric. Surely, one might argue, the advance of science has enabled us to recognise that concepts such as the Inner and the soul are unnecessary; indeed, that they are illusions to protect human vanity. On this approach, consciousness is merely the subjective aspect of brain activity – the brain is as it were the real Inner and one of which science will eventually be able to offer a complete explanation in causal terms. Advances in computer science seem to offer additional support for this view, for our ability to produce computers which replicate some of the functions of the mind seem to underline the claim that the brain is simply a sophisticated form of computer whose operating principles we have yet to master. Taken together, developments in neurology, physiology, computer science, etc. may seem to make this approach unassailable; indeed, its influence is so pervasive that the identification of the brain and the mind has entered into common parlance. Nowadays, it is not uncommon for people to say 'My brain feels tired' or 'My brain is not working properly today' or even 'My brain accidentally added the two numbers together instead of multiplying them'. While there is nothing wrong with such statements (Wittgenstein himself used them on occasion), it would be wrong to treat them too seriously. Generally, they function as jokey paraphrases of normal expressions, and we would certainly be worried about the mental health of anyone who seriously attributed thoughts, feelings and intentions to her brain rather than to herself. Despite such expressions, we shall argue that the reductionism of materialism is just as unattractive as the mystification of idealism.

Before directly considering the relation of the mind and the brain, it is worth underlining the difference in category between psychological concepts and those used in science. Take the example of intention. As we have seen, the key point about intention is the agent's role in expressing it: the language-game of intention is based on the fact that people can generally offer explanations of why they acted and say what they are about to do before doing it. Given that this is our language-game, however, is it conceivable that science should discover as it were the real essence of intention, of which the individual's statements offer a subjective account? The hypothesis itself misrepresents intention, for expressing an intention does not involve giving a description, let alone a subjective one. Leaving that to one side, however, it is also important to recognise that nothing a scientist might discover could play the role intentions currently play in our lives. One aspect of our language-game of intentions is that we can question the agent about her intentions, so that if she says 'I intend to visit a friend this evening', we can ask an indefinite number of questions about that intention (e.g. why do you want to see her? How much do you like her? Would you still go if there was a good film on TV? Is part of the reason you want to see her a desire to boast about your new job? etc.). The answers to these questions clarify the individual's intention and in that sense show more exactly what her intention was; however, it is hard to imagine how any brain state could capture or correspond to this. The problem is the mismatch between the grammar of any physical event or process and that of psychological concepts such as intentionality. If a scientist discovered a connection between brain activity and how people act, this might enable us to predict how someone will act or even to cause her to act in a certain way, but it would neither introduce an alternative to our language-game of intentions nor give an insight into its real basis. Although it is conceivable that the study of brain activity might turn out to be a more reliable predictor of human behaviour, the sort of understanding of human action it gave would not be the same as that involved in the language-game of intentions. Whatever the value of the scientist's discovery, it could not be said to have revealed what intentions really are.

As this example suggests, our psychological concepts, including the concept of the Inner itself, are not in need of, nor susceptible to, scientific elucidation or justification. This is not to rule out the possibility of scientists making interesting discoveries in this area. In particular, it may be possible to establish correlations between applications of our psychological concepts and physiological or neurological phenomena. For example, it is conceivable that good memory is associated with the presence of larger than usual quantities of a particular chemical in the brain or that destruction of a certain part of the brain causes loss of memory. However, the larger and more controversial scientific claim comes with the idea that all aspects of the mind must ultimately be reducible to (i.e. causally explicable in terms of) events occurring in the brain. From a Wittgensteinian perspective, the first response to this idea is to ask why we find it so compelling: why before we have even started to look at the evidence, are we so convinced that this huge generalisation must be true? The form of this statement ('the mind *must* be reducible to the brain') already suggests that it is not an empirical claim but embodies a commitment to a certain approach, and, as we shall see, part of that commitment may reflect philosophical misunderstanding.

Let us begin, however, by considering the example of thinking. Suppose someone claims that what really happens when someone thinks is that a particular chemical reaction takes place in her brain. This unsophisticated approach directly equates thinking and a reaction in the brain, and this creates problems because the concept thinking is self-evidently not about brain reactions – when we say 'She thought . . .' we do not mean 'Such-and-such a reaction took place in her brain'. The differences in the two concepts mean it is not difficult to refute their direct equation. Since they are defined in quite different ways, it is in principle possible that someone should think something and there be no reaction or that the reaction should take place and the individual be unable to express a thought. Similarly, it is conceivable that we should encounter an apparently normal person who we later discovered has no brain. In such a case, we would have no difficulty in applying the concept of thinking and yet *ex hypothesi* there would be no reactions taking place in her brain. Thus it would be wrong to claim that thinking is simply a certain reaction in the brain, for far from being identical the two concepts are of quite different kinds. For the same reason, the mind cannot be straightforwardly equated with the brain; rather what is the real issue is whether the former can be entirely explained in terms of the latter.

Once again, the first point to be considered is why we should think that the mind has to be explicable in terms of the brain – given that science hasn't actually proved this contention, why do we nonetheless still assume that it must be the case? One reason is the assumption that there must be a causal explanation for everything, and yet the basis of this assumption needs careful investigation, for it is by no means clear that the demand for explanation is always appropriate. Consider, for example, the fact that people can often tell the time without consulting a clock. How, one might ask, do we do this? One possible explanation would be that we subconsciously note the position of the sun in the sky and deduce the time from that. However, such an explanation would be wildly implausible, for it is clear that we sometimes accurately estimate the time when there are no indications of this kind accessible to us. Having ruled out this sort of explanation, there is a strong inclination to say that what we do is consult an inner clock; indeed, if we make a mistake, we may even be inclined to say that this shows that our inner clock is running fast. Here then we reach an explanation and we may suspect that science will later flesh out its details, delving as it were into the inner clock's inner mechanism. But what does the reference to the inner clock actually tell us? The inner clock is supposed to explain our ability to guess the time correctly and yet the only reason for postulating the clock is that ability itself. In fact, reference to an inner clock is unnecessary and misleading, for guessing the time does not necessarily involve imagining a clock, still less looking at one, and there is certainly no such thing as glancing at one's inner clock and accidentally misreading it. So what does happen when we accurately guess the time? Well, perhaps nothing except that we say the time that seems right to us and this often turns out to be correct. Here the source of confusion is the desire to explain. Starting from the slightly surprising fact that we can often more or less accurately guess what the time is, we suddenly end up postulating strange inner entities the details of which we misguidedly believe science will later clear up. If, however, we look at the case with an unprejudiced eye, quite different questions emerge, for what makes us think our ability to guess the time can or needs to be explained? Why shouldn't we just accept that human beings who spend so much of their time governed by the clock eventually develop an ability to estimate its course unaided?

Against this, one might object that, while the idea of an inner clock is wrong, the demand for some form of scientific explanation must be right; after all, if one person can accurately guess the time and another can't, there must surely be some scientifically detectable difference between them. This form of argument is a general one; for example, Wittgenstein mentions Russell's claim that the brain of someone who knows French must differ in some way from the brain of someone who doesn't. Once again, however, it is important to ask what justifies the claim that this must be so. Even if we had made a huge number of correlations of this kind (which we haven't), there would still be no guarantee of a correlation in every case. Despite this, we are still inclined to say there must be one. This inclination has two basic sources – one is the success of science and the scientific approach to phenomena and the other is fear that giving up the search for explanation introduces a 'new and unpredictable power, the soul' (*WLPP*, p. 330). We shall consider the first point shortly, but the second is a philosophical misapprehension; as this book has tried to show, talk of the Inner involves very different types of concepts from the simple concepts which tend to dominate philosophical thinking, but it does not involve invoking any mysterious forces or ghostly entities.

Having made this point, we still have to consider the claim that, like everything else, there must be a causal explanation of the abilities of the mind and that this explanation must focus on the brain. The force of this claim results from the past success of science and it expresses the basic scientific approach to the world, for central to that approach is the assumption that all phenomena – no matter how baffling they appear – are ultimately explicable in scientific terms. However, this assumption is a postulate; what it reflects is a particular attitude, more specifically, a commitment to look for causal laws even where none are apparent. Since we apply this principle elsewhere, it seems natural to apply it to the mind and the only plausible way of doing so is to seek to explain the mind in terms of the brain. To object would seem not just narrow-minded but biased, for why, one might ask, should we suddenly set limits to causality just because the object of investigation happens to be ourselves?

The Wittgensteinian response to this challenge is to begin by underlining the assumption on which it is based. The idea that everything must have a causal explanation is not a sempiternal truth, it is a postulate reflecting a commitment to look for causes even in the face of apparent defeat. Clearly if we want to explain (and manipulate) the world, this attitude is appropriate and it has certainly proved astonishingly fruitful. However, the possibility of continuing the search indefinitely does not guarantee that everything will indeed one day be explained.[1] On the contrary, if one were to make any general prediction, it would surely have to be that, even on the most optimistic basis, success is unlikely to be 100 per cent. In fact, the success of science has been so great that we take it for granted that everything must be predictable even if as it happens we haven't the slightest idea how this might be done. In part, this conviction reflects an uneven diet of examples, for certain types of case dominate our thinking, e.g. the classic case of one billiard ball hitting another. As Wittgenstein points out, however, there are other types of case, and it is salutary to remember that science might have been far less successful than it has been.

> Had the case always been that of the apple tree with the leaves dancing about, don't you think we would have had a different idea? – As things are now, you might say: 'if only we knew the velocity of the wind, the elasticity of the leaves, etc. then we could forecast the movement of the leaves.' But we would never dream of saying this if we hadn't already been successful and colossally so. (*NFW*, p. 3)

The success of science encourages us to assume that there is an explanation for everything, that the whole world is a pattern of causes we shall one day track down. But why must this be true? What justifies us in claiming that, in every case where we currently don't have an explanation, one will eventually be discovered?

The general argument that there must be causal explanations is reinforced with respect to the mind by the progress in understanding the brain that has actually been achieved this century. But here again a handful of examples blinds us to the wider picture, for what we can explain is tiny in comparison with what we can't. Thus it is misleading to say everything points to the mind being explicable in terms of the brain; 'in fact, everything you *notice when* and *where* you *look* points to it; no more' (*WLPP*, p. 320). One might also note that the form of the brain itself encourages us to suppose that there are explanations there waiting to be discovered. As Wittgenstein notes, 'the brain looks like a writing, inviting us to read it, and yet it isn't a writing' (*LW1*, para. 806). Here it is interesting to note how easily superstition can influence our approach. For example, despite the evidence to the contrary, there is a strong temptation to claim that a larger brain must mean greater intelligence or at least potentially greater intelligence. If, however, the sheer size of the brain is not correlated with its abilities, why are we so sure other more sophisticated correlations work? Furthermore, even if brain size and mental ability were correlated, it is conceivable that no further correlations might be obtainable. Wittgenstein illustrates this point by considering an apparently absurd example. 'Suppose humans became more intelligent the more books they owned – suppose that were a fact, but that it didn't matter at all what the books contained' (ibid.). The point of this example is that, were it the case, there would be an almost irresistible inclination to say that what's in the books *must* matter. *Ex hypothesi*, however, this would be wrong. Similarly, although we may have a strong inclination to believe that investigation of the brain will ultimately yield causal explanation of all mental activity, it is quite conceivable that one day we should conclude that this is quite simply not the case.

As we have seen, the claim that the mind must be explicable in terms of the brain is misguided; to what extent mental activities can be correlated with brain activity is an empirical matter and not one which can be decided on purely conceptual grounds. This implies that assessing the claim is a question of plausibility. What is interesting, however, is that once one drops the assumption that the mind must be reducible to the brain, the whole idea suddenly seems extremely implausible. The sciences investigating the brain are of course quite right to assume that there is more to be discovered (and more certainly will be), but whether explanation will one day be total is a different matter. Consider the example of thought. If we treat thinking as the occurrence of a particular inner event, it may seem plausible that this will one day be correlated with a change in the brain. As we have seen, however, our concept of thinking does not function like that. To say that an individual had a thought does not imply that anything particular happened within her; it may sometimes mean she said something to herself, sometimes not, it may involve an image or it may not. Furthermore, the intentionality of thought makes it hard to see how any correlation with brain states would be possible. The difficulty here is that the notion of one thought is a highly artificial concept. How many thoughts are there in the *Tractatus*? And when the basic idea for it struck Wittgenstein was that one thought or a rash of them? The notion of intention creates similar problems. If someone says 'I intend to go to the bank', we can ask her which bank she means and she may specify a particular bank or say she is ready to go to any bank but Barclays or that she isn't sure but she knows that she

only has ten minutes to look for one. These subsequent statements can all be seen as amplifications or explanations of the
original thought, but how are we to suppose this relates to the
brain state? Are we to imagine that it too will somehow contain
the answer to every possible question about the thought? This
does not seem to make sense, and yet if the state does not, we
would have to allow that two significantly different thoughts
might be correlated with the same brain state and so we would
have conceded the original issue.

A similar difficulty arises from the nature of language, for, as
we saw in Chapter 4, words may in one sense be interchangeable
and in another sense not. This creates problems for the attempt to
correlate brain states and thoughts because it underlines the
haziness of the concept of identity in relation to the latter. Two
thoughts may be the same in one sense and different in another.
For example, the statements 'she's a fool' and 'she's an idiot'
might roughly speaking be said to express the same thought. On
the other hand, each has a different tie-up with the rest of
language and as such can be used to express a unique nuance of
meaning. So how should this be translated into brain states?
How is the brain state to reflect the fact that the thought is both
the same and not the same? The difficulty here is that the criteria
of identity for thoughts (what counts as one thought as opposed
to another or as opposed to several) are not rigidly defined, for it
is not often an issue and where it is, what is at issue – and hence
the appropriate criteria – may vary. Thus the notion of one
thought is a fragile and artificial one and for that reason it is hard
to see what sense it could make to talk of a one-to-one correlation
with brain states.

The case of memory can also be used to undermine the claim
that every aspect of the mind must be explicable in terms of the
brain. The idea that there must be something in the brain which
corresponds to the memory seems overwhelming, but this
Wittgenstein denies.

> An event leaves a trace in the memory: one sometimes imag-
> ines this as if it consisted in the event's having left a trace, an
> impression, a consequence, in the nervous system. As if one
> could say: even the nerves have a memory. But then when
> someone remembered an event, he would have to infer it from

this impression, this trace. Whatever the event does leave behind in the organism, it isn't the memory. (*RPP1*, para. 220)

Here the postulated trace is like the inner clock, for we no more infer what happened from a trace than we consult an inner clock to guess the time. Furthermore, Wittgenstein argues that the fact that we can correlate damage to the brain with loss of memory does not show that some form of trace theory must be correct.

> Imagine the following phenomenon: If I want someone to take note of a text that I recite to him, so that he can repeat it to me later, I have to give him paper and pencil, while I am speaking he makes lines, marks, on the paper; if he has to reproduce the text later he follows those marks with his eyes and recites the text. But I assume that what he has jotted down is not *writing*, it is not connected by rules with the words of the text; yet without these jottings he is unable to reproduce the text; and if anything in it is altered, if part of it is destroyed, he gets stuck in his 'reading' or recites the text uncertainly or carelessly, or cannot find the words at all. – This *can* be imagined! – What I called jottings would not be a *rendering* of the text, not a translation, so to speak, in another symbolism. The text would not be *stored up* in the jottings. And why should it be stored up in our nervous system?.
>
> (*RPP1*, para. 908)

In fact, there is no reason for assuming that there must be a trace or that what we remember must in any sense be stored up (apart, if you like, from in our minds). The normal functioning of certain parts of the brain may be a prerequisite of memory, but this does not mean that the correlation can be continued in ever greater detail.

The example of memory leads Wittgenstein further, for he goes on to confess that:

> nothing seems more plausible to me than that people some day will come to the definite opinion that there is no copy in either the physiological or the nervous systems which corresponds to a particular thought or a particular idea of memory. (*LW1*, para. 504)

This implies that there can be psychological regularities to which no physiological regularities correspond; and, as Wittgenstein provocatively adds, 'if this upsets our concepts of causality then it is high time they were upset' (*RPP1*, para. 905). Here Wittgenstein argues that in investigating the mind there may be limits on how far causal explanations can go. Returning, for example, to the case of memory, he asks 'Why should not the initial and the terminal states of a system be connected by a natural law, which does not cover the intermediary state?' (ibid., para. 909). According to this view, certain correlations would be possible, but not complete correlation in all details. Take the example of thinking. According to Wittgenstein, it is quite likely that:

> there is no process in the brain correlated with associating or with thinking; so that it would be impossible to read off thought processes from brain processes. I mean this: if I talk or write there is, I assume, a system of impulses going out from my brain and correlated with my spoken or written thoughts. But why should the system continue further in the direction of the centre? Why should this order not proceed, so to speak, out of chaos? The case would be like the following – certain kinds of plants multiply by seed, so that a seed always produces a plant of the same kind as that from which it was produced – but nothing in the seed corresponds to the plant which comes from it; so that it is impossible to infer the properties or structure of the plant from those of the seed that it comes out of – this can only be done from the *history* of the seed. So an organism might come into being even out of something quite amorphous, as it were causelessly; and there is no reason why this should not really hold for our thoughts, and hence for our talking and writing. (*RPP1*, para. 903)

Confronted with this example, we may still be inclined to claim that there must be a full causal story both in the case of the mind and in the case of the seeds. However, there are no grounds for saying that this must be so. In both cases, Wittgenstein outlines something that is conceivable and hence something that must at least be accepted as a possibility. Furthermore, in the case of the mind, Wittgenstein's account is not only possible but also plausible.

Against this, someone might object that Wittgenstein's

221

account involves treating living beings and, in particular, humans, in a preferential or biased manner. The argument can, however, be turned on its head, for why should we treat the animate and the inanimate, the living and the mechanical, in the same way? Surely what is most striking is how different the two are, for it is not just that we view the animate as more complex than the inanimate, rather we see the two are separated by an unbridgeable gulf. Since this is so, one might well argue that it is the idea that the two are the same which requires support, not its antithesis. To illustrate this point, consider a problem in the study of vision.

> How does it come about that I see the tree standing up straight even if I incline my head to one side, and so the retinal image is that of an obliquely standing tree?' Well how does it come about that I speak of the tree as standing up straight even in these circumstances? – 'Well, I am conscious of the inclination of my head, and so supply the requisite correction in the way I take up my visual impression.' – But doesn't that mean confusing what is primary and what is secondary? Imagine that we knew nothing at all of the inner structure of the eye – would this problem make an appearance? We do not in truth supply any correction here – that explanation is gratuitous.
>
> Well – but now that the structure of the eye is known – how does it come about that we act, react, in this way? But must there be a physiological explanation here? Why don't we just leave explaining alone? – But you would never talk like that, if you were examining the behaviour of a machine! – Well, who says that a living creature, an animal body, is a machine in this sense? (*RPP1*, para. 918)

Wittgenstein is not claiming that this phenomenon will never be explained; rather his point is that the absence of an explanation is not necessarily a problem. Although we can make certain tie-ups between the psychological and the physiological, there is no reason for assuming that these have got to go all the way. In fact, what is important to recognise is, first, that there are good reasons why explanations may come to an end here and, second, that admitting this does not imply recognising some strange metaphysical power or cause.

In conclusion we can see that the claim that all aspects of the mind must be explicable in terms of brain activity has two basic components. First, it reflects the philosophical idea that talk of an Inner, a soul or a mind implies a belief in a ghostly entity. Second, it involves the substantive belief that because one or two highly limited correlations have been made a hugely large number of infinitely more sophisticated links will one day be found. Wittgenstein's account of the Inner undermines the first idea and also makes the second claim appear rather questionable. Once we have abandoned the idea that a non-reducible mind would be some form of ghostly metaphysical entity, there is no reason for supposing that everything we want to say about the mind and the Inner will one day be rewritable in terms of the brain.

In the previous sections, we have often referred to the mind, but how, one might ask, does this idea relate, on the one hand, to the Inner in general and, on the other, to the religious or ethical concept of the soul? This question is clearly related to the previous discussion, for an important reason many people want to reduce the mind to the brain is their rejection of the idea of the soul and their fear that failure to explain the mind in terms of the brain will be the thin end of the wedge. It is important, therefore, to recognize that these three ideas – the Inner, the mind and the soul – are far from being identical, for each arises in a different context and has a different significance. The idea of the Inner is a feature of our everyday discourse and part of the psychological concepts we all share. As we have seen, it expresses our relation to others as experiencing beings: as beings with an Inner, we treat their non-informational utterances as expressions of experiences (and not as meaningless) and expect them to be able to offer a more or less continuous account of their waking actions. Thus talk of an Inner brings into play a distinctive array of concepts and expresses the fact that we relate to other human beings in a way we do not to machines or even to other animals. By contrast, the concept of the mind is much more specific – it is one of a number of possible ways of dividing up the various aspects of the Inner. One might, for example, see the Inner as made up of the mind and the heart, i.e. of a thinking part and a feeling part. Alternatively, one might divide it up into a part concerned with perception, a rational part and an irrational part. Differences between these classificatory schemes may simply reflect the purpose in hand, but, as these examples suggest, they may also express a specific view of human nature and so tie in with a wider account of the nature of the world and humanity's place in it. The degree to which these concepts are shared will vary from case to case. The concept of mind, for example, is not particularly contentious, although it is not shared by all outlooks or all cultures (witness the difficulty in translating it into foreign languages). By contrast, the concept of an immortal or God-given soul is a highly substantive idea – it belongs not to the concepts we all share but to a specific and highly controversial view.

From a Wittgensteinian point of view, the different provenance of these concepts is crucial, for our aim is simply to clarify concepts we share, not to suggest that a particular set of concepts is in some sense the right one. For this reason, distinguishing between the concept of the Inner and that of the soul is particularly important, for one is part of our psychological concepts and hence shared by us all, whereas the other is the subject of fierce dispute. Here it is also worth noting that talk of the concept of the soul is itself slightly misleading, for there are as many concepts as there are views of Man's essential nature. How then are we to decide between these different views? Wittgenstein certainly did not believe that our choice must be arbitrary, but he did believe that it was not a matter for philosophy, since there is no means of deciding between them on purely conceptual grounds. According to Wittgenstein, philosophy should be concerned with clarification and with the elimination of conceptual confusion; its role is to clarify the concepts we share, but in the field of ethics or religion this is not always the case. In these areas, use of particular concepts expresses a particular outlook and may therefore be highly controversial. For this reason, Wittgenstein denied that philosophy had a special adjudicatory role in relation to them.[2] While our possession of common psychological concepts means that it is possible to clarify the conceptual difficulties surrounding the notion of the Inner, the same is not true with respect to the soul. With the soul, the problem is not one of clarification, but involves substantive disputes, for while the believer and the atheist may both wonder what is going on in each other's heads, only the believer is concerned about the future of their souls.

Against this, one might argue that recognition of the Inner is itself already a substantive moral move and so at least one step on the road to recognising the existence of the soul itself. For example, if we consider Wittgenstein's fiction of the soulless tribe, one of the clearest expressions of the change in our relation to them if we did decide that they had souls would be that we might take a more moral attitude towards them. For example, as Norman Malcolm suggests, we may no longer treat them as worn-out machines when they are past work (*WLPP*, p. 42). But this argument is too quick. Although the recognition of a group of people as conscious beings may be the basis for seeing them as entitled to special treatment and as having special rights and responsibilities, recognition of them as conscious does not *eo ipso* involve taking up a particular moral attitude towards them – witness the variety of moral attitudes people do take up. Indeed, it does not even imply taking up a moral attitude at all; recognition that another person is also an experiencing subject may be an acceptance of similarity but it is not an expression of fellow-feeling. The sadist is in no doubt that her victim is conscious and experiences the same pain she would if situations were reversed, but this does not stop her inflicting pain. On the contrary, the whole point of her activity is that she does not see her victim as a machine, but as a human being capable of pain and other experiences. Thus use of the concept of the Inner is completely distinct from the taking up of a moral attitude or the use of an ethical concept such as that of the soul. Whether one wants the notion of the Inner to be the thin end of the wedge or not, the idea that it might serve this function is misguided. The notion of consciousness governs our mutual interaction, but recognition of the particular grammar of the concepts relating to consciousness does not involve a commitment to any particular way of understanding the human condition.

To illustrate these points, it is worth considering the work of Freud, for his position challenges most of the distinctions we have made in this chapter. On the one hand, he claims that science can give us an insight into our psychological concepts;

indeed, can show that they are defective and misleading. On the other, he presents a particular breakdown of the Inner which he claims is simply factually correct. Take the basic notion of the unconscious. Freud treats this as a scientific discovery and claims that contrary to what everyone had believed, not all thoughts and desires are conscious. This implies that the conventional view of the mind (and of the Inner in general) is simply mistaken. His approach is therefore a major challenge to our existing language-games. In our language-game of intention, for example, the individual is given a privileged role as the person who states what her intentions are. By contrast, Freud suggests that the individual's real intentions may be hidden from her, so that what she is really trying to do may be less accessible to her than to outsiders in general and the analyst in particular. Thus Freud's work challenges Wittgenstein's account, first, by suggesting that the nature of the Inner is an empirical not a substantive issue, and, second, by suggesting scientific discoveries may overturn our psychological concepts.

In response to these points, the first issue to consider is the scientific nature of Freud's claims. To what extent, for example, does he follow the experimental method? In comparison with natural science, one striking point is that he rarely makes predictions and that all his explanations are backward-looking. What is even more striking, however, is the disparity between the size of the generalisations he makes and the evidence on the basis of which he makes them. He claims, for example, that every dream is a wish-fulfilment, or more generally still, that the key to psychology is the sexual drive and, in particular, the sexual experiences of children. Given the scale of these generalisations, Freud's evidence is slender to say the least. Furthermore, at first glance much of his evidence actually goes against his claims. For example, many of the dreams he describes (e.g. anxiety dreams) would not normally be thought of as wish-fulfilment dreams and only a fair amount of ingenuity on his part succeeds in presenting them as such. In fact, the role of evidence in Freud's work seems illustrative rather than anything else. Similarly, his generalisations seem to rest on plausibility rather than exhaustive research. As an example, Wittgenstein considers Freud's remarks on hallucination.

> Freud wants to say the hallucination of anything requires tremendous energy: it is not something that could normally happen, but the energy is provided in the exceptional circumstances where a man's wish for food is overpowering. This is a *speculation*. It is the sort of explanation we are inclined to accept. It is not put forward as a result of detailed examination of varieties of hallucinations. (*LC*, p. 43)

Freud's argument seems to be that, since an hallucination is something out of the ordinary, something out of the ordinary must have caused it. But this is not necessarily so; the claim seems to be empirical, but in fact simply describes the form which we, like Freud, would want an account of hallucination to take.

As a scientific investigation, therefore, Freud's inquiry looks rather strange. In fact, his explanations have an attraction which is totally unrelated to the evidence which supports them. What happens is that we are presented with a particular picture or way of explaining things and the power of this picture convinces us that it must be right. Consider the parallel case of the Darwinian upheaval. In the face of these theories, some people accepted them enthusiastically, others equally vehemently rejected them, and yet the evidence for them, while interesting, was hardly overwhelming. As Wittgenstein notes,

> the evidence is just a drop in the bucket. But there were thousands of books in which this was said to be the obvious solution. People were certain on grounds which were extremely thin. Couldn't there have been an attitude which said: 'I don't know. It is an interesting hypothesis which may eventually be well confirmed'? This shows you how you can be persuaded of a certain thing. In the end you forget entirely every question of verification, you are just sure it must have been like that. (*LC*, pp. 26-7)

To make this point is not to say that Freud and Darwin were wrong; rather the aim is to highlight the fact that the attraction of their theories does not lie in their empirical basis. What makes their work so interesting is not so much that it brings to light new evidence or demonstrates particular causal correlations, but rather that it presents a new picture and a new way of looking at an issue.

The suggestion that Freud's explanations have an appeal which goes beyond the evidence for them may seem paradoxical, for Freud himself often makes the opposite claim, emphasising that his explanations are disagreeable because they undermine the picture we would like to have of ourselves. According to Wittgenstein, however, the very features which make them 'disagreeable' also give them a perverse charm. To illustrate this, consider the claim that a human being is really only a certain amount of chemicals structured in a particular way. This claim seems as it were to offer a scientific meditation on mortality. In fact, however, it is only a provocative way of presenting the fact that we have been able to isolate the chemical components of the human body. Paradoxically, what makes some people want to present the fact in this way is its disagreeableness. Like Freud's account, the claim attacks our view of ourselves and this gives it a certain charm, for embracing the thesis seems a testimony to our courage and intellectual rigour. The attraction of the thesis is precisely its disagreeableness, for it seems to show us overcoming our deepest prejudices. In relation to our earlier comments, one might also note that another set of claims which could be said to have this attraction is the claim that the mind can be reduced to the brain and that human beings are essentially no different from complicated machines.

To return to Freud, one way of exploring the nature of his claims in more detail is to consider his account of dreams – what he called 'the royal road to the unconscious'. Freud treats dreams as a puzzle both in the sense that they are the key to the state of the patient and in that they are an unexplained phenomenon in need of scientific investigation. But to what extent must there be a science of dreams? Freud assumes that where there is an event, there must be a cause, but, as we have already argued, in this area that is very much open to question. Maybe dreams just happen, or sometimes have one type of cause and sometimes another. Or maybe there is a causal explanation of the general type of dream an individual has or of some elements of that dream but not of every single detail. The point here is not to deny that what we dream often connects up with what we are feeling or with what is happening to us, but to question the idea that one day we will have a causal theory which will explain (and predict) every aspect of a dream and why it occurred at that particular time. If, however, one accepts that there may be some aspects of dreams which do not have a causal explanation, one must surely also accept that quite possibly there is no single causal explanation of dreams as such.

In fact, Freud was not concerned with causes in the normal scientific sense; rather what he wanted to do was to unravel the mystery of dreams and develop a systematic way of interpreting them. The notion of interpretation, however, takes us away from the normal field of science; it opens up questions of meaning, not causation. For centuries, people have been explaining dreams, not because they wanted to isolate their scientific cause, but because they wanted to know their significance. In fact, one of the interesting things about dreams is that, even at their strangest, they do not simply strike us as nonsensical but rather as containing a concealed message. It is to this puzzlement that Freud's explanations of dreams respond for, in place of earlier *ad hoc* interpretations, they offer a systematic account. From this perspective, the claim that all dreams are wish-fulfilments is better seen not as an ill-founded scientific generalisation but as the foundation of an interpreting system, a criterion for what is to count as an acceptable interpretation (*LC*, p. 47). But this does not mean that Freud's principle is arbitrary. Such a system will only be of interest if the explanations it provides justify our sense of dreams as important. More specifically, they must connect the dream up with other aspects of our life in a way that is interesting or illuminating and few would deny that Freud's explanations do that. However, that is rather different from saying that Freud discovered the truth about dreams, let alone the scientific truth.

To explore this point further, it is worth noting that Freud actually offers a variety of possible criteria for the correct interpretation of a dream. According to one way of looking at his work, his approach can be seen as a highly original modification and extension of our existing language-games. On this approach, the subject's central and privileged role in the language-game is not entirely rejected. On the contrary, just as the content of the dream is given by what the individual says she dreamt, so too her agreement is taken as crucial in interpreting the dream. The correct interpretation is the one the individual endorses either immediately or in the course of analysis. Sometimes, however, Freud seems to be suggesting that the correct interpretation is the one the analyst gives regardless of how the patient reacts to it. This constitutes a quite different criterion, for the 'accuracy' of one interpretation over others is no longer established by reference to the views of the patient but in terms of its relation to the interpretative canon and the professional's view of other aspects of the patient's conduct. If one asks which of these criteria is the more scientific, the answer is neither and one could certainly imagine other approaches to dreams which could have an equal or better claim to be scientific. For example, if one defines the aim of analysis as successful treatment, one might draw up a number of interpretative frameworks and test to see which had the 'best' effects in some objectively definable way (e.g. fewer suicides over a given timespan or the greatest reduction in socially condemned behaviour, etc.). This would provide another means of generating dream interpretations, but one might argue that the very idea that dreams have a meaning is itself unscientific. One might argue, therefore, that the 'true' scientific approach would seek to explain dreams by correlating them with, say, chemical activity in the brain. As far as philosophy is concerned, there is no basis for endorsing or rejecting any of these approaches. What is important is to note, first, the different types of claim they involve and, second, the fact that none of them are guaranteed to be successful in every case. *Pace* Freud, there may be dreams for which we can find neither an interpretation nor an explanation.

To underline these points, let us consider a different example, that of intention. As we noted earlier, here Freud's explanations seem to challenge our existing language-games, suggesting that their basis may be misguided. Wittgenstein considers a particular example.

> Suppose Taylor and I are walking along the river and Taylor stretches out his hand and pushes me in the river. When I ask why he did this he says: 'I was pointing out something to you', whereas the psychoanalyst says that Taylor subconsciously hated me. (*LC*, p. 22)

Here we have two explanations and it seems therefore that we must choose between them. Wittgenstein, however, denies this. Since the explanations belong to different games, they can both be 'right', i.e. the appropriate answer within that particular game. This can be seen by considering the significance of each game. As we have seen, part of the interest of an expression of intention is that it gives the individual's own account of her action. Of course, if that account only rarely connected up with what she did, our language-game of intention would fall apart. As things are, however, people generally can give a coherent account of their actions. By contrast, what Freud proposes is a different type of account and one which can also explain actions which we would normally describe as accidental or involuntary. This approach offers a new perspective on human action and to be interesting it must connect up with other things we do in an illuminating way. It would be wrong, however, to see it as offering the truth about intention. One reason for this is that our language-game of intention is only partly about prediction. Even if the Freudian account provided a far more accurate guide to how people will act, we might still be interested in expression of intentions simply because we are interested in others as human beings and hence interested in their own accounts of their deeds. Furthermore, Freud's account is not really a rival to our language-game; in fact, generally speaking, where it has a role it is that of a supplement. Far from abandoning our language-game of intention, we use Freudian explanations to extend that game and to explore the idea that actions which traditionally would have been thought of as having no significance might actually have a meaning after all. What Freud offers is a new perspective on human action, but of its nature it is not something that can either be empirically true or scientifically proven. Finally, it is significant that our reaction to Freud has not been simply to abandon our existing game. We do not always look for unconscious intentions and where we do, our purpose is usually to throw new light on the individual's own account, not to replace it all together.

––––––––––––––

Having made these points, it is worth taking a more general look at Freud's work. In particular, we need to examine how it stands in relation to our claim that an account of the make-up of the Inner can only reflect one particular substantive point of view rather than the scientific truth. As we have seen, Freud's approach can be seen simply as a technique for looking at our actions in a new and surprising light. His purpose, however, was to do much more than this and, as well as asking a new set of questions, he also outlined a framework within which the individual can view her life. Presented in this way, the substantive nature of his claims becomes more apparent. An individual's frustrations, doubts, anxieties and uncertainties can obviously be interpreted in various different ways and, to each of these, there corresponds a particular anatomy of the Inner. For example, one story might tell of the struggles of the rational part of the soul to free itself from the delusions of sense, another will speak of the voice of conscience urging the individual to spurn the temptations of the flesh and of the spirit, while the analyst will speak of repressed ideas and desires re-emerging through the unconscious. From this perspective, what Freud is doing is presenting a particular substantive account of the human condition and Wittgenstein has no objection to this as long as it is made clear what is going on. The way Freud presents his work, however, is fundamentally misleading. For example, he suggests he has unearthed the scientific truth behind ancient myths, whereas in fact all he has done is present a new myth. Take the example of the *Urszene*.

> This often has the attractiveness of giving a sort of tragic pattern to one's life. It is all the repetition of the same pattern which was settled long ago. Like a tragic figure carrying out the decrees under which the fates had placed him at birth. Many people have, at some period, serious trouble in their lives – so serious as to lead to thoughts of suicide. This is likely to appear to one as something nasty, as a situation which is too foul to be a subject of a tragedy. And it may then be an immense relief if it can be shown that one's life has the pattern rather of a tragedy – the tragic working out and repetition of a pattern which was determined by the primal scene. (*LC*, p. 51)

There is nothing in principle wrong with offering people this way of looking at their lives, but it is misguided to present it as the scientific truth. The questions at issue here are not ones which can be solved by science. At most, science could assemble evidence which shows that people who see life in a particular way are less likely to commit certain kinds of behaviour. However, even that would not show any particular approach to be correct. On the contrary, someone might argue that the truth just is hard to bear, so that adverse effects would be a hallmark of correctness, not of error.[3]

In conclusion, therefore, Freud can be seen as making a variety of claims of varying status. Some of his theses are stipulative in that they lay the foundation for a discipline, e.g. laying down the parameters for a dream interpretation. Others combine to form a powerful and plausible mythology which offers people a way of understanding their lives, but one which is just as substantive as the Christian talk of body and soul or the fivefold division of the Buddhists. Freud's idea of the unconscious offers a new way of looking at human action and one whose power lies precisely in the fact that it involves an approach very different from the normal one. However, it does not provide the truth about the Inner, nor does it show that all our psychological concepts are based on a mistaken empirical premise. In fact, Freud's work underlines the necessity and fruitfulness of Wittgenstein's approach; in particular, it demonstrates the importance of distinguishing between the conceptual, the scientific and the substantive. In this chapter and in this book as a whole, we have tried to show how Wittgenstein's account of the Inner can resolve many of the difficulties that arise in attempting to understand our psychological concepts. The aim, however, has been to clarify the relations between concepts we all share, and we have argued that these relations neither constitute nor are based on empirical truths. Furthermore, in clarifying the Inner we have sought to avoid any substantive theses. Concepts such as the soul (or the unconscious) embody claims that we do not all share and therefore the clashes and conflicts they provoke cannot be resolved by conceptual clarification. Here the Wittgensteinian task comes to an end for, having clarified the Inner, it is a substantive question which more specific concepts we use to describe our essence and in so doing relate it to a wider account of the nature of this world.

———————————

CONCLUSION

In this book we have sought to give an account of Wittgenstein's solution – or rather dissolution – of some of the classic philosophical problems thrown up by the attempt to understand the concept of the Inner. As we have seen, Wittgenstein does not set out to answer the mind–body question nor does he advance any theses on the existence of the soul or the meaning of consciousness. These latter issues are substantive – they raise questions about how we should understand ourselves and the world around us, and so relate to the fundamental ethical problem of how we should lead our lives. Such questions are not answerable on the basis of philosophical expertise but require the individual herself to take up a position which, although not arbitrary, cannot be given an unchallengeable foundation.[1] By contrast, Wittgenstein's aim is clarification – he seeks an *Uebersicht* (overview) which will give a better understanding of how our concepts work, so eliminating conceptual confusion and rendering certain questions otiose. The apparently modest nature of Wittgenstein's enterprise and its consequent definitive but frustratingly non-substantive character may be one of the reasons why its author has been praised but largely ignored. The problem is that Wittgenstein seems to rob philosophy both of its grandeur and its point.

One version of this criticism is advanced by Antony Kenny[2] who notes Wittgenstein's suggestion that philosophy eases a particular type of mental cramp and attacks the implication that philosophy only has importance for that blighted section of humanity who suffer from this sort of disability. Wittgenstein claims that 'a philosopher is a man who has to cure many

234

intellectual diseases in himself before he can arrive at the notions of common sense' (*CV*, p. 44), so is philosophy therefore simply a detour which an unfortunate few have to make? If we consider the case of the Inner, we can see that this is not the case. Although Wittgenstein's account is purely clarificatory, it does provide an insight into the operation of our psychological concepts and this can enable us to avoid a variety of widespread confusions and conceptual mistakes. The source of difficulty is that learning to use a concept such as thinking involves acquiring a practical mastery rather than a theoretical understanding of it; since such concepts are important, the scope for confusion when we come to reflect on them is correspondingly great. Although the philosopher ends up where she started, this does not mean she has not travelled – the house may be the same, but it looks different to the stay-at-home and to the round-the-world voyager.

Consider the example of Freud. The theories he produced have been so influential as to seep through to the everyday lives of many individuals who would never think of undergoing psychoanalytic treatment. Many therefore who do not suffer from the cramps of philosophy will have been convinced on the authority of science that the unconscious exists and that our lives are to be understood as the tragic consequence of the difficulty each of us had in piloting our ego through the dilemmas of the Oedipus complex. As we have seen, however, Freud's understanding of his own enterprise is deficient and the conception of the Inner he advances, although interesting, is not justifiable on empirical or scientific grounds alone. His claim that the unconscious is a discovery obscures the fact that it involves a modification of our language-game, and in this way an interesting new perspective on human action is misleadingly presented as a scientific truth about the nature of that action. What this illustrates, however, is the value of a Wittgensteinian philosophical training. Although he does not present philosophy as the privileged source of truth, Wittgenstein does not deny that it is an important asset in many forms of intellectual inquiry.

People sometimes say they cannot make any judgement about this or that because they have not studied philosophy. This is irritating nonsense because the pretence is that philosophy is some sort of science. People speak of it almost as they might speak of medicine. – On the other hand, we may say that people who have never carried out an investigation of a philosophical kind, like, for instance, most mathematicians, are not equipped with the right visual organs for this type of investigation or scrutiny. Almost in the way a man who is not used to searching in the forest for flowers, berries, or plants will not find any because his eyes are not trained to see them and he does not know where you have to be particularly on the lookout for them. Similarly, someone unpractised in philosophy passes by all the spots where the difficulties are hidden in the grass, whereas someone who has had practice will pause and sense that there is a difficulty close by even though he cannot see it yet. (*CV*, p. 29)

A glance at some of the recent speculative works by highly distinguished mathematicians and scientists is enough to underline just how true this remark is.

The importance of a proper understanding of the Inner could be illustrated across a range of disciplines from psychoanalysis to scientific investigations of the brain and from aesthetics to artificial intelligence. It also ties in with more everyday puzzles and perplexities. Although only the philosopher seeks to develop it in a rigorous form, there are surely many people who have at some time or other been attracted by solipsism and unable to work out what they should think about it. Or take the issue of language – how easy it is to view it as purely informational and, forgetting the existence of poetry, to conclude that words are an inadequate vehicle for our emotions and experiences. Here we encounter confusions and uncertainties that are by no means the preserve of a few and, although the touchstone of common sense (and the guiding hand of practical reality) may preserve the non-philosopher from the absurdities to which her more rigorous theoretical counterpart is led, the importance of philosophical clarity is again underlined. The best general illustration of this is the question of the Inner itself, for a lack of understanding about our concepts can create the impression that one must either accept a religious ghost in the machine or conclude that a human being is simply a vastly complicated and as yet not fully understood mechanism. Such a dichotomy raises real substantive issues and how the individual resolves it may be crucial in determining how she leads her life and how she understands the world. The value of Wittgenstein, however, is to show that neither the scientific investigation of reality nor the philosophical analysis of concepts can decide the issue for us. A proper understanding of the Inner may be an effective prophylactic against the snares of rival metaphysicians, but we distort and abuse the treatment if we expect it to be an escape from the need for individual moral decision-making.

Wittgenstein's philosophy in general and his account of the Inner in particular might therefore be said to have a Kantian value. Not because of detailed similarities to Kant, but because it sets limits on the speculative enterprise of resolving all issues from reason alone. In contrast with Kant, however, Wittgenstein's emphasis on simply resolving conceptual confusions means that his philosophy contains no substantive doctrine at all. Clarity, however, should not be seen as a negligible or irrelevant virtue; indeed, if we contrast Wittgenstein's approach with that of the metaphysician's arrogant claim to absolute truth, it is the latter that comes to seem faintly ridiculous.

> I read '. . . philosophers are no nearer to the meaning of "Reality" than Plato got . . .'. What a strange situation. How extraordinary that Plato could have got even as far as he did! Or that we could not then get any further! Was it because Plato was so *extremely* clever? (*CV*, p. 15)

Wittgenstein's 'modesty' is not an abdication of a philosopher's proper ambition, but a belated recognition that the philosopher's claim to special authority and metaphysical insight is the product of a confused self-understanding.

As this suggests, the key difference between Wittgenstein and his great predecessors is the abandonment of metaphysics. Wittgenstein held that the attempt to reach profound truths on the basis of purely conceptual investigations was futile – according to him, grammar is autonomous and conceptual analysis can teach nothing about reality nor resolve the puzzle of how we should understand the world and how we should live. The philosopher is like the thumb-catcher who believes that speed and dexterity will enable her to overcome the impossibility of her own task (*AWL*, p. 166). In its own terms, therefore, Wittgenstein believed metaphysics was doomed to failure. But paradoxically he did not reject the work of previous philosophers as empty nonsense – on the contrary, he once told a friend that he considered it among the noblest products of the human mind (*RW*, p. 105). The key to this paradox is to recognise the substantive (i.e. moral or ethical) nature of metaphysics. The work of a great philosopher such as Hegel does not have the status he claimed for it; it is not the indisputable truth about reality and our place in it. However, it is a powerful vision of the world and one which has considerable intellectual and moral force. The point is that although metaphysics is in part a response to conceptual confusion, it also fulfils other needs and in so doing takes on a different quality. A philosopher's vision is like any other value-system and as individuals we may find it profound or shallow, noble or debased; indeed, we may even be convinced that it is essentially right, that is to say the best (or even the only correct) way of understanding the world and our role in it.

So where does this leave philosophy after Wittgenstein? What is there left for the philosopher to do? Here the first point is that Wittgenstein's activity is still a form of philosophy and one he saw as an enduring necessity. Mastery of our concepts does not presuppose a philosophical understanding of how they function and, since that functioning is often more complicated and less orderly than we imagine, language will always lay traps for us, creating puzzles and confusions we need to dissolve. This is particularly true when we engage in any theoretical discipline, for there the danger of getting tangled up in our concepts is even greater.

> In the course of a scientific investigation we say all kinds of things; we make many utterances whose role in the investigation we do not understand. For it isn't as though everything we say has a conscious purpose; our tongues just keep going. Our thoughts run in established routines, we pass automatically from one thought to another according to the techniques we have learned. And now comes the time for us to survey what we have said. We have made a whole lot of movements that do not further our purpose, or that even impede it, and now we have to clarify our thought processes philosophically.
>
> (*CV*, p. 64)

The discipline of Wittgenstein's method and his technique of unravelling conceptual knots is therefore one strain of philosophy which has a future, both as a training for individuals and as an essential part of the system of academic disciplines.

Philosophy, however, has also always been an attempt to answer certain fundamental substantive questions and, even if we recognise that such questions cannot be answered on the basis of conceptual analysis, this does not mean that they are meaningless or unanswerable. The human need for an account of the world and our place in it will not disappear because traditional metaphysics has been shown to be flawed. A new non-dogmatic or rather avowedly substantive enterprise would be possible, but it would have to recognise that proof was impossible and that no aspect of any account could make itself logically immune to challenge from a different substantive position. As I have argued elsewhere, accepting these points does not involve embracing relativism and is in fact closer to the nature of moral argument as we actually engage in it. Certainly a direct profession of faith can often be more convincing than a supposedly watertight argument and there is no reason why a developed and intellectually compelling account of 'The world as I see it' should not replace the conceptually confused 'World as Philosophy shows it must be'. Whether such an avowedly substantive and challengeable project would produce accounts as baroque as those of traditional metaphysics is questionable. (Furthermore, if one accepts Wittgenstein's personal view of our culture, one might argue that it is in fact for the best if we recognise that the great cathedrals are things of the past and that rather than trying to ape them we would do better to aim for less grandiose but not necessarily inferior structures.)

The conclusion of a Wittgensteinian investigation still leaves all the great questions open. As far as the Inner is concerned, in one sense it will always remain as mysterious as life itself. What Wittgenstein's analysis does, however, is to strip away the conceptual confusions from the real uncertainties we face. Having attained clarity about our concepts, we are now confronted with the real problems, the answer to which each must work out for him or herself.

239

APPENDIX
Seeing As and Perception

In Chapter 2, we claimed that the basis of both continuous aspect perception and aspect-dawning is the specific nature of our relation to pictures. We also argued that our relation to language and to human beings provides the basis for sets of concepts which are in some ways analogous. Some will argue, however, that in doing so we have placed undue limits on the concept of aspect perception. Gestalt psychologists, for example, hold that seeing as is involved in all perception. Similarly, Stephen Mulhall, one of the few commentators on Wittgenstein's work in this area, claims that the notion of aspect perception captures the basic nature of our relation to the world and that this is also what Heidegger was getting at in his conception of human existence as Being in the world.[1] Why then have we restricted ourselves to more modest claims? And what is the truth of the matter?

Let us start with the Gestalt theorists. Citing various phenomena associated with perception, including our reaction to pictures such as the duck–rabbit, they argued that what we really see are patterns, not shapes and colours. This argument seems attractive; indeed, it ties in with much that Wittgenstein himself said. It is true, for example, that our reports of what we see usually employ concepts other than simply those of colour and shape. We say 'I saw a table', not 'I saw a brown rectangular object, supported by four cylindrical forms'. Similarly, if we represent our perception, the manner in which we do so (and the sort of mistakes we will and won't make) will reflect our conception of the object. These points seem to suggest that concepts are a part, indeed a dominant part, of our perception. But such grandiose claims can be dangerous, for it is easy to read

240

more into them than their basis justifies. The points we have noted undermine the sense-data theorist's claim that what we 'really' see are shapes and colours, but they should not be taken as the basis of a new dogmatism. On the contrary, what Wittgenstein emphasises is the variety of ways we represent our visual experience; on some occasions we describe it in terms of shapes and colours and on others in terms of particular objects. Concepts are 'part of perception' only in the sense that we use concept words to describe what we see, and it would be misleading to infer from this that we only really perceive a conceptualised reality. The implied contrast is empty, for any description will necessarily employ concepts. Our concepts do not stand between us and reality, rather they are the tools we use to describe it.[2]

But what of the Gestalt psychologists' more specific claim that all perception involves seeing an aspect? The first problem is that it is not at all clear what would be involved in seeing a chair, say, as a chair. This is certainly not how we normally use the phrase 'seeing as' and so the meaning of the claim is uncertain. However, on the basis of the points above, Wittgenstein suggests one way of giving the phrase a meaning.

> A man might be highly gifted at drawing, I mean he might have the talent to copy objects, a room for instance, very exactly, and yet he might keep on making small mistakes against *sense*; so that one could say 'He doesn't grasp an object as an object'. He would never, e.g. make a mistake like that of the painter Klecksel, who paints two eyes in the profile. His *knowledge* would never mislead him. (*RPP1*, para. 983)

This contrast would be one way of defining the notion of seeing an object as an object, but how similar is it to what we normally call seeing as? One difficulty here is that so far only one criterion for the concept of seeing an object as an object (or as a unit) has been specified. It is therefore unclear what else the concept should be seen as entailing. However, the new concept differs from aspect perception in that it neither defines a relation (i.e. something that has a variety of manifestations through time) nor an experience that can be continuous. By contrast, the relation of regarding a picture as the object it depicts manifests itself in a variety of ways. It shows itself in the utterances of aspect-dawning ('Now it is a duck') and those of continuous aspect perception ('I saw it as a duck, then the aspect changed and I saw it as a rabbit'). It also shows itself in other aspects of our behaviour – the delight we take in the pictures, our sensitivity to small changes and the claim that even a minor adjustment fundamentally changes the picture. This set of reactions underlies the picture of the aspect-blind as a type of person whose relation to pictures is quite different from our own and who lacks experiences we have. But there is no equivalent to this in the concept of seeing an object as an object; the concept does not define a particular relation, nor does it provide the basis for talk of a particular momentary or continuous experience.

At this stage, a different objection arises, for there is another sense in which someone may claim that seeing as is involved in all perception. Here a different grammatical point is emphasised, viz. the fact that any difference in reaction can be used to justify the claim that the individual in some sense sees the object differently. It might be argued, for example, that a chess player and a non-chess player in a sense see something different when each looks at a chess position. Similarly, the eyes of a lover might be said to see differently from those of the unmoved. Such examples underline the flexibility which characterises our notion of seeing and a range of concepts and distinctions is possible. Certainly there are some cases where we shall be more inclined to say that people see the same thing but react differently (or simply know more about what they see, are able to make more finely tuned comments about it, etc.) and other cases where the notion of seeing differently will seem more appropriate. However, there would seem little point in suggesting that every kind of difference involves perceiving a different kind of aspect. Furthermore, even if we did make this claim, doing so would once again introduce a different kind of concept. An ornithologist who can instantly tell the species of a bird, its age, gender and state of health would not normally be said to be having a particular set of experiences denied to the layperson, nor would it be clear what was meant by suggesting that she had some sort of special relation to birds. Even if she made judgements without always being able to specify their precise basis, this would not justify the notion that she continuously sees birds in a specific way.

As the above example suggests, we are reluctant to talk of someone seeing differently, if the only grounds for doing this are that the individual knows more about the object than we do and is able to make judgements we cannot. It is also not sufficient that she is able instantly to make distinctions which for us require more roundabout investigation. The situation changes, however, if the distinctions are purely or essentially couched in visual terms and go together with a distinctive set of reactions and judgements. Take the case of seeing an object as typical of a particular style or as expressive of a particular time. Here the individual is not simply adept at recognising particular factual differences, rather her reactions themselves usher in a new set of distinctions. Objects that are similar in geometric terms are treated as quite different, while objects with no formal similarities are said to look similar. Against the background of these utterances and the other reactions that go with them, we might well talk of seeing the objects in a particular way, and someone may know that certain objects are held to be similar without herself being able to see the similarity. However, this sort of example only underlines the difference between aspect perception and normal perception, for once again it shows that the concept of seeing as only really makes sense in certain specialised contexts.

Stephen Mulhall's claims raise different but related issues. His basic argument is that the fact that we can see an object as something else shows we must already see it in one particular way. In his words, 'any particular experience of aspect-dawning, in making us aware that we can see a given entity as a *new* kind of object, thereby highlights the fact that we are *already* regarding it as a particular kind of object'.[3] Mulhall specifies what he means by treating aspect perception as a two-place schema (seeing A as B) and arguing that, although only certain concepts can fill the second place, there is no such limitation on the first place. According to him, regarding a picture as a picture is just one example of treating an object as a particular type of object. But this argument rests on an ambiguity. In the case of the duck–rabbit, experiencing the change of aspect involves switching from seeing the picture one way to seeing it the other. It shows that we see the picture in a particular way, viz. either as a duck or as a rabbit. It might also be said to show that we see the picture in a particular way in the sense that our relation to the picture can be contrasted with that of the aspect-blind. However, it does not show that seeing the picture as a picture is one possibility among others. There is no contrast with seeing the picture as a table, nor does it reveal that if we see pictures as pictures, we must also see tables as tables. Our relation to pictures with its specific manifestations gives content to the notion of seeing or regarding as picture as a picture, but because the notion of a special relation makes sense in one context does not mean it can be generalised. To justify the concept of seeing an object as a particular type of object, e.g. seeing a table as a table, some new and separate definition is required.

It might be argued, however, that Mulhall does precisely this, for he emphasises that our relation to the world is not that of an interpreter and suggests that the immediacy of this relation is what Heidegger was trying to bring out. But the two parts of this equation are quite different. The criticism of interpretation is correct if all it means is that philosophers are wrong to claim we construct the world from sense-data. Heidegger, however, has rather different objectives: his vision is a substantive one and is essentially linked to the ethical question of how we should understand the world and how we should act. These divergent sources come together in Mulhall's account of what is involved in relating to a particular object as an object of that type. From Heidegger, he borrows the idea that our primary relation to objects is in terms of their use and, applying Wittgenstein's account of aspect perception, he argues that this relation is characterised by immediacy and smoothness. He then links this with Wittgenstein's claim that irregularity and unpredictability are essential for us to recognise behaviour as human, i.e. as the manifestation of the Inner.

> The readiness-to-hand of objects reflects the seamless, unhesitating way in which those objects are taken up into our practical activity, i.e. it reflects the particular grace and smoothness of the human behaviour involved, features which should be seen as defining characteristics of human practical activity *per se*.[4]

But this passage runs together logically distinct issues. Furthermore, against the background of the references to Heidegger, it continually threatens to transform grammatical points into empirical or substantive claims. Is it true, for example, that human behaviour has a particular grace and smoothness? One could surely argue that there are many types of animals that possess more grace than Man. And what should we say of the clumsy, are they less human than the rest of us? The claim that an unhesitating relation to objects is the essence of the human and that being at home in the world is the defining feature of our lives cannot fail to be substantive rather than grammatical. One might argue, for example, that it is the unnaturalness of Man, the problematic nature of his interaction with the world, that offers the better insight into the real nature of the human condition.

But what about Mulhall's specific claim that all perception involves aspect perception? Here it is significant that the notion of seeing as has actually been replaced by a much more general concept of relating as, for what is true of vision is implicitly seen as holding for all the senses. Despite this, the earlier points we made still apply, for what does continuously relating to a table as a table involve? And how does the presence or indeed absence of this 'aspect perception' manifest itself? If, for example, we bump into the table does this involve or imply a momentary spell of aspect-blindness? In the case of pictures, the special relation of standing towards a picture in some ways as towards the object it depicts provides the basis for distinguishing between someone who knows that it is the picture of a certain object and someone who does not just know it but sees it that way. However, with normal perception there is no parallel contrast.[5] The only basis for claiming that aspects are involved in all perception is either the specific empirical reactions focused on by the Gestalt psychologists or the grammatical point we noted earlier. We do use concepts to describe our perceptions, but that is a necessary feature of any perceptual report; the fact that we use object concepts undermines the claims of the sense-data theorist but does not justify a new dogmatism. It certainly does not reveal that we continuously see and relate to objects as objects of a particular type.

NOTES

PREFACE

1 A.C. Grayling, *Wittgenstein*, Oxford University Press, Oxford, 1988, p. 112.

1 THE PROBLEM OF THE INNER

1 *Wittgenstein's Lectures on Philosophical Psychology 1946–47*, by P.T. Geach, K.J. Shah, A.C. Jackson, ed. P.T. Geach, Harvester Wheatsheaf, Hemel Hempstead, 1988.
2 We shall examine the issues this raises about language and our relation to it in Chapter 4.
3 Cases where the individual later 'corrects' one of her own utterances do not undermine this point, for in those cases we are simply presented with two divergent accounts and, if we allow the second to amend the first, this reflects a decision on our part. It would, for example, be possible to imagine a people where the earlier, not the later, utterance was taken as authoritative, so that the second was treated as an aberration, not the first.
4 This stress on language may seem to clash with the fact that we also talk of non-language-users as being in pain. The point, however, is that the language-game is based on primitive pain-behaviour and insofar as that is evident in non-language-users we can extend the concept to them.
5 Of course, the fact that the Outer is the criterion of the Inner does not mean the Inner can never be concealed. Our talk of a specific experience only makes sense where there are criteria for saying it occurred, but once these have been defined, it is quite coherent to suggest that the individual had the experience but did not manifest it, e.g. that she was in pain but did not cry out.
6 A more sophisticated version of behaviourism holds that pain is the cause of pain-behaviour, but this misses the point of W.'s argument. Pain and pain-behaviour are not separate entities which turn out to be causally linked. Rather the latter is the criterion of the former. If someone behaves in particular types of way, we say she is in pain, but

this does not involve speculating that the same cause lies behind all these appearances. Rather it is the concept itself which groups the types of behaviour together. By contrast, in a causal story the various elements must be independently identifiable and would therefore invlove concepts different in kind from that of pain, e.g. the subject would have no privileged role in identifying them.

2 THE WORLD OF THE SENSES

1 Examination of what occurs in the individual's eye would not solve this question, for a scientific concept such as that of the retinal image is a very different type of concept from that of an inner picture. The latter is supposedly the content of the individual's experience, while the former is part of a scientific account of what literally goes on inside the eye.

2 Of course, just as the individual can claim to have an impression of one colour when she is actually having the impression of another, so too she can claim to be seeing the duck aspect when she is actually seeing the rabbit aspect. In both cases, however, her statement is not wrong, but insincere: she is lying, not making a mistake.

3 For a fuller discussion see the Appendix.

4 So what of non-language-users; surely animals also see? Wittgenstein would not deny this, but the point is that we extend the concept to them because of similarities between their behaviour and our own. The primary use of the concept is in the human context and it is characterised by the fact that it includes a first person use 'I can see . . .' or 'I am seeing . . .'.

5 For a further discussion of the significance of this usage see Chapter 6.

6 There are also genuine visual experiences, e.g. being dazzled. For a fuller discussion of the categories of the Inner see Chapter 5.

7 This test can also be used to illustrate the difference between aspect-seeing and perception, for it is perfectly intelligible to order someone to try to see an aspect or, in the case of ambiguous pictures, to switch from seeing the picture in one aspect to seeing it in another.

8 If she was unable to do this, the familiar problems of private ostensive definition would re-emerge, for without a connection with the outer paradigm her inner sensation would be undefined and indefinable.

3 THE MYSTERY OF THOUGHT

1 The same point of course also applies to her actions.

2 See Chapter 4.

3 Of course, if her account is incoherent or does not tie in with her actions, we will not be able to treat her as a normal person and so the assumption will lapse.

4 THE MUSICALITY OF LANGUAGE

1 Cf. Chapter 2, pp. 42–5.
2 It might be argued that our response to, say, classical music is anything but spontaneous. However, even if we must be schooled in a particular culture before we can appreciate it, the point is that we must eventually go beyond what we have been told. We do not say someone appreciates classical music because she has memorised a set of appropriate comments; rather the sign that the music is starting to mean something to her is when she begins to make comments of her own.
3 Cf. Chapter 3, pp. 82–3.
4 'Heaven be praised! Another little something's slipped – from the clutches of the Croats', Schiller, *Wallenstein, Die Piccolomini*, Act 1, Scene 2.

5 THE COMPLEXITY OF THE INNER

1 See pp. 33–7.
2 See pp. 115–16.
3 This reflects a general point about emotions, for, in contrast with sensations, emotions and thoughts interact. On the one hand, there are thoughts typical of, e.g. sorrow and, on the other, the individual's emotions colour her thoughts, so that in sorrow a person's whole thinking may as it were be tinged with sadness.
4 Is losing a lover a greater or less source of sorrow than losing a parent? And if greater, would losing both parents make the blow more equal? The point here that our sorrows are specific and that it already demeans them to suggest totting them up like items on a bill. With pain, although there are also qualitative differences, the notion of a scale of bearableness is less problematic.
5 See pp. 129–30.
6 The term 'disposition' comes from Gilbert Ryle and is misleading insofar as Wittgenstein uses it as a technical term and so in a specialised way which differs from its normal use.
7 There are more sophisticated language-games where this is not the case and hence where the notion and role of the subject changes. But these language-games are simply different from the basic one, not improvements or corrections of it. See pp. 158–64.
8 The point here is that some emotions have objects, while others do not. For example, we feel joy or grief over something, while happiness or sadness need not have any particular focus. With directed emotions, the cause and the object can be different. We might cause someone to be joyful by secretly injecting her with a drug, but the object of her joy would obviously not be the drug itself.

6 THE INNER/OUTER PICTURE

1 That lying about the Inner belongs to a different category from lying about the Outer is illustrated by the fact that in lying about the latter we may accidentally tell the truth. For example, someone may mistakenly believe something did not happen and may mendaciously but correctly maintain that it did. In relation to the Inner, however, this possibility does not exist, for, while our utterances may be insincere, they cannot be mistaken.
2 In German, *Schmerz* (pain) and *Verstellung* (pretence).
3 'That is the expression of a heart truly in love.'
4 For a discussion of the issues involved in breaking the Inner up into mind, soul, spirit, etc. see Chapter 7.

7 THE MIND, THE BRAIN AND THE SOUL

1 It is also unclear what complete explanation would be, for even in science there comes a point where reasons run out and the demand for further explanation is simply rejected.
2 For an exploration (and attempted justification) of the logic of this position see *Wittgenstein and Moral Philosophy* by the author, Routledge, London, 1989.
3 Here it may be tempting to reject the idea of correctness altogether, but we do not have to do so; indeed, doing so is just as much a substantive move as endorsing a particular view as correct. See *Wittgenstein and Moral Philosophy*.

CONCLUSION

1 For an exploration and justification of these distinctions see the author's *Wittgenstein and Moral Philosophy*, Routledge, London, 1989.
2 In Brian McGuiness (ed.), *Wittgenstein and his Times*, Blackwell, Oxford, 1982.

APPENDIX

1 S.J. Mulhall, *On Being in the World*, Routledge, London, 1990.
2 It would also be misleading to say that an element of cognition is involved in all vision. If we ask someone who is seated at a table what she sees in front of her, she will reply 'A table', but this does not necessarily mean she has been thinking about the table or meditating upon its tableness. Although our representation of what we see necessarily involves concepts, this does not mean that all vision is preceded by a process of cognition.
3 *On Being in the World*, Routledge, London, 1990, p. 136.

4 Ibid., p. 198.
5 Wittgenstein does draw a contrast between the irregularity and unpredicatability of human behaviour and that of robot-like beings whose movements are geometric and he suggests that we would have difficulty in seeing the latter as possessing an Inner. However, the issue here is not how they perceive or relate to objects, but what character their behaviour would have to have for us to be able to see it as that of a being with an Inner.

ABBREVIATIONS AND BIBLIOGRAPHY

AWL   *Wittgenstein's Lectures, Cambridge 1932–5*, ed. A. Ambrose (Blackwell, Oxford, 1979).

BB   *The Blue and Brown Books* (Blackwell, Oxford, 1958).

CV   *Culture and Value* (Blackwell, Oxford, 1980).

LC   *Lectures and Conversations on Aesthetics, Psychology and Religious Belief* (Blackwell, Oxford, 1970).

LE   'A lecture on ethics', *Philosophical Review* 74 (1965).

LLW   *Letters from Ludwig Wittgenstein (to Paul Engelmann) with a Memoir* (Blackwell, Oxford, 1967).

LW1   *Last Writings on the Philosophy of Psychology* vol. 1 (Blackwell, Oxford, 1982).

LW2   *Last Writings on the Philosophy of Psychology* vol. 2 (Blackwell, Oxford, 1992).

MS 110   Manuscript 110 in the Von Wright catalogue.

NFW   'Notes on the freedom of the will' – notes taken by Yorick Smythies of an unpublished lecture on free will given by Wittgenstein in Cambridge in 1936.

PI   *Philosophical Investigations* (Blackwell, Oxford, 1958).

RPP1   *Remarks on the Philosophy of Psychology* vol. 1 (Blackwell, Oxford, 1980).

RPP2   *Remarks on the Philosophy of Psychology* vol. 2 (Blackwell, Oxford, 1980).

RW   *Recollections of Wittgenstein*, ed. Rush Rhees (Oxford University Press, Oxford, 1984).

TLP   *Tractatus Logico-Philosophicus* (Routledge & Kegan Paul, London, 1961).

WLPP   *Wittgenstein's Lectures on Philosophical Psychology 1946–47* (Harvester Wheatsheaf, Hemel Hempstead, 1988).

Z   *Zettel* (Blackwell, Oxford, 1967).

INDEX